MID-AMERICAN
★ FRONTIER ★

A

SUMMER JOURNEY IN THE WEST

[Eliza R.] Steele

ARNO PRESS

New York Times Company

New York — 1975

Editorial Supervision: ANDREA HICKS

———◆———

Reprint Edition 1975 by Arno Press Inc.

Reprinted from a copy in The State
  Historical Society of Wisconsin Library

THE MID-AMERICAN FRONTIER
ISBN for complete set: 0-405-06845-X
See last pages of this volume for titles.

Manufactured in the United States of America

———◆———

Library of Congress Cataloging in Publication Data

Steele, Eliza R
    A summer journey in the West.

    (The Mid-American frontier)
    Reprint of the 1841 ed. published by J. S. Taylor,
New York.
    1. Middle West--Description and travel. 2. Steele,
Eliza R. I. Title. II. Series.
F353.S75 1975   917.7'04'20924 [B]   75-123
ISBN 0-405-06888-3

A SUMMER JOURNEY IN THE WEST.

A SUMMER JOURNEY

BY

Mrs. STEELE.

NEW-YORK.

PUBLISHED BY JOHN S. TAYLOR,

145 Nassau Street.

A

SUMMER JOURNEY IN THE WEST.

BY MRS. STEELE,

AUTHOR OF HEROINES OF SACRED HISTORY.

" I write that which I have seen,"—LE BAUM.

———————————

NEW YORK:

JOHN S. TAYLOR, AND CO.
(Brick Church Chapel, 145 Nassau-St.)
1841.

PREFACE.

THIS little book assumes to be nothing more than a note book of all that passed before the observation of the author, during a summer tour of four thousand miles, through the great lakes; the prairies of Illinois; the rivers Illinois, Mississippi, and Ohio; and over the Alleghany mountains to New York. Since she has been 'urged by friends to print,' the author has added to her notes and letters, some little information regarding the western States, in hopes her book may be of use to future tourists and emigrants, who will here find an account of the distances, prices, and conveyances, throughout the author's route. Anxious to guard against errors, information acquired upon the road, has been compared with the best Gazeteers. Accuracy, in a newly settled country, is difficult, and accounts differ much; still the author trusts the traveller who may honor her by taking her book for his guide, will not be far mis-led.

New York, May, 1841.

A SUMMER JOURNEY.

"I write that which I have seen."—LE BAUM.

LETTER I.

JUNE 14th, 1840.

My dear E.—The variety of scenes which have passed before my eyes since I last beheld you, and the crowd of new ideas acquired thereby, have not obliterated your Shaksperian adieu from my mind:

> "Think on thy Proteus, when thou haply see'st
> Some rare note-worthy object in thy travels,"

were your last words—in consequence of this desire, I hereby send you all I deem note-worthy. With what delight did I find myself once more upon the Hudson! Although so often seen, to me it is still lovely, for custom cannot stale its beauties. I pass along this river as through a gallery of cabinet pictures. The sunny vista and romantic glen of Gains-

2

borough—the frowning cliff and murderous dell of
Rosa—the Dutch cottage of Teniers—the Italian villa
and graceful trees of classic Weir—cattle, as if just
sprung from out a Berghman and grouped upon the
shore, or standing in the cool translucent wave,' their
'loose train of amber-dropping hair,' not being 'braided
with lilies,' but occupied in flapping the flies away!—
all these, and many more are placed side by side before me as I float along.

You have never seen this famed stream, and I will
therefore describe it to you minutely. Mine will not
be 'notes by the way,' nor 'crayoning,' nor 'pencil
sketches,' but perfect Daguerrotype likenesses of all I
see.

With a bold rush our steamboat was free of the
wharf and out into the stream. Ascend now to the
upper deck with me and you will obtain a fine view
of the city of New York and its noble bay. Upon
one side lies the city with its mass of houses, churches,
and vessels; beyond is Long Island. Observe what
a pretty back ground is Staten Island: its numerous
white buildings show well against the green elevated
ridge behind them; then turn your eye to the opposite side and you will behold New Jersey, with its
pretty city, and villages, and churches; and in the
center of all this is the glassy water covered with
steamboats, brigs, ships of war, and vessels of all
sizes, and dotted with pretty fortress islets. Ho-
boken with its neat church and romantic colonade
are passed, and the rugged cliffs of Weehawken rise
upon our left as we ascend the river. These cliffs are
the commencement of the Palisade rocks, which soon
retreat into the interior to arise again above. Bull's

Ferry (worthy of a better name,) next appears, with Fort Lee, pretty rural retreats, whose white houses, churches, and fences, are pencilled as with white chalk upon the river's green and sloping bank.

From the east side, turret and spire have passed away, and villages and country seats adorn the shores until we arrive at Spuyten Duyvel creek, rendered famous by the redoubtable Van Corlear, who swore he would pass it in spigt den Duyvel; and also as being the boundary line of Manhattan Island. To a hasty observer, the shores beyond this are as lonely and wild as if we were hundreds of miles from any city; but if you will fix your eyes steadily upon the wood-lands which line the river banks, you will catch glimpses, between the trees, of Grecian portico, Yankee piazza, or Dutch gable, telling of many a summer haunt of the city's 'tired denizen.'

Upon the west side the Palisade commences, a perpendicular wall, or to speak more scientifically, 'a columnar escarpment,' from three to eight hundred feet high, and two miles broad, thus continuing for twenty miles along the New Jersey side of the river. As you dabble in geology, I must not forget to tell you these rocks are of the trap formation, passing into green stone. Under it are layers of slate, sandstone, and grey limestone, much of which is used in the city and its neighborhood. Sloops were lying at the foot of the rocks, as we passed, taking in their load of sandstone flagging, or roofing slate for the use of the citizens. These sloops, which carry masts sixty or seventy feet high, show the height of these cliffs, as when seen anchored below them they appear like skiffs. A few stone-cutters have erected

cottages upon the rocks, which might be taken for
children's houses. Shrubbery is seen in some spots,
while a green fringe of trees is waving from the summit. These rocks have stood the brunt of that mighty
torrent which wise men tell us once rushed over the
country from the north-west, as if some lake had
burst its barrier—for bowlders washed from the Palisades are seen in various parts of Manhattan Island
and Long Island. To the alluvium brought down by
this flood, we are indebted for Manhattan Island and
Staten Island. What a pity 'wise saws' are out of
fashion, or I could lengthen my epistle by telling
what 'modern instances' these islands are, of the
'good' brought down by 'ill winds.'

As we are both now tired of these Palisades, it is
very pretty of them to retire as they do, into the
country, making a fine back ground to the rich land
lying upon the river's bank, adorned with several picturesque townlets. These are Nyack, reclining upon
a verdant slope; Haverstraw, nestled under a high,
green promontory; and Tappan, which ought to have
been first mentioned. This is, however, but the
'landing' of the town of that name, lying a few miles
in the interior, and whose 'heavens' ought to be
'hung with black,' for the sake of the talented and
unfortunate Andre, whose silver cord was here un-
timely loosed.

The river swells out into a broad lake, called Tappan sea, which ought to be spelled Tap-pann Zee.
The west side I have described, except that from
these towns the ground rises into an elevated green
ridge of Haverstraw, and then descends gracefully to
the water, ending in a low level spot, covered with a

rich velvet sward, dotted with groups of oaks, and evergreens, among which a silver rivulet winds its happy way. This is very prettily called Grassy Point.

Upon our right hand we have smooth, lawn-like slopes, over which the buildings of Yonkers, Tarry-town, and Dobbs' Ferry (harmonious sounds,) are straggling, or reposing in graceful groups upon every gentle swell. Sing Sing, with its long range of prisons, is before us; so called, I suppose, that the inhabitants of those abodes may have something cheerful about them. It is a lovely spot commanding a beautiful view of the river scenery—so lovely that I am almost tempted to be *wicked*, that I may be ordered to reside there, and sit like a Naiad sing singing upon a

> "diamond rock,
> Sleeking her soft alluring lock."

That is all very well, you will say, when the rock is already cut out for you to sit upon; but where one is obliged to hew out one's own rock, as do these woful sing-singers, it would be as well to abandon the place to the heroes who there do congregate. They quarry a white granular limestone which is used as building material. The antique Dutch church looks very well, seated upon an eminence; and Wolfert's Roost, with its Dutch points and gables, the residence of the cele-brated Irving, is another interesting object upon this shore.

Look behind you quickly, if you would take a last farewell of Staten Island, whose dark outline has, until now, filled up the back ground, although we are thirty miles from it. As we turn towards the narrow outlet between Stoney and Verplanck's Points, the Palisades are sweeping around to the east, and rapidly shoving

2*

in their side scene between us and the Island.   Now
it is gone, and the Narrows are fast being covered,
through which you might, if your eyes could see so
far, descry the green ocean and its gallant barks.
The river now seems a lake behind us, upon whose
bright bosom a fleet of vessels, like a flock of birds,
are skimming, and ducking, or reposing upon the
water. Two *Points* defend the entrance to the Highlands: Stony Point on the west, a bold rocky promontory, formed of fine horneblend granite rock, and surmounted by a light-house; Verplanck's on the east
presents a small village, containing a pretty fanciful
hotel, and some lordly dwellings upon the elevated
ground above.   These are now behind us, and we find
ourselves in the Grand Pass of the Highlands.   Beautiful creations they are—high, green cones, sweeping
gradually down to the water's edge, where they sometimes appear a verdant precipice nearly two thousand
feet high; or projecting their spurs into the river, and
crossing each other so that the Hudson must wind
hither and thither to follow the tortuous path between
them.   Various lights give new beauties to these hills.
It is pleasant when the sun shines broad and bright
upon them, to penetrate with your eye their green
recesses, or endeavor to distinguish whether those
bushes on the summit are indeed trees or no; and
again when a cloud passes, running rapidly over the
surface, the effect is very beautiful.   As we were near
the centre of the Pass, the sun was obscured, and a
heavy shower clothed every thing with gloom.—
Through the sombre light they seemed like giant
mastadon or mammoth of olden times, couching down
upon each side, musing upon the changes which have

taken place upon this diluvial earth. The rain has ceased, and the mist has all retired into the mountain caves, save on one spot near the summit, where it lowering stands, like one of Ossian's ghosts, whose wont it is, he tells us, to ' fly on clouds, and ride on winds.' Or, it may be the wandering spirit of some red warrior who has perished on these shores, and now haunts the scene of his former triumphs.

Upon a promontory jutting out from the river, are situated the Military Schools of West Point. It is a summer's day well spent to ramble over that pretty spot. If you care not for the Schools, nor to see the orderly young cadets, you may admire the monument dedicated to Kosciusco, or walk in his garden as they call the spot where he used to ' sit on rocks' and muse upon the sweets of Liberty—or you may climb up to that ruined fortress crowning the summit of the mountain which overhangs the Point. From thence you have a fine view of all the rugged, cultivated, wild, adorned and varied country for miles around—and of that broad silver stream bearing upon its waters many a graceful vessel. The dusky peaks and dells, and undulations of the several mountains around are here distinctly seen.

The Dunderberg, where is the thunder's home, raises its frowning head at the right, followed by Bare Mountain, Sugar Loaf, Bull's Hill, Crow's Nest, Butter Hill, Breakneck Hill, and many others bearing designations equally euphonius. Among these hills, beside West Point, are many spots famous in the history of our country. Do not be afraid, I am not going to begin ' In the year 17—' nor tell of the iron chain which bound Anthony by the nose to the Fort opposite; nor arouse your indignation by pointing to the chimneys of Arnold's house; nor make you sad by speaking again of Andre; nor arouse your patriotism by relating the deeds here done in times of old. Let the past be *by-gones;* and turn to the present whose sun is shining down upon the pretty village of Cold Spring opposite to us, and upon that romantic white chapel dedicated to ' Our Lady of Cold Spring,' which is so tastefully perched upon a rock washed by the Hudson's waters. At West Point is a depot of fossil enfusoria, and sulphur has also been found. Shooting out of the Highland Pass, we find ourselves in a broad expanse of water, presenting some of the prettiest views to be seen upon the river. Seated upon the elevations of the left bank are many towns; Newburgh being the most conspicuous as it is the largest: and it is built upon a high cliff of argillaceous slate, thus displaying its numerous houses and churches to advantage. The opposite shore presents a beautiful green mountain wall, the highest peak of which is 1689 feet above the river. At its foot reposes the smiling town of Fishkill.

I must not linger thus by the way. Remember I have four thousand miles to travel and the summer is passing. Imagine then to yourself a broad and beautiful river, skirted with cultivated country with often a mountainous back ground, and rich with ' summer's green emblazoned field'—and wafting upon its waters river-craft of all forms, from the lazy whaler returning after a four year's cruise, to the little pleasure yacht. There are many towns on this river, one of which, Poughkeepsie, is rendered famous as being the place where Washington, Hamilton, Jay and Chancellor

Livingston met, to compose the Constitution of the
United States. The city of Hudson is agreeably situated upon the summit of a slaty cliff commanding a
view of the Catskill mountains, and the town of Athens
on the opposite bank of the river. Imagine, scattered like gems upon the borders of the stream, pretty
villas of Grecian, Gothic and nondescript styles, the
homes of the Livingstons, Dewitts, Ellisons, Ver-
plancks, Van Renselears, Schuylers, and other gentlemen of taste and wealth. I saw nothing of those
Dutch elves and fays which the genius of Irving has
conjured up, among the dells and rocks of the Hudson—those creatures are unfortunately out of fashion ;
and one might as well look for them as for high heeled
shoes. Perhaps they will come in with the ancient
modes. If I thought so, I would immediately order
hoop, train, cushion, buckle, high heel, and all the odi-
ous costume which rendered my ancestresses so hideous. Alas I fear the 'mincing dryades' with high
crowned hats, are all departed—and no more—

> " On the tawny sands and shelves,
> Trip the pert fairies, and the dapper elves."

Albany appears at great advantage seated upon a side
hill, presenting a mass of imposing buildings surmounted
by many a tall steeple, and crowned by the Capitol
and City Hall, from whose gilded dome the evening
sunbeams are brightly streaming.

I have said nothing about my gallant bark, nor my
company—the first a large and rapid steamboat, arranged with satin cushioned and canopied saloons—
the latter a mixture of all countries and sexes.

But we are at the wharf and I must put up my papers. Adieu.

LETTER II.

June 15th, 1840.

My dear E.—We shall of course remain in Albany during the Sabbath for the pleasure of worshipping that kind Friend, who has showered upon us the blessings we are now enjoying. In the morning we walked to the church of a Baptist clergyman, Mr. W——h, who has been long celebrated as a very interesting preacher. This church is a handsome marble structure, surmounted by a dome, and adorned by a colonade of pillars in front. The lecture room is below, and we ascended to the chapel, a neat apartment with a good pulpit and commodious seats. Mr. W. sprang from an obscure station, being a mechanic, and therefore could only obtain a common education. What he is, he has made himself, or rather was made by the Holy Spirit; for we all know how religion refines and elevates the intellect of man, as well as his affections. After his conversion he rapidly improved, and now one is astonished at the beauty and purity of his language. He is not an animated preacher, nor does his *forte* lie in arousing a sinner; but he shows forth the

truth and beauty of religion, and expounds the Gos
pel doctrines with a power and grace, and clearness,
which fascinate the hearer.   This church is always
crowded by the *elite* of Albanian society of all sects,
and by the strangers who are in the city.

In the afternoon we attended service in an old Dutch
church, one of the oldest in the city.   It is built of
brick, and boasts two spires which give it a singular
appearance.   The interior is richly fitted up, with
gilded chandeliers and many comforts and elegant
conveniences.   Here we found ourselves surrounded
by the old Dutch families, whose fathers emigrated
from Holland and settled themselves here; among
them were the family of the Patroon.   I looked around
with pleasure upon the sober benevolent faces of the
congregation, for I have always felt a very kindly sen-
timent toward our Dutch brethren.   The peaceful,
even tenor of their lives; their contented spirit, their
industry and integrity entitle them to our most ‘golden opinions.’   The Rev. Mr. Y——,who officiates
here, is an able, solid, preacher, well versed in the
fundamental truths of christianity.

I am happy to say, the people of this city, are a
very moral and religious people.   This applies also to
the ‘first society’—which is a singularity in city history.   Beneath their influence theatres, dissipation,
and extravagance cannot thrive.   Already I seem to
breathe freer, although so little distant from New
York; whose atmosphere, rank with foreign luxuries,
is like a hot house over-crowded by fragrant exotics;
stifling us with perfume.

We admire this city, which however we have only
been able to see in our odds and ends of time.   Its

situation is very fine, it contains many handsome buildings, and it is generally kept very neat. A broad street through the centre leads up to a pretty square, surrounded by several imposing buildings—the Capitol occupies a fine position here; it is of dark stone, with a neat marble portico supported by four ionic columns. The City Hall on the opposite side of the square, is a noble edifice, built of white marble from the quarries of Sing Sing, surmounted by a gilded dome. The view from this dome is beautiful; embracing the city at your feet—green hilly country, dotted with country seats and towns, among which is the city of Troy— the noble Hudson, winding among this country and a back ground of mountains. The new State Hall is a pretty building—the Exchange, is a huge mass of granite, giving one a great idea of the extent of business which requires so large a structure for its merchants.

What a different place is this to the town which stood upon this two hundred years since. Then the only public building was a quaint old Dutch church, with painted glass windows; adorned with the coat of arms of those ancient worthies, who, clad in trunk hose and steeple crowned hats, sat demurely below. There are but few of the ancient dutch houses left, and these are daily falling before the yankee spirit of improvement—which improvement by the bye sometimes merely amounts to *alteration*. At this city is the southern termination of the great Erie Canal.

LETTER III.

My dear E.—We arose at an early hour, and after looking into some of the public buildings we returned to breakfast. This dispatched, we drove to the rail road depot, an ugly building at the head of State Street where we alighted and stood in a large barn-like apartment, among men and trunks and boys—the latter screaming, Albany Argus'—'Evening Journal!'—and among all sorts of confusion, until we were seated in the cars. Soon however, two fine horses, to whom I render my thanks, dragged us out of the barn into open day—up through the square, over the hill, to the Locomotive Depot, giving us on the way many sweet little back views of Albany and its pretty country and river, and the round tops of the Catskills in the blue distance beyond. The snort of a steampipe, and perfume of grease and smoke, announced the vicinity of our locomotive; and, as if to show off its paces, the engineer whirled the hideous thing back and forth before our—at least my—nil admirari eyes.

3

Our horses were unhitched—the engine attached, and away we rushed, leaving our fine steeds gazing after us with tears in their eyes, to see themselves outdone by a great tea-kettle.

There are many pretty villas along the road; breathing places for the heated citizens below, which I would describe to you; but dashing along at sixteen miles an hour speed I can only catch a glimpse of white pillar and portico when the next minute we are three miles away. You must expect no description of the country when I am on a rail road, for the scenery is all blurred, like a bad lithograph. I only saw groups of pine trees rushing past and several bright dots which I suppose meant wild flowers when we came in sight of Schenectady, an antique dutch town. Before entering it I was struck by the vision of two immense tarred ropes walking deliberately beside our car, and discovered we were upon an inclined plain, descending which, cars of stone were brought up at the other end of our ropes. Our steam horse was once more exchanged for one of flesh and we set off upon a jog trot. Near the city we passed a canal basin in which lay several canal boats, for the Erie Canal passes through here. We entered the city, crossed the end of a long street filled with bright looking shops, where people and horses were frisking about in the morning air,—when another large depot received us in its barn-like expanse. The Ballston and Saratoga train entered at the other end, and you may imagine the charming confusion as the people of both trains jumped in and out the carriages, marched and counter marched until they had settled down into their several seats.

We were not suffered long to look upon this pleasant picture, for at 9 o'clock we were on our way to Utica. We could see but little of Schenectady while passing through it, but it looked well at a distance. Upon an eminence above the town stands Union College a fine building of grey stone.

Schenectady, is an Indian name spelt by them Schan-naugh-ta-da; meaning 'the Pine Plains,' a fitting name, for the pine is universal here. This town has been the property of many different nations—the Mohawk, the French, the Dutch, and the English having each in succession ruled its destinies.

After leaving the town, we entered at once the glorious valley of the Mohawk which runs nearly westerly, and whose course we followed eighty miles to Utica. There may be lovelier vallies in the world, but certainly not another like this, for it is unique in its kind. Imagine a long green valley covered with rich farms—through its centre a bright transparent river, having a rail road on one bank and a canal on the other; while a range of hills frame in the picture on each side. So straight is this valley, that canal, river, and rail road run parallel, and within sight of each other nearly all the way.

It was one of June's sweetest mornings when we passed the shores of the pretty Mohawk, and I was never weary of gazing down into its smiling face, as we glided along; or of watching the lazy canal boat dragging its rich freight at the foot of those soft green hills opposite; or, of peeping out the coach at the rugged cliffs, which reared their bare heads far above our road.

There are many little villages on this route, where

we stopped to refresh ourselves, or to fill the engine.
The first was Amsterdam a small Dutch settlement.
Near this place stands a handsome stone edifice which
is renowned in the annals of New York as the residence of Grey Johnson and his brother Sir William,
the dreamer.   At these towns there are hotels, and at
other spots refreshment houses, built at the road side,
where you are allowed a few minutes to rest.   You
are shown into large rooms set out with long narrow
tables, bearing loads of coffee, oysters, cakes, pies,
fruit lemonade, etc.,—you pile your plate with good
things, stir around your coffee or tea, when tingle!
goes the bell 'all aboard!' rings in your ears, and you
have just time to put your 25 cents into the attendants hands and yourself in a car when puff! and away
you go.   Some of these towns are pretty, as St Johns,
Fonda, Canajoharie, Herkimer, and many others.—
What hungry people these travellers are! at every
refreshment station the tables were crowded and at
the signal they rushed into the cars each with a cake
or pie, or apple, to finish at his leisure.   We may say
with Horace,

'At Fundi we refused to bait.'

One would imagine he was speaking of our little Fonda,
which is here pronounced as Horace spells it.   It was
named after the celebrated Col. Fonda.

Fort Plain is a pretty place on the other bank of
the river; here I longed to 'stay one turn' to hammer a specimen from the encrinal lime-rock which is
found there.   The little falls of the Mohawk is a delightful place.   The river here forces its way through a
rocky country and falls over successive ledges of rock
in pretty cascades.   The beauty of the scene does

not consist in altitude, but in number and variety of
these saults; and the foaming river rushing over its
rocky bottom or winding around its tiney islets, and
in the towering cliffs around it. The village is seated
upon each side of the river, connected by a handsome
marble aqueduct leading to the canal basin, and by
a neat bridge for carriages. The scene as we approached was very pretty. You see a frame work of
rugged cliffs, enclosing a noisy rushing river with
numerous cascades, its shores crowned with white
buildings, and spanned by a noble bridge ; the canal
boat is seen creeping at the foot of the hills opposite,
while the steeples, court house and hotels, are peeping from the trees which cover the sloping bank at
our right. Perched upon every jutting point and
grouped around the shores were many shanties occupied by the children of Erin who have kindly volun-
teered to make our rail roads and canals.

When the train stopped before the hotel, instead of
the usual sound of 'Newspapers,' or 'Nuts,' or 'Apples to sell,' I heard young voices asking if we wanted
some diamonds ! Surprised, I looked out and beheld
several little girls holding up small boxes containing
Quartz Crystals. We of course became purchasers,
and found among them some very perfect and pure.
'Where do you find these ?' I asked. 'Oh, all
among the cliffs ma'am,' she answered in the Hibernian
tongue—'and if its stop ye wud, I'd show ye to the
diamond holes where I often dig up the *ful* of my
pocket.' We observed this was a large town, having
several churches, dwellings, a handsome court house,
and many large manufacturers. Geologists tell us
this was one shore of that lake of which the high-

3*

lands were the southern boundary. How it came to wear through these hills and run away to the sea no one can ever know. The rocks here are limestone, principally; but I observed there was with it some fine granite. There was an old man among our passengers, who had lived here 'when all this was a wilderness.' He amused us with some stories of past times; one of which I think interesting enough to tell you. Here it is to fill up the page.

During the War of Independence there were two brothers, who, although they were brothers, could not think alike; they joined opposite sides in the war. It happened while the Division under Gen. Herkimer was destitute of arms, ammunition and clothing, he heard of the approach of the English troops. Fight he could not; fly he would not; and he was seeking some stratagem to better his situation, when fortunately, for him, the English brother having strayed too near his camp was taken up as a spy. The brothers, who had been long separated met once more; but it was a bitter meeting, for one was a prisoner and condemned to die. In spite of their different sentiments they loved each other. The prisoner earnestly entreated his brother, who was the General's Aid, to use all the influence in his power to save his life. The Aid was conscious he could not succeed unless he made the 'worse appear the better reason;' for his brother had been fairly captured as a spy, and in consequence of some bloody deeds of the enemy, his life was to be forfeited. With a heavy heart and darkened brow he entered the General's tent.

'I know what you would ask ere you speak' said his commander.' 'I have expected you and have determined upon my course. You come to ask your brother's life—it is your's upon one condition.' 'Name it! I am not afraid to agree to any thing my General may propose!' 'I require you to go over to the enemy as a deserter—tell them exactly of our numbers; for I have learnt they do not imagine we are so strong; conceal the state of our arms and provisions; and if I am not much mistaken, they will immediately withdraw when they know how large is our force. You are then to find your way back again as you can. When you return your brother shall be free.'

For one moment the Aid hesitated. To appear as a deserter—to act the spy—to deceive even an enemy, was adverse to his open noble nature—there was also danger of discovery when returning, which would lead to disgrace and death.

'Well young man! what is your determination?' asked the General. 'I will go, and trust in heaven and in you.' He sought the enemy's camp, was imprisoned as a spy—but his feigned tale procured his liberation. The enemy retreated before so large a force, which they could have conquered if they had known their distressed condition. It was many months ere the Aid rejoined his General. His brother was released, and after a parting full of sorrow they separated never to meet again.

We arrived at Utica at three o'clock, and repaired immediately to Baggs's hotel. Here we found an excellent dinner, just ready, which to hungry travellers is a cheering sight. As I promised to put down our expenses, we pay $3,75 each, from Albany to Utica, eighty miles. We here concluded to leave the train, and spend a few days at the celebrated Trenton falls. After partaking a very nice dinner at Bagg's hotel, we entered a neat carriage for Trenton falls, 14 miles north of Utica. The drive is a pretty one, and up hill all the way. We arrived at dark at a small inn in a forest, and were obliged to defer our visit to the cascade until the next morning.

After breakfast we walked out to visit the falls. Our way was through a deep forest breathing forth sweet fragrance in the early morning air. Suddenly, in the midst of the woods, we found ourselves upon the brink of a precipice, one side of a narrow chasm two hundred feet deep, while, too far below to be heard, a mountain torrent was rushing and foaming over the rock. A range of five ladder stairways led down the steep,—and as we thus hung over the water, we felt very much like some of Shakespear's samphire ga- therers, and thought what a 'dreadful trade' was hunting waterfalls. Safely down, we found a narrow ravine, so filled with the roaring torrent, that there was scarcely room for a pathway beside it. Part of the way a chain was inserted into the rock that we might, by holding upon it, pass the boiling whirlpool, if our nerves are strong enough to command our hands and feet—so scrambling, climbing, swinging, we contrived to reach the uppermost cascade, which is two miles from the last one. This stream, called the West Canada Creek, falls down a deep ravine over successive ledges of rock, in six small cascades of great beauty. The highest is only fifty feet high. The sides of the ravine are precipitous, and covered with the beautiful foilage of numerous trees. Among them are many evergreen trees—of these I remarked the stately white pine, which grows over one hundred feet high and perfectly straight; the red pine, with its dark green leaves, and yellow cones; the black spruce and the lofty birch. The rocks are slate and transition lime stone of the silurian series, abounding with petrifaction, of which many are perfect trilobites. Quartz crystals are also found here in great beauty and profusion. This place has been the scene of some tragic events—one of them most pitiable. A young girl sat out upon a pleasure tour, accompanied by her mother, father, and affianced husband. They came to this place, no warning spirit pressing them back, no drear omen warning them away, and no dream or presentment checking their steps. Gaily they descended the stairs, and clambered the rocks—the lover with the hand of his betrothed in his; the father and mother behind. Being thus led along, did not accord with her playful spirit, and telling him she could take care of herself, she in an evil moment withdrew her hand. His charge to be careful was answered by smiling asseverations of her sure-footedness; he turned with another admonition and she was gone! Where is she? He looks in every direction. She has hid herself in play; he calls; no answer but the torrents roar; she has rejoined her parents; he turns towards them and sees them quietly reposing together upon a rock. His pallid look—his wildness, as rooted to the spot, he gazes upon them, tells them the tale of woe, soon bitterly confirmed by her pretty bonnet of straw, which was at that moment whirled past their feet. Oh, the agony of those hearts as they stood beside that dark torrent, away from all help, and powerless to save their beloved one. The guide was despatched to the village for help, but not until three days after was she found a mile below ; her tender form having been thus far carried over rocks and whirlpools.

Another family party came to view these scenes. A tender girl of eleven years was for security consigned to the valets arms.   One false step plunged him into the torrent—he struggled to the shore, but the parent's pretty fondling was lost to them in life.   The body was the next day found.

As I stood upon the slippery rock, while these events were floating through my memory, their scenes pointed out to me by the guide ; the place lost all its beauty, and the dashing torrent seemed some huge monster, seeking whom he might suck beneath his horrid depths.   I grew nervous, and much to my companions surprise, begged him to return.   He, rejoicing in the fresh country air, and released from the city's dust, ran over the rocks with, to me, an alarming quickness, and I turned to depart.   Why these beloved ones should be thus snatched away from their fond relatives ; taken from their homes to find their death in this wild spot, is to us unknown. He who commanded this, has purposes, to, us unscrutable ; perhaps it was to read a lesson to those who hear the tale, to teach them the uncertain hold they have upon life, and all its pleasures, and to fear that power which can in an unlooked for moment, bear them from life to eternity.   There are hundreds every season who stand upon this spot, and hear this story, and the heart which is not affected by it must be as the hearts of the petrified animals around them.

We spent several days here, riding and walking among the romantic scenery.

The village of Trenton Falls is a small one, containing a few shops, and cottages and two churches, one of which is quite pretty. The ride towards Utica is very beautiful. The ground descends on each side to the Mohawk valley, and while our road wound down this side, we had the whole slope of the other side before our eyes, covered with orchards and fields, and dotted with villages. The town of Clinton with Hamilton college, stands upon elevated ground, while, below, at the river's brink is spread the city of Utica. Here we spent a day looking about its streets and shops. The ground slopes down to the river, near which are the business streets, while most of the dwelling houses are upon the more airy and elevated portion of the city. Genessee street is a fine wide avenue leading up the hill, lined upon each side with shops, hotels, churches, libraries, museums, &c. The canal is here crossed by a pretty bridge. The houses were substantially built, surrounded, many of them, by gardens, and appeared very comfortable residences. The business part of the city show rows of well built ware-houses, and were filled with people and carts passing to and fro, as if their trade was an active one and their city thriving. The Erie canal has brought much trade to this place, which now is one of the most flourishing inland towns in the State. The canal boats, stages, and rail trains which are constantly arriving and departing give a stirring appearance to the place. Religion, education, and literature, engage the attention of the inhabitants who support sixteen churches, and many seminaries and literary institutions. The population in 1835, was 10,183, to which now of course, several thousands must be added. It is situated in Oneida County, which was selected by the celebrated Baron Steuben as his retreat, and here he was buried.

June 21*st.*—We left Utica to-day in the three o'clock train for Auburn. About four miles from the city we passed a small town called Whitesborough, a pretty place, with two churches, an academy, and a building called the Oneida Institute. There is also here a manual labor school. A large unfinished building just outside of Utica, we learned was to be a lunatic asylum, calculated to accommodate one thousand patients— God pity them.

Several pretty towns lay upon our route : as Rome, Manlius, Canastola, etc. Sweet retreats from the con-fusion of a city without the solitude of the country. The canal and railroad which run through or near these towns present facilities for trade or travelling. Rome is a place of considerable importance, contain-ing five churches, a court house, academy, several shops and dwellings. The population, five years since, amounted to 4,800. When arrived at Syrac se we drove up to a large good looking stone building bear-ing the name of Syracuse House. There we stopped to take tea. This place is sixty miles from Utica ; enjoys considerable trade, but is still in its teens, having arisen since the canal passed through that part of the country. The Oswego canal joins the Erie here, which, with the salt works near, brings them much business. The population is 7,000. We ob-served in passing through it, several good churches, a pretty court house, substantial ware houses, numerous shops and dwellings, with a lyceum and high school, so that it would seem the inhabitants ought to be wealthy, refined, and well educated. The salt springs are at Salina, one mile and a half from Syracuse, where there are eighty manufactories of this material. These salt springs flow from beds of slate, in some places two hundred feet thick. Among the layers are masses of vermicular rock, whose interstices are supposed once to have been filled with salt. In this region of country are extensive gypsum beds; water lime is also found in profusion. Sandstone, generally old red, and lime-stones, are the prevailing formations of the county.

It was a beautiful evening when we left Syracuse. The sky, every where of a clear deep blue, paled gradually as it approached the west, where it was lost in a rich golden glow. The spires of the town behind us, reflected this brilliant hue, and the country as we passed, looked like one of Turner's *one colored* pictures. Onondaga lake with the pretty village reposing upon its shore, and the rich fields around it, were all touched with this golden pencil. The fields were strewn with salt vats, where the salt was undergoing evaporation, which were covered with low sheds, probably taken off in the morning, as it was now late Saturday afternoon, and this might have been to protect them from the weather. It was quite dark when we reached Auburn. We left the cars at the railroad depot, and were provided with carriages to the American Hotel. Here, large commodious bed rooms, and luxurious mattrasses, received your weary friends. I lingered a while to write you the events of the day, but must now hasten to bid you—adieu.

Sunday, June 22d.—This morning we visited the first presbyterian church, a large handsome edifice of brick. The pulpit was neat, and the seats and backs of the pews comfortably lined with horse hair. From Mr. Lathrop, the clergyman, we heard a very good discourse. The baptist and several other churches struck us as very neat and tasteful. The episcopal is in the gothic style, the interior lined with oak, and containing a handsome monument of Bishop Hobart, who died in this place. The hotels are showy handsome buildings, particularly the Auburn House, and the American, where we have taken up our quarters. This last is built of grey limestone from that neighborhood, and is surrounded by two rows of piazzas supported by handsome pillars. Opposite to it is the court house, quite a little palace in appearance. It is in the Parthenon form with a portico and high pillars, with the questionable addition of a large dome. From the cupola of an hotel, we obtained a charming view of this beautiful town and its environs. 'A palace and a prison on each hand,' I exclaimed as I glanced around, for behind was the grand court house, and in front arose the gloomy walls and towers of our famous State Prison. We saw from here the Theological Seminary, several handsome churches, hotels, elegant private dwellings, and streets of shops; while the outside of the circle presented a charming and varied range of fields, and hills, and groves and streams. It seemed indeed the loveliest village of the plain around, and I expressed my surprise at seeing so large and

well built a town ' so far off.'   My companion told me
it was too near the commencement of our journey to
be astonished yet, I had Rochester, and Buffalo, and
Cincinnati to see.   This town has a population of
nearly 7,000, I do not know exactly, but refer you to
the Gazetteers.   Those of our friends whom we visited
gave the place a fine character for good society, and
told us they enjoyed all the conveniences and elegan-
ces of life, with good pastors and good books.   In
twenty-four hours any thing can reach them from
New York.   The prison presents an imposing appearance.   It is built of dark stone with gothic ornaments,
and consist of first, a high wall enclosing a large
square, in the centre of which, rises a massive pile of
building surmounted by a cupola.   This building is
arranged on three sides of a square, the centre 276,
the other 242 feet long.   In this are the eating rooms,
hospital, chapel, and cells.   The work shops are
erected against the wall leaving a space for the keeper
to walk around and gaze upon them through holes for
the purpose, himself unseen.   It is a dismal life these
poor creatures lead, not only encarcerated from the
world, but confined alone, and forbidden even to speak
to a fellow prisoner when they meet at table or in the
shops.   They pass the life of La Trappe monks, except that it is against their will.   At table they sit in
rows with their faces one way, so that they cannot
even see each other.   However, this solitary and silent existence is said to be the best and most successful method of restraining and reforming the unhappy
convict.   In solitude they have time for reflection, and
silence prevents corruption from their fellow crimi-
nals.   They have religious instruction, which has con-

verted several. I cannot but think it a very efficient arrangement. The guilty man is stopped in his mad career, and solitude, silence, and time for reflection, and religious counsel, are blessings placed in his path. In the mean while his bodily wants are attended to, he is supplied with nutritious food, well ventillated rooms, with nurses and physicians. He is obliged to work, and the fruits of his labor go to defray the prison expenses. We saw carriages, shoes, cabinet-ware, and various other articles made by them, offered for sale in the shops of the village.*

* Sunday schools have been maintained; and in pursuance of my recommendation, the cell of each prisoner is always supplied with a volume
of the School District Library.   The measure was followed by a gratifying
improvement in the conduct of the prisoners. Many wearisome hours of
solitary time are beguiled,; resolutions of repentance and reformation
are formed, and the minds of the unhappy convicts, accustomed to the
contemplation of virtue, and expanded by knowledge, are gradually prepared to resist the temptations which await them on their return to society.—Gov. SEWARD's MESSAGE, JAN. 1841.

LETTER IV.

June, 23d, 1840.

Dear E.—At ten o'clock, we entered the stage coach for Rochester, 70 miles distant. Among our passengers were two whom we had found extremely interesting, while journeying from Utica here—a clergyman of Massachusetts and his daughter. The Rev. N. T——r, was about seventy, but extremely active, and very cheerful. His conversation was instructive and agreeable and of course in a pious vein, for he had occupied the pulpit 47 years, as had his ancestors for 230 years back. There was such simplicity of heart about him, such piety, and kindness of manner, joined with elevated thought and deep learning that we lent a charmed ear to his discourse, during the whole day.

Our route lay through an exquisitely beautiful country, covered with cultivated farms and varied with pretty lakes and towns. The first lake we saw was Cayuga lake. It is from one to four miles broad, and thirty-eight long. It is a bright sheet of water,

4*

lying in a deep valley and from its surface its shores
gently rise, covered with a fine farming country. We
crossed the end of the lake over a bridge more than
a mile long. So pure was the water that as we
looked down upon it, we plainly beheld the trout
swiming beneath.

Leaving the lake we passed through the pretty villages of Waterloo and Seneca Falls. Here the dark
green Seneca river rushes foaming over a bed of rock,
in a fall of forty seven feet. There are several mills
and manufactories upon its borders, and we observed
several churches, an academy, and many shops. Seneca! fair Seneca Lake, how can I describe the gentle
beauties of thy varied shores, and of that pretty
town which so adorns thy banks. This lake and its
surrounding country, present a very lovely scene.
There is nothing grand about the lakelet; you must
not imagine it enclosed in the moutains of lakes George
or Champlain; the style is petite and delicate. Its
Indian name was Jensequa, which has been modernised
into its present appellation. It is a placid, transparent
sheet of water, of very great depth, 4 miles by 35
long, and is said never to be frozen over in the coldest
winter. The road lay around the end of the lake,
from whence the eye wound over its fair pellucid
waters to its cultivated shores, adorned with handsome farm-houses, and country seats, and the massive buldings of the college which occupies a commanding elevation near the town—and the towers
and steeples of the village peeping through the
trees, as if to catch a glimpse of the waters below. We stopped at a small stage house in the lower
and business end of the town, where we all descend-

ed from the stage while the operation of changing
horses and stages was going on. A good sized parlor furnished with gay landscape paper received the
female part of the passengers, while the restless
mankind part, repaired to the shops, to inspect
the manufactures of the town, or to refresh themselves at the soda-water, and ice-cream shops. Once
more seated in our stage coach we ascended the hill,
to the better portion of the town, where we passed
through the principal avenue of the place, upon each
side of which were arranged those pretty villas and
gardens for which Geneva is so justly celebrated.
There were several churches in view, and a new pres
byterian half built. This, to us, was an interesting
object, a token God was not forgotten by the busy
people below, or the wealthy ones around us.

Canandaigua with its lake and street of villas received
our commendations.   There we dined at a very pretty
and commodious Hotel, having a fine view of the lake
from its windows.   Some of the lake trout which appeared upon the table we found very fine.   This lake
is smaller than those we have passed being 14 miles
long.   The main street is nearly two miles long, and
we drove through a mile of tasteful ' garden-houses,'
surrounded by grounds laid out in a pleasing manner,
adorned with flowers and fine shade trees.   The country from thence to Rochester is very beautiful.   Spotted with farms and villages, and woodlands covered
with groves of maple, hickory, bass-wood, elm, and
evergreen trees.   It was nearly dark around us,
when we were told the city was in view, and against
the bright evening sky we beheld in the distance the
towers and spires of Rochester.   When we arrived we

drove to the Rochester House. After some refreshment we bade our companions adieu ; promising to
meet at an early hour the next morning and drive
over the town before we left it for Lockport—and then
were glad to rest, for we had come a long day's journey
and in spite of good roads and commodious coaches,
fine spirited horses, and good drivers, we were very
much fatigued.

Well do the inspired writers compare man and his
brief existence to a flower that early withereth—to a
shadow—a cloud that quickly vanisheth—one day
here, and the next gone. Truly saith Job, ' thine eyes
are upon me and *and I am not,*' a just figure of man's
fleeting life. Never have I found the truth of these
comparisons more striking than at the present moment.
I told you of the amiable intellectual clergyman, who
with his daughter agreed to meet us early this morning—when that morning came he was in eternity ! At
two o'clock last night we were aroused by a messen-
ger from Miss T. saying her father was very ill. We
followed the servant through the dark and lonely halls
into the chamber where ' the good man met his fate.'
Yes, all was over. Around the room in attitudes of
mournful musing sat the keeper of the Hotel, some
servants, and several ladies who had arisen to do all
in their power to soothe the sufferer's pains. All had
been done that was possible, but in vain. Upon the
bed, lay a silent corpse, whose countenance bespoke
a death of agony—it was all that now remained of
that good and kind old man, that tender father, whose
refined manners and intellectual conversation, had
charmed us so much the day before. But his high intellect, his talents, his agreeable converse, of what

avail were they all to him now, had they not been joined to deep heart-felt piety, and been devoted to the interests of religion. He had died far from his home, with no friends near him except his daughter—his last hour passed away in a hotel among strangers—yet spare your sympathy, for he died happy. The everlasting arms were supporting him, a tender father was waiting to receive him in those heavenly mansions where death and sorrow can never come. He was going to no unknown region, he was to meet no stranger face, for his mind and his heart had ever been familiar with that celestial home, now to be his eternally—he knew a welcome awaited him from that Savior and that God, with whose spirit he had ever held communion through a long life spent in devotion and in acts of beneficence. It was the wish of the celebrated Archbishop Leighton that he might die at an inn, thus to be more forcibly reminded he was a pilgrim upon the earth—his wish was fulfilled, for he died at the Bell Inn, London.

With what terms of praise high enough shall I speak of the people of Rochester. When the news of this sad event spread, they surrounded the bereaved daughter with sympathizing hearts, and offers of service. The persons belonging to the house, and the boarders, with many physicians and clergymen with ther families, were anxious to cheer the heart of the sad survivor, and to lighten her mournful duties. The services of the Episcopal church were read over the body by the Rev. Mr. W. a young English clegyman of great talent and piety. The persons assembled near, seemed much affected with this solemn event. May God bless this sudden providence to them and to us. Uniting in a procession we accompanied the corpse to the canal boat, where bidding adieu to Miss T. we left her to pursue her dreary journey of five hundred miles, accompanied only with hired attendants. With what comfort did we see in her the power of religion elevating the soul above the trials and sorrows of life. Nothing else could have supported this bereaved daughter through so heart-rending a dispensation. But she knew in whom she believed. She saw from whom the blow came, and her faith told her it was done in mercy. As we were to leave Rochester the next morning, some of our kind friends called that afternoon and insisted upon driving us through the town. It being our only chance of seeing this celebrated city, we accepted their kindness, although the scenes of the morning had unfitted us for any thing but retirement.

As we drove along we were astonished at the extent and beauty of this city. It was you know founded in 1812, and now contains 22,000 inhabitants. We had heard of its rapid rise, but supposed it must consist mostly of wooden buildings as is often the case in new settlements, and our surprise was the greater to find it built in the most solid manner. Churches, houses, hotels and banks, court house and arcade, markets were all of marble or stone. There are here fourteen churches* some of them quite handsome. The Episcopal Church of St. Paul's, is a fine gothic edifice of grey stone—the church which enjoys the ministration of the Rev. Mr. W. mentioned above, is also handsome, of gothic form, neatly edged with brown free stone—the pres-

*Chapin's Gazateer.

byterian is of grey plaster supported by substantial
abutments—the baptist, where Mr. C. officiates, one
of our active friends of the morning ; a neat brick
edifice—also catholic, methodist and bethel for the canal men.   The streets are many of them McAdamized.
There is a fine park here surrounded by neat rail-
ings where the children of the neighborhood are
brought to take exercise.   But what most elicited our
admiration were the private dwellings, which in number and beauty are seldom equalled in our cities.
They are spacious, built of marble or stone, in gothic
or grecian form surrounded by wings and piazzas, and
out-buildings and grounds handsomely laid out, adorn
ed with shade trees, shrubbery and flowers.   They
are delightful retreats from the city's dust and noise ;
make fine play grounds for the children, and altogether
evince much taste and wealth.   How much better
is it for men of fortune, to secure for themselves and
families, pure air and room for exercise, instead of
squeezing, as they do in our city, into houses only 30
by 100 feet, as is too much the custom in our cities.
The wealth lavished upon gay entertainments would
procure space where their children might gain health
and strength.   A frolic upon the green sward is much
more conducive to health, than a sober city walk beside a nurse.   I often see these palid pitiable little
creatures in our streets walking as gravely and demurely as some old octogenarian.   A child without
gaiety is as cheerless as a landscape without sun.

The Genesee river divides the city into two parts, and
is crossed by three bridges and the two aqueducts of the
Erie canal.   The oldest of these is a very fine piece
of hewn stone work 804 feet long supported by eleven
raches.   They were building another aqueduct, which

is 858 feet long and 28 in height,* and the music of
the rushing river was almost drowned by the mason's
hammer.

Beside this canal there is another called the Genesee valley canal from Rochester to Olean, 119 miles.
The Genesee falls are very pretty, consisting of rapids
through the city, and in the suburbs it plunges over a
circular rock into a deep dell.   The whole fall through
the city is 268 feet; 97 at the cascade.   There
is another cataract farther down the river, which falls
106 feet.   This is at Carthage, two miles below, and
here is the port at which the lake steamboats stop.   A
rail road runs to this place.   There was not much
water in the river, and we did not see the falls in their
greatest perfection, but still there was great beauty in
the feathery foam which fell in snowy masses over
the dark rock.   These cliffs are old red stone and
limestones—with feruginous sand rock, and argillaceous iron ore; supposed by geologists to be equiva-
lent to the Caradoc series.   Upon the summit of the
cliff opposite to us was a range of solid stone mills,
from whence we obtain that fine Genessee flour,
ground from the wheat in the fertile region around.
Five hundred thousand barrels of flour are turned out
in a year.   There are twenty-two of these mills.   The
little streams which trickle down the rocks, are stolen
from the river to turn the wheels.   Our kind friends
were anxious to drive us to Mount Hope, a celebrated
cemetery a few miles from the city, but time was
wanting for this and many other proposed pleasures.
A distant view of Lake Ontario is said to be obtained

*Tanner.

from this hill. We returned home through some of the business streets, which, particularly Maine and Buffalo, were filled with busy people, waggons of home or foreign produce, while the long ranges of shops were gay with dry goods hanging from the doors, and piled with every comfort and luxury. Stages were landing or taking up passengers, canal boats were arriving and departing and every thing we saw denoted a strirring and thriving population.

5

LETTER V.

Dear E.—We left Rochester this morning at eight
o'clock, in a fine stage and four horses, for Lockport,
64 miles distant, for which we were to pay two dollers
and fifty cents each, dinner on the road, included.   It
was with much regret that we parted from this interesting city, for, although we had been there but a
short time, we had seen enough to be able to appreciate its beauties, and the sterling qualities of its beneficent and refined inhabitants.   We passed through
several pretty villages, and observed with pleasure the
farm houses and even the meanest cabins were deco-
rated with roses, geraniums, honey-suckles and other
flowers ; a pleasing custom which I wish was more
followed among us.   In one of the villages, I think
its name was Greece, I observed a neat grave yard
enclosed in a handsome stone fence and iron railing,
where ' the rude forefathers of the hamlet sleep,' while
around the tombs the kind hand of surviving friends
had planted roses and drooping willows.   A great part

of our way lay over the famous ridge road, an elevation of ground about as wide as a common road formed
of sand and shells. and which is supposed once to
have been the shore of Lake Ontario, now about ten
miles distant.   The ground has very much this appearance as the land between us and the lake is much
lower, and level, with marshy spots.   It is in some
places covered with a dense forest.   There is one
thing however, which struck me as singular, the land
declines the other side of the road also, in some places leaving a narrow ridge to ride upon, which is not
the ordinary form of a lake shore.   Why may it not
have been a public road, formed by that indefatigable
race of diggers, the *mound builders*, as a thoroughfare
between two of their cities.   It might still have been
the border of the lake, but swampy and marshy ground.
If we are to believe Mr. Delafield* these people were
the descendants of the builders of Babel, and wher
dispersed by the confusion of tongues wandered about
the world and at last found themselves in America.
Here they have thrown up pyramidial mounds in imi-
tation of their ruined tower on the plains of Shinar.
The Arabs have a tradition that Nimrod, disappointed
in his purpose of reaching heaven by building a tower,
constructed a chariot, to which he placed a pair of
wings, and thus hoped to enter the celestial regions.
Alas ! since the days of Nimrod how many like him,
have sought to attain the courts above, by their own
strenuous exertions.

Dear me, how I have wandered from the ridge road.
The celebrated traveller, McKenney, believes this to

* Antiquities of America.

have been the border of the lake, which broke away
and ran over the State of New York, thus scooping out
the earth at the other side of the ridge. The lakes
Geneva, Canandaigua, Cayuga, etc., he believes to
have been left by this flood. This agrees with Dr.
Mitchell's theory of a vast lake having been once in
this part of the state, which burst through its southern
shore at the Little Falls of the Mohawk, and through
the Highlands, flooding the coasts of New York with
alluvion. De Witt Clinton also, in his Canal report,
remarks: ' The general position of the Little Falls,
indicate the former existence of a great lake above
connected with the Oneida lake ; as the waters forced
a passage here and receded, the flats were formed
above, composed of several acres of alluvion.' In
this alluvion trees are often found twelve feet under
ground. Darby observed marks upon the rocks at
Little Falls fifty feet above the river, showing the
water had once stood so high.

At a distance we saw Brockport upon the canal,
and soon after, at Gainesville, we dined. We reached
Lockport at five o'clock in the afternoon and were
shown into a neat comfortable hotel where we awaited
the time of starting in the cars. Lockport is a town
of the mushroom order, having arisen around the
locks of the canal within a few years. The churches,
houses, and hotels, looked very respectable, and the
rail-roads and canals gave it quite a stirring appearance.
The locks at the canal here are a great curiosity.
There are five double combined locks which carry the
canal over the ridge. There is also a deep cutting
through the solid rock for some miles which is very
interesting. Many specimens of minerals have been

discovered here, as carbonate of lime, selenite, dog-
tooth spar, petrifactions, etc. I promised to give you
an account of all our expenses, so I will mention now,
we are to pay ninety-four cents each to Niagara,
twenty miles, as I shall not think of such mundane
affairs while there. Our expenses at the hotels have
been two dollars a day each, and meals fifty cents
each at all our stopping places. Seated in the rail
car we were soon on our road, and fast dashing
through a tolerably cultivated country, with several
neat mansions peeping through the trees. I trembled
lest the land should remain thus until we arrived at
Niagara, for I could not bear to approach it through
petty villages and farms, but we soon left all cultiva-
tion behind and found ourselves in a deep forest.
While gliding rapidly along, the engineer's bell rang to
scare some cow or other animal, as we thought, from
the rail track. Several of the passengers looked out,
one pronouncing it a man, another a cow, until, as we
approached, we discovered it was an Indian female.
She was enveloped in a dark mantle from beneath
which could be seen her scarlet leggins richly embroidered with beads. With a slow and stately step
she paced the rail-track, the engineer's bell and shrill
whistle unheeded. That she heard them was evident,
for another Indian woman, her companion, who walked
outside the rail, stretched forth her hand as if in ear-
nest appeal, but the haughty young princess scorned
to fly before her country's foe. The engine with
slackened speed came near her and stopped; then,
and not until it had quite stopped, she condescended
to walk off the rail-way. As we passed I saw she was
young and pretty, and her dark eye flashed with a

5*

triumphant expression which said, 'You dared not drive over me! I scorned to be forced from the road by your bell, like an animal!'

'Look out for the Falls! Prepare for Niagara!' is the cry of all in the coach. My heart began to beat— does not yours? Do be a little romantic, and feel some emotion, while about to behold one of Nature's greatest wonders. I looked out; we were on the river's bank, a high precipice of about two hundred feet Far below rushed the river, of a green copper hue, or verdigris; far up through the defile I caught a view of a mountain of mist, but I resolutely turned away, for such snatches of views I have been told to avoid, as bringing disappointment with them. The road swerved from the river, and in a few minutes we found ourselves in the midst of the little village of Niagara. When the train stopped we were surrounded by a host of porters, struggling to secure us for their several favorite hotels. We chose the Cataract house, from a friend's recommendation, and from its appropriate name. We had no cause to repent our decision as its accommodation and attendance were every thing we could wish. We were shown into a neat chamber, which to my delight looked out upon the rushing rapids. The tea bell rang as we entered, and much to the annoyance of my impatient spirit, my companion made it plain to me I should refresh myself before visiting the Falls. Tea over, I had leave to go, and we were soon upon the pathway. Shall I take you at once into the presence chamber of the divinity, or shall I describe the halls and corridors as I pass through them to her throne? I think a minute description will best please you. Niagara river, just

before it reaches the fall is divided into two parts;
one rushing past the Canada shore, plunges over the
rocks making the crescent, or horse-shoe fall—this
fall is about one hundred and sixty feet high.   The
other half of the river passes around an island, called
Goat, or Iris island, and falls from the American side.
This island has been sacred from the foot of man until
a few years since, when a bridge was thrown across
the rapids with much dexterity and daring.   Upon
this bridge we will walk if you please, stopping one
moment to view the rapids.   These constitute a very
beautiful feature of the scene, and, were it not for the
falls, would be well worth a visit on their own account.
The river is a mile wide, and comes rushing and
foaming over rocks some ten or twelve feet high,
looking, sea-faring men tell us, very much like breakers, or a sea in a storm—the green waves heightening
the illusion.   One is glad to be safely over this tumul-
tuous water, especially as the former bridge has been
carried away.   From the bridge you land upon Bath
island, containing about two acres of land, upon which
is erected a toll-house, and shop for the sale of Indian
curiosities and canes.   There are also bathing houses
here. A short bridge brings us to Goat Island, one-half
a mile long and a quarter wide.   It is also called Iris,
and as such I shall designate it.   The increased roar,
the mist rising above the trees, urge you on, and
you pass the 'curiosity shop' and refreshments here
offered, and hasten on through many a winding forest
path, until you gain the opposite side of the island,
where you find yourself upon the brink of a deep gulf
into which an ocean broken loose from its bounds is
precipitated with astounding noise and violence!....

This is the crescent fall on the Canadian shore. But linger not here. Descend the island to the brink of the river, and cross the rapids over a tottering, frail bridge, to the tower, which stands upon the precipice at the edge of the falls! Ascend to the top, and lean over the railing, look calmly down if you can, into the fathomless abyss of ocean, where the waves are dashing; the foam whirling, and the winds rushing, amid the roar of a thousand thunders eternally ascending. Deafened, confounded, bewildered, you retreat in haste, fearful every moment the breakers which are dashing against the tower, will tear it away from its foundation, and plunge you into the fearful ocean depths below. At this place, and upon table rock opposite, you see Niagara in all its power and terror. But if you would behold it in all its ravishing beauty, you must go as we did, the next morning before sunrise, and view it from the ferry house. To reach this spot, you do not cross to Iris island, but follow the river bank to the American fall, near which is the ferryman's cottage, and at a little distance the ladder which leads you down to the boat. Seated upon a rock, in front of the cottage, we feasted our eyes with unearthly beauty. Beside you is the American fall, tinged with a delicate apple or beryl green hue. One delights to follow with the eye this fair translucent arch, as it plunges far down into the water nearly two hundred feet below us. You have but a sideling view of this fall here. Looking past it you see the dark foliage of Iris island, and beyond, the Canadian fall. This immense mass of water falls over rocks in the form of a crescent, and is tinted with an elysian loveliness which you have never beheld, and never can

conceive, let me write pages upon it. Earth has
never produced water of the like hue : something of
the emerald, but more rich, more vivid. This green,
spotted, and embroidered as it is, with wreaths of
snow white foam, presents the most charming and
unique effect imaginable. In some places the water
pitches over perfectly smooth, as if an emerald arch ;
and so pellucid, that you may distinctly see through
it the white foam that is churned from the rocks over
which it flows. As we reached the spot from whence
this is seen, the sun arose above the trees, and immediately two glorious rainbows spanned the river from
shore to shore ! and the mist which was rising high
in the air, took the tint of the rose, which faded, only to
be replaced by the most gorgeous prismatic hues.
Never had imagination pictured any thing so glorious
as that scene : a tremendous fall of green and white
water ; a gay colored rainbow ; rosy mist ; azure sky,
and shores of various shades. It was a creation which
belonged not to earth. It seemed as if the celestial
city was before us, with its gates and walls of sap-
phire, of emerald, of ruby, and of gold. The waters
of life that flow through the city of God, seemed
rushing past us, for the scene was altogether unearthly,
and our feelings were elevated to that sublime architect, who could create such surpassing beauty. Earth
and its cares, home and its joys are all forgotten, and
we feel as if we could ever recline before the throne
of that mysterious presence, and watch untiring those
clouds of incense which are rising before it forever.
When we left the scene, we trod in solemn silence, as
if on holy ground. The violence with which the
water pours over the rocks has worn them away,

and the river has broken its way up from Lake Ontario at the rate of a rood in three years. It is supposed, when first discovered, to have been near the
Clifton House on the Canadian shore, and the ferry
house at the American.

June 26th.—Thi smorning we descended the cliffs by
a staircase and crossed to the canadian shore. The boat
was tossed about like a shell upon the whirling waves,
and as they looked up at the mass of water tumbling so
near them, and at the boiling water two hundred and
fifty feet deep, under us, some of our fellow passengers became a little nervous. My whole soul was so
absorbed in contemplating the wondrous scene, that I
felt no terrror. A sentinel in the scotch costume
greeted our eyes when we landed telling us we were
now in a strange land among another people. A
winding walk up the cliff, leads you to Clifton House,
a celebrated Canadian hotel. From the balconies of
this house, is one of the most imposing views of the
Niagara falls. You see the whole at once, while from
the American side you see only a part at a time. Still,
if not so grand, the view is more varied and more
beautiful upon the opposite shore and from Iris
lsland. Every one says it is ridiculous to attempt to
describe these falls, but, I have promised to give you
daguerreotype views, and will endeavor to sketch the
outlines—the shading, and the *impressions* of the
scene can only be given by the place itself. Imagine
a crescent of water a mile long, plunging with awful
violence as if the foundations of the great deep had
broken up again, from a cliff nearly 200 feet high.
According to McKennney 15,000,000 tons of water

are poured over the rocks in 24 hours. A green island divides this fall into two unequal parts. Table rock, upon the Canadian shore is at the edge of the falls, and projects over the cliff where you may stand with nothing between you and the boiling ocean below. So close is it to the water that the waves wash over part of it, and it is almost always covered with mist and spray. If it be glory to be buried in Niagara, you may here hope for that fate, as a portion of the rock has already fallen, and a large crack shows you the remainder will soon follow. From this spot, is said to be the finest view, as the eye embraces the whole circle of waters; but, as it was one of the days when the mist takes that direction, I saw but little of this. I found myself upon a slippery rock, a shelf between heaven and earth, with waves of spray breaking over me, and a furious mist dashing into my face—a noise of waters was in my ears, a white foam rushed wildly past, and I felt as if caught up in the sky in a whirlwind and driving snow storm. We waded back through the wet grass and ran into the Pavilion to avoid the spray dripping from the eaves. This house besides being a curiosity shop is the residence of the guide who will conduct you down a long staircase, and behind the fall if you wish—as I had no penchant for being drenched, half drowned and suffocated I did not attempt this exploit. We descended this morning the American side and ventured a little behind that fall. One feels very much as an Israelite making his *exode*, with a wall of water at his side ' where the flood stood upright.'

When once in, you see a glorious chamber with dome and walls of emerald rendered transparent by

the morning sun.   You might imagine yourself in one
of those crystal caves where the sea nymphs congregate, beneath the arches of the sea.   On the road
from table rock to Clifton House, there is another
building where there is a fine museum containing
4,000 specimens of indian curiosities, animals, minerals &c., many of them from that region.   The trees
about here are most of them evergreen.   The regular
yellow pine grows here and the silver fur with its
white lined leaves and purple cones and the fan leaved
larch growing 100 feet high.   The rocks of Niagara
are secondary limestone and sandstone, abounding
with veins and nodules of various minerals—among
them selenite, calcareous spar—petrifactions—tufa
from the cave, and many others.   I believe I have
sketched for you every thing regarding these falls—
gigantesque phenomene as La Vaseur calls them.
Still I do not expect to give you any idea of them, for
no one who ever wrote, conveyed an impression of
the reality to me.   I might make a pyramid of exple-
tives, and when all the superbs beautiful's, majestic's
and touching's are expended, you will say when you
come, 'the half has never been told me !'   Many have
been disappointed here chiefly because the scenery
around the falls is not as imposing as they had imagined.   Some would have a range of lofty mountains
as a back scene ; or a crest of naked rocks towering
above the falls ; but I fancy these are of the class of
contradictionists who make a respectable figure in
conversation merely by opposing every thing.   They
thus obtain a hearing, are able to enter into an argument, when no other means would gain them a listener.
He who formed this imposing scene is a better judge

of the sublime and beautiful. A range of mountains would materially injure the effect, as it would by contrast take away from the height of the water. The cataract would be a secondary object, but seated as it is in a level region of country, it is the first object that strikes the eye—a gem on natures forehead. There are many drives in this neighborhood to various interesting places, such as springs, whirlpools, battlefields &c. The parade ground is also a favorite place of resort. A regiment of 700 soldiers are reviewed upon the Canadian shore. We hired a carriage at the Clifton House and after a short drive found ourselves upon a beautiful plain above the falls, surrounded by guard houses, and barracks. The plain was soon filled with soldiers, who came marching up in seperate detachments from every direction. They were tall fine formed men, all of one height dressed in the Scotch costume, consisting of the short plaid skirt, stockings laced with red, cap and a cloud of black plumes. They were well drilled, and marched, counter-marched and went through all their evolutions as one man. The dress is picturesque, but must be a cold one in these regions. A pantaloon over the naked knee, I think would be an improvement. I could see soldiers, although not as well drilled, at home, so I was glad to turn my course towards that rolling flood below. From this plain is a fine view of the rapids above the cataract, and of Iris Island, which seems to have floated to the brink of the precipice, like one of the Mexican floating islands. We spent the afternoon upon Iris island. In the little curiosity shop we refreshed ourselves with delicate white strawberries grown upon the island, covered

with rich cream. Here also we added to our stock
of Indian bags and moccasins. Among the articles in
the shops at the village I admired most a large living
eagle which was chained to his perch. His feathers
were black and white, and his beak and claws yellow,
with a ruff of grey about his neck. I pitied the poor
captive as he stood gazing sadly out apparently listening to the roar of the falls, and longing to be at
large in his native forest once more.

The village of Tuscarora Indians is sometimes visited, much against their wishes however. The Indian
nations have never lost the remembrance of their
former power, and their present degradation. They
look upon us as usurpers, who have wrested from
them the land of their fathers, and have never forgiven
us. They count themselves our prisoners, and are
indignant that we should come and gaze upon them
in their fallen state as objects of curiosity. Their village is built upon the high shore of Niagara about
eight miles below the falls, commanding a fine prospect of the river and lake. They are under the care
of a missionary who has been the means of converting
fifty out of the three hundred. This tribe once belonged to the confederacy of five nations, but came
originally from North Carolina, and are living upon
the proceeds of the sale of their land there and their
trade. Some of them are prosperous, industrious farmers, while the women embroider beautifully, with
beads and stained porcupine quills, upon birch bark
and deer skin. These they dispose of at the shops,
and to strangers at the Hotels. Upon these occasions,
I am struck with the difference between this proud
race and our own   A pedler or travelling shopman

comes in, unpacks his wares, holds up every article, insists upon its worth and beauty, and urges you to buy—with the Indian it is otherwise. At our hotel, while ascending after dinner to the dining room, one is struck by the sight of a row of dark beings sitting upright upon the settees in the halls envelloped in cloaks of scarlet or black, richly embroidered with beads or adorned by peices of tin cut in flowers and tacked on. Their eyes are fixed upon the ground, their long hair falls over their faces, and an expression of profound melancholy sits upon every countenance. You stand before them and gaze upon them, but silent, grave, and motionless they sit, like the band of conscript fathers awaiting the approach of Attila. You at last ask, 'Have you any moccasins!' with a dignified motion they throw open their cloaks, and their laps are filled with articles for sale. You ask the price—a low musical voice tells you the amount in a very foreign accent, and that is all I could ever obtain from an Indian woman although I made many efforts while at Niagara, and they can both speak and understand English.

I never saw but one of them smile. I asked her what she had for sale in her lap—she threw it open, and behold a pretty Indian cupid asleep in a birch cradle, swathed and bandaged in their peculiar fashion. Titania would have quarrelled for it. At my start of surprise and admiration, a moonbeam smile flashed over her face and then all was dark and gloomy as before. The celebrated Timothy Flint tells us, 'the Indians are a melancholy musing race; whatever emotion or excitement they feel, goes on in the inner man.' So close an observer as he was, and living so long among them, his views can be relied on as being correct. The Indians have always been noted for their strong attachment to their children, and a stranger among them has only to praise the papoose to win his way to the parents heart.

June 27th.—I could not have believed parting with Niagara would have caused such sorrow. The lofty, and celestial emotions which are produced when in the presence of this one of God's most beautiful creations you are unwilling to lose. You feel ' it is good to be here'—and you dread to leave this holy ground to enter again into scenes which will do much to efface these pure emotions. A glimpse of heaven has been vouchsafed you, and most reluctantly you return to earth again. Slowly we sat out this morning to take a last farewell. We had seen it in all its brightness and we now beheld it in a sombre hue. The heavens were overcast, the mist, once of a dazzling whiteness now took a dusky tint, and hung over the cataract like a mourning veil. It was more in accordance with my feelings than to have bade her adieu while she was smiling in the ' bright garish eye of day'—one might fancy she was sad at losing such true worshippers. But you cannot understand such feelings now, they no doubt seem ridiculous—come here, and you will experience the truth of such emotions. At two o'clock, soon after dinner, we sat out on the rail road for Buffalo. The road for some time is laid along the river bank, and gives us a fine view of the islands, rapids, and other objects of interest, as Fort Schlosser, and Chippewa,—and then a long low wooded island floating upon the bosom of the broad stream was shown, as Navy island, the head quarters of the Canadian revolutionist in '37 and '38. The band have however now dispersed, and the island has returned to its parent, promising never to do so any more. It contains 700 * acres of good land. The river now begins to expand from one mile to eight, including Grand Island in the centre. This is twelve miles in length, and contains 17,384 acres of rich land and stately timber. A neat village called White Haven stands upon its shore, containing among other buildings, a steam saw mill which furnishes ship stuff from 20, to 70 feet in length. A fine situation, for such an establishment, as there is plenty of the raw material for this manufacture in sight all around.

There are 15 or 20 islands between the falls and Lake Erie, some of them very pretty, adorned with clumps of maple, oak, or cedar. Upon one of them, Tonawanda isle, is a fine mansion with cultivated grounds and fields around it. Our road lay through a village of the same name situated upon Tonawanda creek, a small place through which runs the Erie canal. We had sufficient time to survey the beauties of Rattle-snake Island at our leisure, for, when just opposite, a part of our engine gave way, and we came to a sudden pause. The male passengers were soon out, to discover the cause, and came back with a report that we could proceed no farther, as the injury was very great. We were declared to be ' in a pretty fix.' A horse was procured from a house in sight, and a a man was despatched upon it to Buffalo about eight miles distant. Many of the passengers sat out to walk to Black rock 4 miles a head, where they could

* Gazetteer.
6*

procure carriages to take them to Buffalo. The rest
of us remained seated in the coaches, with a hot July
sun streaming through the windows. What should we
do—scold at the road, or the train, or the engineers ?
No, an American never vexes himself about such
things—he is calm and indifferent under every circumstance. Some of us fell to reading, some to napping
and some to rambling. We undertook the latter, but
as we were only surrounded by ploughed fields soon
returned to the coach, where I busied myself in writing the above. Pray read on if it is only to repay
me for my sufferings those two hours in the heat. I
think I had better abuse this rail road a little, for it
deserves it. Do not, however, suppose I am vexed at
being left thus ' sitting on a rail !' The iron is ripped
up in several places, causing a jolt when we strike
against these land snags, and a man rides beside the
engineer with a hammer to nail them down. It is the
worst rail road I ever travelled over : however, as it
is only used a few months in the year when Niagara
is fashionable, perhaps it may not yield sufficient profit to allow much expense upon it. Something is seen
coming up the road—all heads are out, and we hope to
be released from our captive state—it turns out to be
the return train which had been waiting for our engine and cars, and now has been obliged to take horses instead. As it was impossible to pass us, the
passengers and their baggage were turned out, and
placed in our coaches, to the Niagara end of which
their horses were fastened. They looked very sourly
at us while this was passing, thinkingperhaps of the
maxim of Pythagoras to his scholars—Do not remain
in the highway. They wondered at us for sitting in

their highway, depriving them of their engine, and condemning them to the loss of a fine afternoon at Niagara. Some of them perhaps might have been of that whisking class of tourists who intended to return the next morning early, and to them it would be quite a loss.

A joyous shout announced the appearance of our horses, and we were soon on our way again. We passed through Black Rock, a considerable village, and then followed the Erie canal for some distance. The last two miles were upon the borders of Lake Erie which stretched away a mighty mass of green waters, to the horizon. As this was our first view of our great ' inland seas, we gazed upon it with much interest. There are many handsome villas in the vicinity of the town commanding fine views of the lake and city ; one of them, a large Gothic stone mansion, promises to be quite an ornament to the country if ever finished. At Buffalo we drove of course to the American Hotel, as its fame had reached us at home. It is a large stone building, well kept, and elegantly furnished. The drawing room is as handsome as any in the country, and the dining room is a large airy commodious apartment lighted with five large gilded chandeliers. The staircases and halls are of oak covered with copper in some places—the bedrooms, private parlors, table and attendance as good as we could find in our boasted city. There is here also a public room, hired sometimes, for concerts and lectures, which is well lighted with chandeliers and set round with green silk couches. In fact every thing is good and neat.

June 28th.—Sabbath morning—that blessed day of rest, given in mercy as a moment of repose in the wearied journey of life to the ' world's tired denizen !' We felt its benefit, and rejoiced no stage horn could hurry us onward, and no bell, save the ' church going bell', could summon us forth. The presbyterian church is a plain building, but handsomely fitted up inside, and very comfortable. Rev. Mr. Lord is the minister, an able and pious man. We heard in the morning a very interesting discourse from Mr. Stilwell of the American Bethel Union. He delivered it in a Baptist church in which the Rev. Mr. Choules officiates when in the city. It is a neat, commodious building, the pews made of the native black walnut cushioned and lined with horse hair. A choir of good singers accompanid by instruments led the music. The society to which Mr. Stilwell belongs devotes itself to the sailor's interest. The state of the boatmen upon the Erie canal he reported to be very wretehed. There are about 25,000 boatmen and sailors employed upon the canal and in lake navigation, who were of the lowest and most worthless class of men ; seeming inaccessable to all efforts for their reformation or conversion. These, mixing with the lower population of Buffalo, and other towns on their route, exerted a baneful influence. The Bethel Union attempted to send missionaries among them, but they were abused, insulted and almost discouraged. Still, as they felt it their duty, these self-denying men persevered every Sunday in addressing the men along the canal, and in presenting bibles and tracts. They soon began however to have some hope, for when the canal closed last autumn there were only two men who had refused tracts, and only three who insulted them. With this success, small as it was, they were excited to go on, hoping the Lord was smiling upon their labors. The minister most successful among them had once been a canal boy himself, and while sitting upon his horse dragging the boat, employed himself for hours in inventing new and strange oaths to surprise his fellow boatmen. The men now readily listened to him. They were conscious of their degradation, knew they were despised by all good men, and never hoped to rise. Seeing now, one of their number so bright and shining a light, they trusted a boatman's name would not always be an object of scorn. These poor men complained to him, that they had no day of rest, as there was as much forwarding upon the Sabbath as upon any other day. The Captains of the lake boats were also obliged to struggle against this evil, and in some instances had renounced their trade upon that account, or upon remonstrance had been turned adrift for some less scrupulous Captain. The fault then seems to lie upon the forwarding merchants, whom Mr. Stillwell addressed, begging their forbearance in this respect.

It is to be hoped this address produced its intended effect, and the merchants who claim a day of repose for themselves, have granted the same to the unfortunate boatmen.*

June 29.—This morning we sent for a carriage and sat out to see the city and make some visits. Buffalo,

---

* I am glad to see Troy, who is ever forward in the cause of religion and morality, has abandoned this practice in some instances. There has been more success in the canal this year. Mr. Eaton, in his report, mentions 150 conversions. A small number among 25,000, but enough to cheer on the pious missionary.

although suffering with all our cities in the stagnation
of trade, seems to be doing a great deal of business.
The rows of shops, and handsome ware-houses, seem
to contain every article necessary for comfort or luxury. It is a larger city than Rochester, but has not
its air of elegance and neatness. The town was burnt
by their neighbors, the Canadians, in 1814, but has
since been rebuilt. The streets are wide and airy,
Maine street, the principal avenue, is more than a
mile in length. The churches are neat buildings, one
of them, a catholic, promises, when finished, to be
handsome. The court house is a solid well built edifice having pillars up to the roof. The markets are
very good also. The city is well situated upon ground
rising gently from the lake, the upper part being
covered with handsome private dwellings, which thus
obtain fine views of the lake and surrounding country,
and secure for themselves room for their gardens
which are very prettily laid out. There is here also
a military station for the United States troops, whose
barracks, comfortable brick buildings, are built around
the parade ground and surrounded by a good wall.
Our friend's cottage was upon elevated ground looking down upon the green Niagara river, and enjoying
a view of the lake in front, and behind an extent of
country covered with the untamed forest. It was the
first time I had seen a forest landscape, and I looked
with much interest upon this vast plain of green
leaves reaching to the distant horizon; a smoke curled
in one spot telling of some settler clearing his way
through the green wood. The handsomest private
dwellings here do not affect the Gothic or Greecian,
which had prevailed along our road, but were substan-

tial square stone or brick buildings, having a marble
portico in front, an cupola upon the top, surrounded
by a fancy railing.   Our drive around Buffalo was very
interesting, and we wondered, as we marked such a
mass of solid buildings, and depots of articles from
every region in the world, and such throngs of human
beings deposited in a wilderness, but a few years re-
deemed from the Indian, the buffalo, and the bear.
What industry, what energy, has been employed to
bring hither all these materials.   Buffalo is a frontier
town, and grand portal of the west, through which is
flowing a constant stream of travellers and emigrants.
This mixture of all nations in the streets, give them
an unique appearance.   Here you see the Indian
beau with his tunic bound with a crimson sash,
his hat surrounded by a circle of feathers ; his
deer skin pantaloons richly embroidered in barbaric
patterns, while ribbons and tassels swing out from
his dress at every step.   After him will pass a
band of United States soldiers ; then a rough back-
woodsman, upon a horse looking as wild as himself, its uncut mane and tail waving in the wind as he
gallops violently through the streets.   Then follows a
party of comical German emigrants ; a scarlet clad
British officer ; a Canadian ; a Frenchman ; a wild
looking son of Erin ; a sturdy ruddy, gaiter legged English farmer ; a Tonawanda squaw with her papoose
upon her back ; and lastly the dainty lady traveller
with her foreign abigal, and fantastically dressed children. Among the crowd I observed a curious figure—
a one legged negro, wearing an old uniform coat with
ruffled cuffs, ringing a bell most energetically.   The
old English custom of sending a bell-man to proclaim

the loss of any article, prevails here, as in some of
our other towns, I believe. 'What is lost, Sambo?'
inquired a person. 'Your wits, massa,' he replied
quickly, setting his juvenile train off in a fit of laughter. To another inquirer, he replied, 'My leg is lost,
don't you see' holding up the stump. He is, I suppose a privileged wit, who, if he cannot set the *table*,
no doubt does the *street* in a roar. The Buffalonians are a
gay social people. The unamiable fashion of exclu-
siveness being very little known here, for, living where
the population is continually changing and where
strangers are constantly claiming their hospitality,
they have acquired an easy *unsouciant* manner, and
are ever forming social meetings to entertain the
stranger. Our letters procured for us much kind attention, and we had an opportunity of witnessing this
free hospitable spirit. In the afternoon one of our
friends called, and we drove down where a fanciful
yacht awaited us, and a pleasant party of ladies and
gentlemen, for the purpose of taking us over to the
ruined fort opposite the city. This is a favorite pic-
nic haunt of the young citizens. Fort Erie is upon
the Canadian shore, opposite Buffalo, just at the point
where the Niagara river runs out of lake Erie. It
was destroyed during the war of 1812.

I have scarcely enjoyed any thing so much as that
sail over Lake Erie. The lake is here five or six
miles broad. The water rushes swiftly past, as if
eager to accomplish its glorious destiny of plunging
over the rocks of Niagara, there to be a spectacle
which nations come from afar to gaze upon. We
caught the excitement which seemed to animate the
water, as we were tossed upon its wavelets with

quick, gay, tilting motion; and gazed with much delight at the novel objects around us. The city, with its numerous domes and spires; the bright Niagara rushing and gurgling at a rapid rate over the ledge of rocks which once was Erie's barrier ere the waters burst their bounds—the gulls wheeling above us, or floating upon the waves; and above all, that immense lake, that mighty mass of sparkling emerald water, stretching far into the mysterious west. The air, breathing from the fresh forest and cool lake, was so refreshing that I was almost sorry when we reached the shore. Landing upon a sandy beach, we repaired to the fort, where under the shadow of a ruined wall, we seated ourselves upon the green sward, and while refreshing ourselves with the contents of our provision baskets, our discourse fell upon the hapless fate of those whose blood had dyed the fair turf around us; or upon other scenes which occurred during that border war. But now all this is over; conqueror and vanquished are both beneath the 'clod of the valley'; the echo of the war trump has died away; the green earth smiles again as peacefully as if it had never drank the blood of the dying, and wall, and bastion, are fast crumbling into their parent elements. The lake, the sky, the shore, are no longer vexed with sights and sounds of strife. Alas! whence come wars and fighting among us? Must these things always be? Must earth's children ever thus hack and tear each other? And we who are brethren, whose homes are in sight upon either shore of this bright lake, can we not dwell in unity? They who have opposite creeds, who differ in dress, in manner, in language, may and will rival, dislike, detest, fight and exterminate each

7

other; but we, who are sons of the same father, who speak the same tongue, Oh, must we be ever thus at enmity?

> * Though ages long have passed
> Since our fathers left their home;
> Their pilot in the blast
> O'er untravelled seas to roam,—
> Yet lives the blood of England in our veins!
>
> And still from either beach
> The voice of blood shall reach,
> More audible than speech,
>   "We are one!"

I have said this is a favorite place of resort, and here a party of gay young people came to avoid the noise of the city, and spend a quiet day with their books and work, upon the fourth of July. Their little feast was spread under the shade of the fortress, and they were in the act of drinking to the day, when they were suddenly taken captive by a band of English soldiers. It was at that unhappy time when Canada was disturbed by revolutionary projects, and it was naturally imagined they had come there purposely to insult them. It was an imprudent frolic, and they paid dearly for it; they were marched off three miles to a military station, where, after being fully examined and no signs of revolution being found upon them, they were suffered to depart and return as they best might. I relate the anecdote to show how easily we may mistake each other's motives, and how soon ill-blood may be brewed between those who are suspicious of each other, and ready to take offence.

While we were thus discoursing, the sky grew gradually dark, and a veil of blackness was let down

* America to Great Britain.—ALLSTON.

over the lake, giving token of a thunder shower. We
were soon in the boat which tossed very much, but
we had able young seamen who landed us safely just
as the sun, bursting forth, smiled at our idle fears. An
evening of social pleasure ended our agreeable day.

June 30*th.*—This morning we were again employed
in rambling about the city. The situation of Buffalo is
calculated to make it a great commercial mart. It is
upon the high road to the west, and will command
much of the business of the lakes, while the great
Erie canal connects it with the Atlantic. This canal
is indeed a 'herculean achievement.' It is three hundred and sixty-three miles in length, forty feet wide,
and four deep ; contains six hundred and eighty-eight
feet of locks; is crossed by several fine aqueducts ;
and all this was completed in eight years. There are
other canals connected with it. This great artery,
bringing up the produce of Europe to the west, through
this city, must increase its prosperity* and population.

At twelve o'clock this morning embarked in the
steamboat Constellation for Chicago, through lakes
Erie, St. Clair, Huron and Michigan, a distance of
twelve hundred miles, for which we are to pay twenty
dollars, ten each. The wharves as we left them presented a busy scene. We counted forty steamboats and
canal boats, beside several large vessels. Among the
latter was the Queen Charlotte, a stately ship of war

* Amount of flour and wheat which entered the canal from Lake Erie
at Buffalo :—

From Ohio,	505,262 barrels of flour ;	72,525 bushels of wheat.
Michigan,	112,215 " "	97,249 " "
Indiana,	13,726 " "	48,279 " "
Illinois,	2,259 " "	10,634 " "
Wisconsin,	1,166 " "	

belonging to Canada, but degraded to the ignoble fate of a Buffalo trader. She had, it is true, lost some of her original brightness ere thus fallen, for she had been twenty-three years under water, having been sunk in a naval fight on Lake Erie, and lately raised. The wharves were loaded with produce and merchandize, while carts, boats, and men, were loading and being unloaded.

We left Buffalo with regret. Its majestic river and noble lake—its back ground of forests, gay streets, and social people, have left a vivid and pleasing picture upon our memories. A fine pier, or breakwater as they call it, of solid mason work extends 1100 feet, protecting the wharves from the waves. A light house stands upon the end of the pier. When the city had completely faded into the distant horizon we turned our gaze on our companions. Upon one corner of the deck was a promiscuous heap of chairs, children, pots, kettles, men and women, being a family moving west. That old man with a cocked hat, and large metal buttons, the young man in a blue frock, and women with embroidered stomachers and indescribable caps, sitting upon a pile of strange looking articles of husbandry, and huge unwieldy chests, is a band of emigrants from central Europe. A party of English gentleman from Canada were there, bound upon a hunting expedition to Wisconsin—another of Buffalo young men, were going to while away the summer months in a fishing excursion upon Lake Superior, a long light skiff being part of their travelling luggage. There were also tourists for pleasure, information and health like ourselves, and some few going to inspect lands which they had bought unseen. Our

steamboat is a very fine one although not of the first
class. There is a handsome saloon for the ladies surrounded by a circle of state-rooms opening upon the
deck—below are the eating rooms and gentlemen's
cabin, the whole fitted up with comfort and elegance.
There are about 53 steamboats upon lake Erie, some
of them of six hundred tons, and fitted up with every
luxury and elegance, many costing from $15,000 to
$120,000 each. They are built upon a fine model,
and are well finished. The upholsterer's bill sometimes amounts to $4,000. They are generally built
very strong to resist the waves that run high here.
The complement of men for one of these boats
amounts to 40 ; the captain receiving $100 a month.
After an excellent dinner we ascended to the prome-
nade deck which, like our Hudson river boats is the
uppermost deck, surrounded with seats. We were
out upon lake Erie, and gazed around us with wonder
and delight. The water was a fine dark green, which
as the wind was high, was tossed in waves crested
with white foam, or sparkling spray. The shores
were in some places low and wooded, alternating with
gentle elevations, at whose foot ran a line of yellow
sand—a sky of purest azure dotted with fleecy clouds
was above. What a lovely scene—

"Where shall we find in foreign land
So lone a lake, so sweet a strand?"

asks Sir Walter. This lake however is rather larger
than his Scottish lake, it being 290 miles long. It has
the character of being the most tempestuous of all
the lakes, a fact we were soon able to verify, for in
the afternoon the wind increased to a gale, and the

7*

waves dashing against our vessel gave us each time a shock as if she had struck a rock.

The ladies soon began to feel the effects of such tossing, and one after another retired to their berths quite ill. Forty-five miles from Buffalo we stopped at the town of Dunkirk, which is the termination of the New York and Erie rail road. It commences at Hudson river 25 miles above the city of New York, a distance of 450 miles from its end. This town, under these circumstances, is rising rapidly. It has a fine circular bay having two projecting points which protect it, one and a half miles across—and is one of the best harbors upon the lake. There is also a pier within the shelter of which five large schooners were moored. We observed a rail road depot ready for the future engines and train—a church, tavern and a few stores. Several little boys came on board with pails of cherries for sale, which they disposed of at four cents a quart. Here we landed a passenger, an inhabitant of Dunkirk, who, during the voyage, had been vaunting the advantages of his town. The day would soon come, he said, when he should no longer resort to Buffalo for his goods, as the new rail road would bring all the trade to Dunkirk. Darkness drove us to our state room, which we found replete with every convenience—a circumstance much to our satisfaction as we were to spend a week in it ere we reached our destined haven. I would recommend you if you ever travel this way, to choose, as we did, a state cabin looking towards the shore, for these boats stop at every considerable town, and of course keep near the coast. In consequence of this arrangement, we could, if inclined, sit in our cabin, and through the open door, or

window, behold the scenery at our ease ; while those
upon the opposite side, gazed out upon an uniform
waste of waters without a shore. I thus obtained a
sight of the town of Erie where we stopped during
the night. Aroused by the noise, I looked from my
window and saw the town distinctly by clear starlight.
This town is in Pennsylvania, and is the termination
of the Pittsburg and Erie canal. In the canal basin,
beside canal boats, I saw a large steamboat and several schooners. Presque Isle defends the harbor. There
was a large hotel brightly illuminated, and some stage
coaches, awaiting the arrival of passengers. Erie
stands upon a high mass of Schistose rock surmounted
by a stratum of clay—the whole forty feet above the
lake.* There is said to be here a neat court house,
and several pretty houses surrounded by trees—the
streets are at right angles, and the trade considerable.
There was a bridge spanning the canal, which I
hoped was the one where the revered La Fayette was
feted. It was formed into a large tent by sails and
flags, which had waved in the battle upon the lake,
under which was a fine collation. Several ships of
war have been built here. You will surely give me
credit of being a first rate correspondent when I leave
my slumbers to collect items for your amusement and
edification.

July 1*st*.—Early this morning we found ourselves
off Conneaut, which we looked upon with interest as
belonging to the great state of Ohio. It is a small
place, at the mouth of Conneaut creek near the boundary line between Pennsylvania and Ohio—is a small

* Darby.

but flourishing place. The next town we passed was
Ashtabula, or rather its landing place, the town being
some miles in the interior. A wooden breakwater
defends the harbor. A river of the same harmonious
Indian designation empties itself into the lake sullying
its pure acqua-marine, with a dark brown tint which
could be distinctly seen a mile from the shore. The
day is lovely—our boat glides swiftly upon her course.
On one hand we have a line of green waving forest
coast, where the oak, the elm, the linden, and the maple, and stately yellow birch are standing in pretty
groups, or gracefully bending over the water—upon
the other we have a shoreless ocean. For miles there
are no signs of human existence, and then some little
village appears with its invariable accompaniment, a
pier, lighthouse and schooner. We passed Fairport,
at the mouth of Grand river, and from thence the
ground begins to rise, being a band of argillaceous
schist, which extends to Cleveland. This is a beautiful town standing upon this formation mixed with
sand and pebbles elevated sixty or seventy feet above
the lake of which it commands a fine prospect. It
was a pretty object in our view as we approached, its
steeples and buildings crowning the summit of the
picturesque cliff. We lay here some hours taking
merchandise, thus enjoying sufficient time to examine
it. The steamboat passed up, the Cuyahoga river
through two piers each 1200 feet in length. Upon
each side the ground arose from the river covered
with the buildings of two rival towns, Cleveland and
Ohio city. The business streets are upon the banks of
the Cuyahoga river, and the wharves were lined with
vessels, merchandise and native buckeyes, as the Ohio

people are called after their beautiful tree. Cleveland is built upon a plain; the streets running at right-angles, wide and airy with a pretty square in the centre. There are six churches, a neat court house, banks, public library, and many handsome dwelling houses. The population is 7,000 and several newspapers and periodicals are published here.* It is 170 miles from Buffalo. We had been a day and a half reaching it, on account of our frequent stoppages. This being the northern termination of the Ohio canal a great deal of business is done here. Their trade in flour and wheat is very great, they having exported nearly a million of barrels of flour in one season—cotton, tobacco and other southern merchandise has passed up from the Ohio river through the canal. This canal runs the whole length of the state of Ohio to Portsmouth upon the Ohio river a distance of 309 miles. It is forty feet wide, four deep, and has 152 locks.† The Cuyahoga river is sixty three miles in length, and running down over the sandstone ledges which abound in that region, it has a fall of 240 feet, affording a fine water power. From Buffalo to the borders of Michigan there is a band of alluvion upon the lake shore from three to twenty miles in width. This is bounded by a ridge of rocks 40 or 50 feet high once, according to Darby and Schoolcraft, the original boundary of the lake, thus giving another proof that these lakes were once higher than at present they are. This ridge is composed of micaceous limestone, and

* Smith's Western Tourist.

† Among the articles arrived at Cleveland from the Ohio Canal this year were—504,900 barrels of flour; 167,045 bushels of coal; 932 hhds. tobacco; 2,252,491 lbs., of iron and nails; besides numerous other articles of merchandise.

schistose rocks, covered with farms, and groves of beech and oak which attain to a large size. Yesterday afternoon while sailing upon the lake, we observed these hills making a pretty back ground to the towns on the shore—now it trends too much to the interior to be seen. In this ridge arise waters which flow each way, some into lake Erie, and others, as the Muskingum and Alleghany, into the valley of the Ohio. This last river, becoming the Ohio, falls into the gulf of Mexico 'upwards of twelve degrees of latitude from its source.' * Successive ledges or *steppes* of sandstone rock lead down to the lake, over which the rivers flow in rapids or falls, making the scenery in that region very beautiful. We took in at Cleveland several barrels of flour, and nails, and Selma salt, and boxes of merchandise,—landed several passengers, and then left this interesting town. It must, I imagine be a very delightful place of residence. The Cuyahoga could be distinctly traced some distance from the shore in a long dark line.

The swell in the lake still continuing, most of our passengers had become too ill to leave their berths. A horse which was at the other end of the vessel also became affected. Our German emigrants felt it least, as they had been seasoned by crossing the Atlantic. I saw them seated upon their packages, eating brown bread and cheese as merrily as ever. Their passage costs them little as they provide their own frugal fare, and sleep upon their goods on the deck. Several others pursued this economical plan. The emigrants from the German and Swiss nations are invaluable to us and ought to be warmly received, for in industry,

* Darby.

economy and patience, they set a very excellent example to our extravagant people. They always succeed; their settlements and farms present an admirable order and neatness, and yield a rich reward to their patient labor. The restless spirit, the excitement, caused by a hope of rising in the world, of seeing no one above him, which animates the American bosom, and many of our transplanted brethren, never agitates them. Where they plant themselves they remain, and in labor and social duties, pass the even tenor of their way. The motion, rendered it impossible to walk, or even stand unless supported, and instead of being unpleasant to me, I have seldom experienced sensations so novel and delightful. My companion being an old traveller felt no ill effects from it either. Leaning over the railing, we watched the vessel as she surmounted one huge wave to sink again as soon. The fresh western breeze, breathing perfume from the forest clad shores, exhilerated our spirits, and spread forth our star-spangled banner in a bright canopy over our heads. Two noble steamboats filled with passengers from the ' far west ' passed us with their banners flying, the bells of the three boats ringing out their friendly salutations to each other. They are gone— the white foam of their track alone remaining to show where so many human beings had just been wafted away. How glorious was that sunset on lake Erie ! Dark and stormy clouds had gradually gathered from every quarter, and now dropped down as a veil over the west concealing the sun from our view, and the lake is one vast gloomy abyss. But see— some fairy hand has touched the clouds with gold and purple and every gorgeous hue—the surface of the water is streaked with rose, and every wave is gilded. The towers of Cleveland now distinctly painted against the dark horizon, are glittering as if cut from jewelry. Our fears of storms are vanishing, when suddenly a black terrific cloud spotted with fiery blood color, appeared in front of us, as if the Indian Manitou had arisen from the lake to arrest our progress and forbid our farther entrance into his dominions. Larger and larger it grew, until the heavens were covered with inky blackness. A terrible blast lashed the lake into fury—the waves arose in their might as if to reject us from its bosom—our vessel careened fearfully upon one side, and confusion ensued. Men hurried forward to remove the merchandise to the other side and trim the vessel—women's heads were, from the cabin doors asking ' what's the matter ' and torrents of rain are surging over the deck. The awnings are buttoned down—all is proclaimed tight and right, and we retired to our state-room to listen to the wail of the wind, and write our promised journals.

LETTER VI.

Dear E.—Rocked by the tempest we slept soundly, but arose in time to witness a glorious sunrise scene upon lake Erie. We were in the centre of the lake—no land was visible on either side, save two lonely islands, one of which was just vanishing upon the distant horizon, while the other one was only a short distance from our vessel. Suddenly a dazzling radiance shot up from the east, and in a few moments the sun came rushing from out the water as if in eager haste to greet his favorite lake. A flood of glory lighted up the green depths of Erie; tinging the foam with a thousand prismatic hues, and tipping with gold the white plumage of the birds which were soaring over our heads. The dark alleys of beech, maple, and hickory which covered the island, and its pebbly shore covered with diamond spray, were illumined with the morning rays, receiving new beauty from every touch. We were stretching from Sandusky bay upon the Ohio shore to the Detroit river; many islands were passed, some of them quite large. Cuningham island contains 2,000 acres. They are of limestone rock covered with forest trees. Here was the scene of the famous naval battle upon lake Erie, and these peaceful glades once echoed with the cannon's roar. I regretted not seeing Sandusky, a large and pretty town, situated upon a river and bay of the same name. Here also is the mouth of the Maumee river, or the Miami of the lakes, northern termination of the great canal which commences at Cincinnati, and is connected with the canals of Indiana.

Land began to appear upon our western quarter, and soon the State of Michigan became visible. The mouth of Detroit river was soon after seen here, five miles wide from the Canadian shore to Michigan. At Amherstburg, a small Canadian town, we stopped about seven o'clock, for the purpose of taking in wood. The flashing of bayonets and the red uniform, as the sentinel walked up and down the wharf, told us we were in a land belonging to another nation. Fort Malden is passed soon after. Upon a platform, in front of the fortress, a file of soldiers were going through their exercises, their brilliant scarlet dresses and arms, prettily flashing back the morning sun. A boat, filled with red-coated soldiers, was passing over to an island to relieve the guard which stood upon a romantic point, near his little sentry box. A large ship came rapidly down the river, with all its sails out, looking like a huge bird of prey winging his flight to the shore, adding to the variety of the scene. Detroit is a beautiful river, connecting lakes St. Clair and Erie. Its width is generally about a mile—opposite Detroit city three-fourths of a mile. The shores are very beauti-

ful, cultivated upon each side, with several pretty
islands in the centre. Upon the Canadian side we
observed several French settlements, their windmills
upon every point giving a novel and unique effect to the
scene. We did not reach Detroit until ten o'clock,
although it is only 19 miles from the mouth of the river,
owing to our delay in taking in wood. The city appeared well, covering a plateau of ground elevated 40
feet above the river. Three steamboats were in sight as
we approached, one being a ferry boat to the town of
Sandwich, opposite. As we were to remain here some
time we landed and walked about the city. The city
stands upon a plain which commands an extensive view
of the river and surrounding country. A broad street
runs through the centre called Jefferson avenue, lined
on each side with shops and hotels. At the upper end
are several handsome dwellings surrounded with gardens. The churches are common in their appearance,
except the catholic, which I must say was uncommon.
It is a large building of unpainted wood, having two odd
looking steeples exactly alike, in the centre of the front;
at the back is a dome having on each side a belfrey. Ad-
joining this is the residence of the Bishop, a large
brick building. I was disappointed in the appearance
of this city. It was built by the French, you know,
in 1670, and being so much older than Rochester or
Buffalo, we naturally supposed it would be larger than
it is. But the same causes do not operate here which
influence the prosperity of the other cities. It has
not the old and settle state of New York behind it,
nor the great canal. Michigan, of which Detroit is
the capital, has been recently settled, and that only in
the southern parts. The fur trade was for years its

main dependence, and that has of late fallen off very much. As man invades the recesses of the forest, the animals retreat before him. Detroit has, however, felt the wind in her sails, and is rapidly following after her southern sisters. Of this, the increase of population is one proof—2,222 being their number in 1830, and 1839, 9,278. Several railroads are planned out, which, when the river and lakes are filled with ice, will be of much service. Of these, the Detroit and St. Joseph are the principal—leading from this city across the State to lake Michigan, a distance of 194 miles ; 33 miles are completed. Many persons take this route to Chicago, in preference to the more extensive one around the lakes. Besides these, there are in contemplation the Detroit and Pontiac ; Shelby and Detroit, &c. Michigan will soon fill up, as its population has increased since 1830, seven hundred per cent. ; then it was 28,600, and now, in 1840, they count 211,205. Detroit will then be the great depot of the lakes, and bids fair to rival the neighboring cities. Here we landed our German emigrants, who were bound to the rich plains of Michigan. Upon the wharf were men busily engaged packing white fish salted, with barrels, fifty of which we took on board. The white fish is a delicious fish, something the form of our shad, averaging from 4 to 10 lbs. and sometimes weigh 14 lbs. There is a great trade of this fish upon the lakes. 30,000 barrels were exported from Cleveland this season. While passing the city, when we had resumed our voyage, we observed several rows of handsome ware houses, many of which seemed as if newly erected. We also noticed a large brick building erected for the hydraulic works which supply the

city with water, it being in these lakes fit for cooking,
washing and drinking.   This city is the scene of one
of Pontiac exploits.   He was one of those brave and
haughty spirits who cannot accustom themselves to
the yoke of the white men.   Of these, a few have appeared in latter years; Black Hawk being the last.
The French he had become accustomed to, and suffered their presence in his realms, but when another
nation appeared he determined to root them out the
land.   They were at peace apparently, but a deceitful
peace, for Pontiac was organizing a confederacy
against the English, who then occupied Detroit.
'There was no sounding of the toscin, no alarm of
war given, no motion of the waves were felt,' to quote
the words of McKenney—'In this moment of still-
ness, a scout returned bringing the intelligence that a
large body of Indians were crossing lake St. Clair in
canoes, and coming in the direction of Detroit, while
numerous bands were appearing at every point.' Pontiac appeared in the neighborhood with 3,000 warriors,
who, in a friendly manner approached the fort, erected
their wigwarms, and commenced their Indian games,
to lull all suspicion.   That very band, unknown to the
English, had just returned from the bloody massacre
of Fort Michilimackinack, which they had surprised
in the manner they now intended.   Major Gladwin,
however, suspected them, and admitted only six Indians at a time in the fort. The wily Pontiac at length
succeeded in having a council held at the fort, and
was permitted to attend with thirty-six chiefs.   Their
rifles were cut short and hid under their robes, with
which they were to shoot down the officers and seize
the fort.   Were it not for the fidelity of a squaw to

her master in the fort, the plan would have succeeded
As it was, they suffered severely from famine, and
many were cut off who came to reinforce them, before
the Indians finally retreated. Ten miles from Detroit
the river gradually expands into lake St. Clair. A pretty
lake—a most sweet lake—appearing small among its
larger sisters, and yet it is 90 miles in circumference.
The waters are cool and transparent, fringed with the
graceful ash, the linden, 'tasseled gentle,' the beech,
and the stately liorio dendron, and many other varieties. We felt reluctant to enter and ruffle the glassy
surface, and disturb the profound repose which reigned
around. The shores are low and there are no houses
in sight. A wood cutter's hut, and at its extremity, a
light-house, were the only signs of life we saw. The
trees were throwing their flickering shadows upon the
placid water, or leaning over, as if to admire their own
reflection so perfectly painted upon the mirrored surface,—

> In which the massy forest grew,
>   As if in upper air;
> More perfect both in shape and hue,
>   Than any waving there.

If you do not choose to emigrate to any of those
charming spots I have mentioned along the road; if Auburn, or Rochester, or Cleveland do not lure you, perhaps yon would like to come to the picturesque shores
of St. Clair, and weave you a bower ' in some sweet
solitary nook' under those trees of ' ancient beauty ;' or
erect a picturesque hermitage with a pet skull, and
moralize and spiritualize your hours away. I have
heard many declare they could better worship their
Creator in the fields and woods than in temples made

with hands, and can 'look from nature up to nature's God.' I fear such are greatly deceived in the nature of their feelings, and many a lonely anchorite has thus mistaken adoration of the beauties of creation for worship of its Creator. His heart may be filled with the most elevated emotions while contemplating the glory and grandeur of God's works, and he may be subdued to tears of tenderness while reflecting upon that kindness and mercy which has adorned the residence of man with such exquisite loveliness; but will that regenerate his heart? will it give him a knowledge of his Savior; shew him the mysteries of faith and redemption, and subject his will to that of Christ? If so, let him live upon a mountain top, and gaze at will; but I much fear these sentiments are but the 'semblance of sacredness.'

The shores of St. Clair, being low, display the rise which has taken place in these northern lakes. That there is a rise and fall in this singular mass of fresh water has been observed for many years; and many opinions have been hazarded as to its cause. Some of the Indians declare there is a regular rise and fall every seven years; while the scientific traveller, Darby, tells us there is a rise once in fifty years. A person, upon whose knowledge we could rely, told us at Buffalo, one year, while he resided upon the banks of the St. Lawrence, the current ran out of lake Ontario at the rate of ten miles, and the next year the lake had unaccountably risen, and ran thirteen miles an hour. It must have been one of those extraordinary floods, of course much higher, which caused the lakes to overflow, as I have mentioned above—that is, if it were not a diluvial torrent. The captain of our steamboat, who had navigated these lakes for several years, a man of intelligence and integrity, agreed with the Indians in the belief of a gradual rise and fall in seven years. During these last two years the water has risen to the height of five or six feet. Our captain pointed to many spots, upon the shore, where the water had overflowed the land. Upon one pretty place a farm house had been abandoned, and a fine apple orchard, standing two years in the water, had been destroyed; and now, while all around was green, their limbs were bare and leafless. A very intelligent man, a settler upon the river St. Clair, pointed to several noble maple and beech trees, as we passed the Michigan shore, whose gradual decay he had watched, while making his spring and fall trips in order to purchase goods in New York. It was pitiable, he said, to behold such goodly trees, 'green robed senators of ancient woods,' sinking beneath the subtle destroyer, as some. noble heart withering away at the touch of affliction! He watched them with an interest he would a friend consuming under a slow decay—their glorious beauty dimmed and faded, until a lifeless skeleton alone remained.

> " a huge oak dry and dead,
> Still clad with relics of its trophies old,
> Lifting to heaven its aged hoary head,
> Whose foot on earth hath got but feeble hold."

This man's history interested us much, and I will relate it for your edification. He was a native of our city of New York, one of a large family straightened for means. While quite young he had married, and struggled for years to support his family respectably, but sickness and 'bad times' rendered his lot a gloomy one. Hearing so often of the happiness and prosperity of 'the west,' he resolved to remove thither, and accordingly bought a tract of land upon St. Clair river, then farther west than it now is. He came here twenty years since, with a wife and several young children, and a mere trifle in money. A little village has now risen around him, of which he is the owner. He has built a good tavern for travellers, which he rents out; has erected a saw-mill; a few shops and houses, and a little church. His children are married and settled around him; and he is, as he expressed himself, 'independent of the world.' Once a year he goes to New York or Buffalo, to purchase goods for his shop. How much better is this state of things than to remain, struggling for a morsel, among the hungry crowd of a large city. I asked him if he never repented renouncing a city life. 'No, indeed!' he answered—'I go there once or twice a year to transact business, but hurry away, for I feel as if in prison. I want elbow room, and never breathe free until threading my green lakes and vast forests again. I am glad to leave such fictitious existence, where each man models his conduct upon that of his neighbor, and dare not act as his spirit prompts him.' We had passed into St. Clair river, and about sun-down dropped this man and his goods at his little village, which was seated upon a green slope, cut out of the forest, upon the Michigan shore. The houses were surrounded by little gardens and seemed comfortable. The sign of the village inn was swinging in the summer breeze; a traveller had just alighted from his horse in front of the piazza, and the steam from his mill was rising high above the trees tinted purple in the evening light. From a shop door a young man, probably his son, accompanied by a neighbor, stepped forth to greet him; while, from the honeysuckle-covered porch of a neat cottage a woman, whom I fancied his wife, was looking eagerly out to watch his approach. Every thing denoted industry, cheerfulness, and independence.

Soon after leaving the village of Clay, we observed a ship at anchor near the shore, quite a picturesque object. It proved to be the Milwaukie, a ship of three hundred tons burthen, bound from Buffalo to Chicago. It was waiting for wind, or steam, to enable it to enter lake Huron, as this lake pours into the river St. Clair with so strong a current, that vessels can seldom stem it without a strong wind. She was soon attached to our steamboat, and we both passed swiftly along. What a superb western sky! The sun has long left us, and yet we scarcely miss its light, so golden and so brilliant is the mantle he has left behind him. It is nearly nine o'clock, and yet I can see to write this; but fatigue drives me to my cabin, and forces me to say adieu until to-morrow.

July 3*d.*—Still in the river St. Clair. We stopped some hours in the night at Newport, to take in a supply of wood. The captain purchased eighty cords at $1,50 a cord. He told us it was his opinion the steamboats upon these waters would soon be obliged to burn coal, although surrounded by such a world of trees, as there is so much time wasted in stopping for it. I did not regret our detention, as I was anxious to lose no part of a scenery to me so novel and pleasing. This is a beautiful river about sixty miles long, and half a mile broad, having several little towns upon it.

Cotrelville and Palmer we had also passed in the night ; the latter a thriving place, from which a rail road is contemplated to Romeo, twenty-six miles, there to meet the Shelby and Detroit rail road. A communication will thus be continued with Detroit through the winter. The country upon the Canadian shore is wild and uninhabited, while the Michigan side of the river is frequently adorned with fields of grass or wheat, or thrifty orchards. The houses are plain, but seemed surrounded by every comfort. Our course ran quite near this shore, so close, that I might fancy myself transported into the midst of a farm yard, with all its morning business going on. A pretty white wood house is before me now, surrounded by fields and barns, having a row of cherry trees in front whose fruit is glistening red in the morning sun. In the barn yard a man is chopping wood, to cook the breakfast, I suppose—another is busy hoeing in a potatoe field—a boy is leading a horse down to the river for water, while numerous other children are arrested in their play and stand open mouthed gazing at us—ducks are dabbling in the wavelets—pigs are rooting up the turf—a flock of geese are running down the bank at us with beaks and wings extended in a warlike attitude—while a sober cow chews her cud under a large hickory nut tree. The next moment all is gone, to give place to the silent groves of oak, maple and ash. Upon a long narrow island near the Canadian shore, my eyes were attracted by what seemed a row of haystacks. I enquired the meaning, and was told I was looking upon an Indian village, and these were wigwams. I was delighted to behold a veritable Indian lodge, and to see *real* Indians, instead of those half

civilized beings I had met at Niagara. They are a
body of Chippeway Indians who reside upon Warpole
Island under the care of a Missionary of the Methodist
church. Their wigwams consisted of poles meeting
at top, around which, coarse matting, formed of reeds
is fastened. From the apex of these cones smoke
was rising, telling of culinary operations going on
within. Around each lodge was a small patch of potatoes or corn. A small church, with the missionary
cottage and a few log cabins, were in the midst.
Groups of Indians were lounging upon the bank gazing
at us, while others unconcernedly pursued their usual
occupations of fishing or hoeing. How much more
graceful were those wild sons of the forest, than the
civilized men I had observed upon the shores I had
passed. Their mantles of cloth or blanket stuff, trimmed with gay colors, were gracefully thrown around
them, and their ornamented leggins or moccasins
glittered as they walked. How dignified is the tread
of an Indian! we remarked as we passed the island,
many in various occupations and attitudes, yet they
never moved awkwardly, nor sprang, nor jumped in a
clumsy manner. The missionary cottage was an object of great interest to us. I had often read of these
self-denying disciples of Jesus, but never before looked
upon the scene of their labors. Here in this lonely
shore, away from all they love—their friends and
home—and almost shut out from the face of civilized
man, they spend their days in laboring to ameliorate
the lot of these unhappy children of the forest. In
bringing them to the feet of their master, they are
indeed conferring a blessing upon them past all return. As a recompense for the bright land their

fathers have taken from the bereaved Indian, they are leading them to another, brighter and more lasting. There is no change, nor shadow of turning—there, no enemy can destroy their homes—there, the tears are wiped from their eyes, and all their sorrows soothed. Noble missionary, who can appreciate thy sacrifice? None but those who have come from a civilized land, where thou hast passed thy early days, and who now sees thee among the endless forests with no associates save those wretched savages, can understand the greatness of thy disinterestedness. During the short summer, a residence may be tolerable, but when the rivers and lakes are choked up by ice, the short glimpse he has obtained of his fellow man, while whirled past in a steamboat, will be denied him. The roar of the winter wind will shake his cottage, and the wolf will scare him from his slumbers. But what are earthly joys or sorrows to a child of Christ? His meat and drink is to do the will of him that sent him, and in return for the comforts and pleasures of civilized life, he receives a peace ' the world cannot give'—a joy, David in all the glory of his kingly life sighed for, when he prayed ' Give me the joy of thy salvation.' A small settlement is formed at the mouth of Black river, called Port Huron, which is to be the termination of another canal across the state.

Here we found another vessel waiting for wind. It was the brig Rocky Mountain, bound to Green Bay, being attached to our other side we passed ' doubly armed.' Near the point where the river leaves lake Huron stands fort Gratiot, an United States military station whose white walls and buildings, over which the

9

American flag was waving, looked out brightly from among the dark forest of the Michigan shore. A line of blue coats were going through their morning drill; and a few cannons looked out fiercely upon us. A small white Gothic church, and a cottage stood near; the whole making a pretty cabinet picture. The river now narrowed to a quarter of a mile, upon each side a point—the American side crowned by a light-house, and the Canadian by a cluster of Indian cabins. A bark canoe, paddled by five Indians, pushed off the shore and came after us with the greatest rapidity, their long black hair flying wildly behind them. Our two vessels retarded our motion a little, so that the Indians overtook us, and kept at our side for some distance. They used their paddles with astonishing quickness, and we were surprised to see them in their 'light canoe,' keep pace with our large steamboat. It was however for a short distance only—they were soon fatigued with such great exertion, and turned towards the point, and sprang out, or rather stepped out with the greatest dignity, drew the canoe to the shore, and then *squatted* down upon the bank evidently enjoying their race. I use the above inelegant word, as being very expressive of their posture. The Indian never sits down as we do—with his feet close beside each other, and his body erect, he sinks slowly down—his blanket is then thrown over his head and around his feet, so that nothing is seen except his dark glaring eyes. Through the narrow pass before mentioned, between the two points, the waters of Huron run with a swift current. Here we were furnished with another evidence of the rise of these waters.

An officer of the army and his wife were our fellow

voyagers, very intelligent and agreeable persons. They had been stationed at fort Gratiot a few years since, and had frequently roved over the beach around the light-house in search of the pretty silecious pebbles, agate, camelian, and calcedony, which are often found upon these shores. To their surprise, they now found their favorite point, 'curtailed of its fair proportions' by a rise of nearly five feet of water. Our steamboat and its two 'tenders,' passed between the points out of St Clair river, and we found ourselves at once in a large and shoreless lake, with nothing in front, between us and the bright blue sky, which touched the green waters in the far horizon beyond. The transition is so sudden from the narrow opening, to the boundless lake as to produce a grand and exciting effect. Once out upon the calm waters of Huron, our two guests were loosened from their tackles, and spreading their huge wings, they passed one to each shore, and we soon left them far behind. About an hour after the bell of our steamboat startled the still lake with its clamors, denoting the approach of some vessel. We looked out in time to see the noble steamboat Great Western rush past us as if upon the wings of a whirlwind. She was on her way from Chicago to Buffalo. Her bell answered ours, and the deck was crowded with passengers. One of these standing alone by himself, and taking his hat off attracted our notice and we discovered in him an old acquaintance from New York. These meetings in a distant land are very interesting, carrying our feelings at once to the home we had left. This steamboat is one of the largest upon the lakes, is finished in a style of great elegance, and is said to be as long as the English steamship of the same name.

This whole day since ten o'clock—we have been passing through Huron under a cloudless sky. The lake is two hundred and fifty-five miles long, and its waters are of a deeper tint than those we have passed, owing to its great depth, as we are sailing over nine hundred feet of water, while in some places it is said to be unfathomable. The color is a dark olive almost black, and it is only when the sun shines through the waves that we can perceive they are green. The cause of the various colors of water has produced many a hypothesis. Sir Humphry Davy tells us the primitive color of water is like the sky, a delicate azure. * He says 'the finest water is that which falls from the atmosphere—this we can rarely obtain in its pure state, as all artificial contact gives more or less of contamination; but, in *snow melted by the sunbeams* that has fallen upon glaciers, themselves formed from frozen snow, may be regarded as in its state of greatest purity. Congelation expels both salt and air from water whether existing below, or formed in the atmosphere; and in the high and uninhabited region of glaciers, there can scarcely be any substances to contaminate. Removed from animal and vegetable life, they are even above the mineral kingdom.' Water from melted snow, then considered as the purest, Sir Humphrey goes on to describe its color. 'When a mass is seen through, it is a bright blue, and according to its greater or less depth of substance, it has more or less of this color.' 'In general when examining lakes and masses of water in high mountains, their

* Salmonia.

color is the same bright azure. Capt. Parry states
that water in the Polar ice has the like beautiful tint.'
The brown, green, and other colors of rivers he imputes to substances over which they flow, as peat
bogs, vegetable and mineral substances. He allows
the sea cannot be colored from any thing upon the
bottom, but imputes the tint to the infusion of iodine,
and brome which he has detected in sea water, the
result of decayed marine vegetables. Of this primitive water are our lakes formed, originating as they
do in regions of snow and ice. Lake Superior, from
whence they flow, is a vast basin of trap rock, of volcanic origin. *   It is the most magnificent body of
water in the world, five hundred miles long, and nine
hundred deep, and perfectly pellucid. Into this pure,
and originally, azure primitive water, there flow forty
rivers, upon the south side alone, according to Mr.
McKenney of the Indian department, who counted
this number from St Mary's to the river St Louis.
These rivers he tells us are all *amber colored*. Why
then may not these yellow rivers flowing into blue
water, produce *green*. You see I like to hazard a
hypothesis as well as others. I hope you will not call
this absurd. Col. McKenney himself, imputes the
green color to reflection of the 'rays of light passing through the foliage of the shores, conveying their
own green hue unto the surface of the water from
which they are reflected.' This might be the case in
small rivers or lakes, but it cannot thus tint such a
vast extent of water. A writer in the American Journal of Science, is of opinion the color of water is
reflected from the sky, and is blue, dull, black, or

* Schoolcraft.
9*

golden, as the sky may be—and that 'green is produced in water, by the yellow light of the sun mixed
with the cerulean blue through which it shines.'   On
the contrary the Count Xavier de Maistre, * does not
impute the color of water to any infused substance,
nor to reflection from above, but reflection from the
surface below, 'as the blue color of the sky is owing
to reflection from the earth beneath.' 'Limpid waters,
when they have sufficient depth,' says the Count,
reflect like air, a blue color from below,—and this
arises from a mixture of air, which water always contains to a greater or lesser amount.   This blue color,
being the primitive hue of water is sometimes clouded
or lost by earthy infusion, or reflections from a colored
sky.   The green tinge which he sometimes observed
in water, he tells us, is occasioned by reflection from
a *white* surface below.   This he proves by his experi-
ment of a sheet of tin painted white let down beneath
the water—and his description of the water in the
beautiful limestone grotto, on the shore of the Medite-
ranian at Capri.   The green tint observed in the
ocean is only seen when it is so shallow, as to reflect
the sun's rays from the earth beneath it.

As the States surrounding these lakes are more or
less underlaid by limestone, we may suppose the bottoms of the waters are in some places paved with it;
and from this, or the shores under the water and
around it, may be reflected, according to the Count's
theory, the light which gives the water a green appearance. But I will not trouble you with any more specu-
lations; they come with an ill grace from me who

* Biblistheque Universelle, translated by J. Griscom, in the American
Journal of Science.

only pretend to describe all that passes before my
eyes.

In the afternoon we were off Saginaw bay, an inden-
tation in the coast of Michigan running seventy or
eighty miles deep and forty wide, making the lake
here very broad; in one spot we were out of sight of
the land.   A river of the same name flows into the
bay, upon which, about twenty-three miles from its
mouth, is a small town.   A canal is proposed from
this bay, across the state to lake Michigan, at Grand
or Washtenog river.   How shall I convey to you an
idea of the loveliness which sat upon earth, air, and
water this afternoon! Certainly that sunset upon lake
Huron is the most beautiful I have ever beheld.   The
vast and fathomless lake, bounded by the heavens
alone, presented an immense circle, 'calm as a molten
looking-glass,'—to quote from my favorite Job—surrounded by a band of fleecy clouds, making a frame
work of chased silver.   Slowly and gracefully sank
the orb, the white clouds gently dispersing at his
approach, and leaving their monarch a free and glorious path.   As he drew near that chrystal floor, all
brilliancy faded from the face of the lake, save one
bright pathway from the sun to us—like the bridge of
Giamschid leading from earth to heaven.   The sun
which I had always been accustomed to see above,
was now below me, near the water, on the water,
under the water! A veil of purple is thrown over it,
and now the sun sleeps on lake Huron.   The gold
and rose which painted the western sky have gone.
Darkness has stolen over the world below, and we
turn our eyes above.   What a high and noble dome
of loveliest blue! Upon one side there hangs a cres-

cent of the purest pearly white, while at its side steals
forth one silver star, soon followed, as, saith Ezekiel,
by 'all the bright lights of heaven,' until night's star-
embroidered drapery is canopied around us.   What
bosom is insensible to this gorgeous firmament?   Who
hath not felt the 'sweet influence of the Pleiades'
while gazing at this starry roof above?   I wish I could
make you a piece of poetry upon this subject, but as
there is enough already composed upon the stars, 1
will send you a bit of Byron and tell you—

> Blue roll the waters—blue the sky
> Spreads like an ocean hung on high,
> Bespangled with those isles of light,
> So wildly spiritually bright,
> Whoever gazed upon them shining,
> And turned to earth without repining.

Do you remember that little hymn our old nurse used
to teach us in our childhood:

> Twinkle, twinkle, pretty star
> Can't you tell us what you are,
> Up above the world so high
> Like a diamond in the sky.

Yes, from childhood to manhood, we wish to penetrate into the mysteries of those golden regions, and
ever ask them to tell us 'what you are.'   We see
them gem the night with their lustrous beauty; we
watch them as they pace their azure courts, and lose
ourselves in high imaginings, too vast for us, while
earth still keeps our souls its prisoner.   How much
deeper must be the interest with which the astrologer
of old followed them in their 'golden tracks.'   In
them he read his destiny, and thought to see the
scenes of earth reflected in their light.   How must
he have gazed upon them, as their rays paled or
brightened, while reading in them ' the fate of man and

empires.' Man's efforts to penetrate the mysteries of these glorious creations have not been all in vain. The Almighty architect, from time to time, graciously bestows upon him, knowledge of 'parts of his ways.' How much more has been vouchsafed to us than to the early nations. Looking back through the vista of the past, we shall see great men appear, as 'stars to rule the night' of our darkness and tell us of creation's mysteries. Solomon, Ptolemy, Gallileo, Copernicus, Tycho Brahe, Paschal, Newton, Herschel, with a host of satellites, have been graciously shown the book of knowledge, to light man's pathway through the earth, and enlarge his ideas of the magnificence and the benevolence of his Creator. 'In the beginning,' it did not enter into God's purpose to tell mankind more of the starry host, than that they were 'lights to rule the night,' and for 'signs and for seasons;' now see what amazing things have been shown to us. We know they are worlds like our own, filled with mountains and seas; having night and day, summer and winter. We see their fields, now white with snow, now dark with returning vegetation. How our hearts bound with hopes of future knowledge; and imagine the time will come, when we can gaze upon their landscapes, and 'listen to the hum of their mighty population.'* We have seen nature in all its power and grandeur, while tossed on Erie's waves, or listening to the thunder of Niagara; but here she is at rest in all her quiet loveliness; and would her worshippers behold her in her fairest mood, let them come and gaze at evening on lake Huron.

* Chalmers.

July 4th.—The sun and I arose at the same time.
When I left my state-room, as if waiting to greet me,
it arose majestically from the bosom of the water,
flooding the lake with light.   No land was descried
upon the east, but we were near the Michigan shore
off Thunder bay.   The Shanewaging islands which
stretch across it were distinctly visible, and presented
various beauties of shape and tint.   All trace of man
has now disappeared, for the northern part of Michigan has never been settled owing to the intense cold
of the winters.   We have passed a long line of coast
without any inhabitant (except a forlorn woodman's
hut in one spot) stretching for two hundred and fifty
miles, covered with boundless forests, in whose green
recesses there are paths ' which no fowl knoweth,
and which the vultures eye hath not seen.'   Here is
the home of the bear, the elk, and the moose-deer—
and upon the aspen, oak, and maple trees, sport the blue
bird the robin, and yellow hammer, undisturbed by
the foot of man.   We have now past the bounds of
civilization, and our vessel is the only spot of life in
this vast region of forest and water.

From the entrance of Lake Huron to Mackinac,
there were but two places where man was visible.   At
the mouth of the Zappa river soon after entering the
lake, there is a cabin where a woodman resides in the
summer season to supply the steamboats; and at
Presque Isle where we stopped in the afternoon there
is another cluster of cabins, and woodpiles.   Our
Captain did not stop at this latter place, as he did not
like their wood, it being chiefly swamp ash.   The
shore is low, covered with trees, having below, a beach
of yellow sand, until just before coming in sight of

Michilimackinac when the land becomes a little elevated. Ten miles this side of the last mentioned place, we passed Boisblanc, a large wooded island, taking its name of ' *white wood*' from the silver barked birch tree. This island belongs to government, and its only inhabitants, save a few straggling Ottowas are the family of the light-house keeper whose pretty tenement, and stately light-house, appear upon a projecting point. There is also a farm upon the island given by government to the Missionaries of Michilemackinac, who sometimes maintain a farmer upon it. O Mackinaw, thou lonely island, how shall I describe thy various beauties! certainly for situation, history, and native loveliness, it is the most interesting island in our States. We approach it through an avenue of islands, Drummond and Manitoulin, dimly seen on our east, and Boisblanc, and Round, in our western side. Stretching across our path, far away in front of us, is Mackinaw, painted against the clear blue sky. The island of Michilimackinac, or Mackinaw, or Mackinac as it is commonly spelt and pronounced, is a high and bold bluff of limestone about three hundred feet above the water, covered with verdure. Its name signifies in the Indian tongue great turtle, as it is something of the figure of this animal. At the foot of the bluff are strewed the buildings of the town. Among the most conspicuous of these are, the agency house and gardens, residence of Mr. Schoolcraft, Indian Agent—and the church and mission house. Along the beach were several Indian wigwams, while numerous pretty bark canoes were going and coming, as this is the Indian stopping place. A very beautiful, and conspicuous object was the United States fort, presenting at a distance

the appearance of a long white line of buildings inserted,
into the top of the island high above the town. As
we approached, its picturesque block-houses and
the pretty balconied residences of the officers, came
out to view, having the banner of the 'stripes and
stars' waving over them. While gazing at this fair
picture, suddenly a brilliant flame, and volumes of
white smoke arose above the fort, while a booming
sound told us they were firing their mid-day salute in
honor of the day. This added much to the beauty
and grandeur of the scene. As our boat was to
remain there for some hours, we disembarked and
ascended to the fort to visit our friends the commanding officer and his family. We found them sitting
upon their balcony, looking down upon the newly
arrived steamboat. After the first greetings and mutual enquiries were over, we were shown all it was
thought would interest us.

The view from our friend's balcony was beautiful in
the extreme. The bay in front, the lovely islands around
covered with a luxurious vegetation—the town spread
out at our feet—the Indian lodges, and the canoes
skimming the bright waters, each called forth our expressions of admiration. Passing into the interior
of the fort, and through the fine parade ground and a
large gateway, we found ourselves upon the summit
of the island. Our path lay through copses of white
birch, maple, and various other trees, and over green
sward covered with strawberries and a variety of wild
flowers. Our friends kindly gathered for me a variety
of these, among which was a fine scarlet lilium super-
bum, blue bells, and kinni kanic, or Indian tobacco,
and a pretty plant called Indian strawberry. Suddenly

the silver tones of woman's voice, sounded near, and
in a fairy dell we came upon a tent, surrounded by a
party of ladies and gentlemen, busily engaged preparing for a fete in honor of the day.   Among them was
the daughter of our host, and some of the celebrated
family of S——t.   We were presented to the party,
and were quite chagrined our limited time would not
permit us to accept their invitation to remain and par-
take of their festivities.   The grace and beauty of
Mrs. S——t made great impression upon us.   To me
she was peculiarly interesting from the fact of her
being descended from the native lords of the forest;
for you know I have always taken the greatest interest in the fate of our Indian tribes.   From the accent,
the deep brunette of her smooth skin, and her dark
hair and eyes, I should have taken her for a Spanish
lady.   From the tent we wound our way up to a high
peak of the island.   When near the summit, we left
a grove, and saw before us one of the most picturesque
and singular objects imaginable.   It was a high arched
rock of white limestone, stretching across a chasm
before us, making a pretty natural bridge, through
which we gazed far down into the waves of Huron, at
least two hundred feet below.   The surprise, the
beauty and novelty of this striking object, brought
forth expressions of admiration from us.   The white
arch was adorned with tufts of wild flowers, and shrubbery.   Ascending the arch, we gazed down upon the
white beach below, whose pebbles could be here distinctly seen under the limpid water although many
feet deep—and out upon the fair waters, and the pretty
islands, which

> "——Like rich and various gems inlay
> The unadorned bosom of the deep."

10

We were obliged to be satisfied with a hasty view of this charming scene, as our time was limited; and we turned reluctantly towards our boat, without visiting the ruins of fort Holmes, upon the high summit of the island. While passing through the town we observed several antique houses which had been erected by the French, who first settled this place in sixteen hundred and seventy three.

These are frail delapidated buildings, covered with roofs of bark. Upon the beach a party of Indians had just landed, and we stood while they took down their blanket sail, and hauled their birch bark canoe about twenty feet long, upon the shore. These are the Menominies or wild rice eaters, the ugliest Indians I had ever seen—also Winebagoes, with dark skin, low foreheads and shaggy hair, and having no pretentions to dress. I saw a chief however afterwards who was gaily bedizened with tinsel, beads, and paint, having one side of his face a light pea green, and the other cheek scarlet. We watched them erect their lodges which was done very soon—a few poles were placed in a circle, one end of each stood in the earth, while the others met at the top—coarse matting was folded around these, leaving an opening for a door, over which a blanket was hung. Some matting being spread upon the floor inside, the children and moveables were placed inside, and the canoe drawn up near it. We visited some of the shops and laid up a store of Indian articles, which are made by these poor people and sold here. Among them were small baskets called Mococks, made of birch bark embroidered with porcupine quills, stained different colors—this was filled with maple sugar. It is pleasant to meet friends so far from home, but I think the pleasure is almost counterbalanced by the pain of parting. This we felt keenly, when the planks had withdrawn, and our friends had been forced to leave us, as we gazed after them winding their way up to the fort, the shores, and waters around seemed more desolate, more lonely than before.

Just before the steamboat started we had an opportunity of judging of the boasted transparency of this water, its depth having prevented this on our voyage. I looked down into it from the boat, where it was twenty feet deep, and could scarcely believe there was anything but air between us and those shining pebbles below. We had also an opportunity of hearing some Indian music. Upon the shore sat a group of unearthly beings, one of whom struck several taps upon a sort of drum, accompanied by the others, in what sounded like a wolf recitative—at the end of this all united in a yell which dyed away over the lake, much in the style of a howling blast accompanied by the shrieks of a drowning traveller. Our fishing party left us here to go up the Sault St Mary, into lake Superior, spending their summer days among the picturesque scenery of that magnificent lake. We bade adieu with much regret to this pretty island, whose green terraces, fort and picturesque town, Indian lodges, and light canoes, made a beautiful scene—but the most interesting point in the view, was that white handkerchief waving farewell from the fortress balcony.

This island is 615 miles from Buffalo ; 319 from Detroit. There are water marks upon the rocks 200 feet above the lake, proving the water had once

stood so high. The scenery here has been prettily
described by an author of talent, Mrs. Jameson ; but,
as much pleased as I was with her book, I must regret
she came here under such circumstances. It is with
reluctance I censure one so gifted, but it is with a
view of warning you, and my young friends to whom
I know you will show my letters, against errors to
which the very witchery of her genius would blind
you. However passionate a desire you may entertain
for the picturesque, I hope you may never leave the
protection of your friends and wander in search of it
alone. May your curiosity to see great men never
lead you to invade the retreat of a world hating bache-
lor ; and may you never stray in wild forests, through
storms and tempests, with no companion save a rude
Indian, or a 'bronzed, brawney, unshaven, back-woods-
man,' 'very much like a bear upon his hind legs,'
and you 'a poor, lonely, shivering woman.' I quote
her words. You had better be a 'tarry at home traveller,' or write ' voyages around my own room.' If
you do thus, you must expect the ladies where you
visit will look ' formal and alarmed,' as she tells us the
ladies of Toronto looked upon her. But now I have
done scolding and will pursue my journey. Upon a
green slope of the Michigan shore, a pile of ruins
were pointed out as the site of old fort Mackinac, which
was taken by Pontiac with a stratagem and afterwards
every one within were massacred. How must those
unfortunates have felt, upon this desolate shore, hundreds of miles away from their country, and at the
mercy of savages. A band of Chippewa's or Ojibwa's
were just passing in canoes thirty feet in length.
This tribe stands higher in rank than the others,

and their language, like the French, is the polite
tongue among the Indian tribes. They have a ruler
whose office has been hereditary for ages. He is called Mudjikiwis, and they pride themselves much upon
his and their own rank and lineage. There is an anecdote, related by Schoolcraft, of one of this tribe,
which, if you have never seen, will amuse you. Chi
Waishki, alias the Buffalo, was presented by the commissioners of the treaty of Fond du Lac, with a me-
dal as a badge of distinction. 'What need have I of
this?' he said haughtily. 'It is known whence I am
descended!' These canoes are the prettiest and
lightest things imaginable. They are formed of the
bark of the birch tree, sewn together with a thread
made from fine roots of cedar split. The bark is
soaked to make it more pliable. Sometimes they are
very gaily painted and ornamented. The paddles are
of light wood. Our Captain placed before us at dinner a very fine lake trout, which he had purchased at
Mackinaw. It was two feet long, and very delicious.
Fine salmon are also taken in these lakes. We were
now upon the great lake Michigan, which stretches
from here three hundred and twenty miles, to the
Illinois shore, and is nine hundred feet deep. Our
course lay near the Michigan shore, which presented
high bluffs and points of limestone, with banks of
pebbles, and high jagged hills, or *dunes* of sand.
These pebbles and sand are said to be thrown up by
the north-western winds, but I should rather imagine
them left up by the floods which have swept over the
land. Upon our right were Fox and Beaver isles, beyond which, Green bay runs into Wisconsin, one hundred and three miles. This northern shore of Michi-
10*

gan is uninhabited, and covered with dense forests.
The ledges and masses of white limestone upon some
of these islands looked like fortresses or other buildings.

July 5th.—Sunday upon the lake.   When I left my
cabin, I found the morning was misty, and the sun
looking like the yolk of an egg, was bobbing up and
down upon the water.   It had just peeped above the
waves, which, dashing about, sometimes obscured it
from our view.   We were lying at one of the Manitou
islands, taking in wood.   This is a pretty crescent shape
islet, covered with trees.   In the centre we were told
is a lake which is unfathomable, and supposed to be
connected with lake Michigan.   It is filled with the
large trout, salmon and white fish of the lakes.
There is a woodman's hut, and several large piles of
wood upon the shore.   ' Oh that the woodman would
spare those trees.'   Soon the pretty island will be de-
nuded and forlorn.   It is a sacred island—the Indians
imagining it to be the residence of their Manitou,
never dare to land there, as they believe such an in-
trusion would be followed by the anger of their Deity.
One Indian, who despised such superstition ventured
upon the shore, and was never heard of since.   The
forests and lake in the interior, they imagine is the
abode of the blessed after death, whose hours will
there pass in hunting and fishing.   The Manitoulin
islands in lake Huron, are also sacred; but they are
much larger than these, one of them being fifty-five
miles in length.   I secured a handful of pebbles from
the shore, which, like those of other lakes, are agate,
chalcedony and other sileceous minerals.   Upon the

shores of lake Superior these are found very fine,
mixed with trachte, lava, and other volcanic rocks,
and with masses of native copper. I had brought
with me a package of well selected tracks, which I
opened this morning, and laid a few upon the table of
the ladies saloon. Soon after, a pretty little girl
knocked at my state-room door, saying her mother
wished to know if I had any more traets, as she should
like to read one. I asked her where were those I laid
upon the table ? those, she replied, some ladies were
reading. I gave her several. The chambermaid next
appeared begging for some; and then the cabin boy
came with the same request. While I was selecting
one which I thought might suit him, I observed a
brawny dusky figure, with his shirt sleeves rolled up,
and his person begrimed with soot and smoke, gazing
earnestly towards us. 'That's Tom, one of the fire-
men,' said the cabin boy with a snigger; 'he heard
you had books to lend and wants one dreadfully.' I
beckoned to him, and he came forward with alacrity,
while behind him I discerned several other 'grim
visaged' beings peeping out from their compartment
towards us. I gave him a package to distribute among
his fellows; and during the day had the pleasure of
observing the greater part of the crew and passengers
busily engaged with my books. During our long
voyage, those who had books had read them out, and
those who had none, were getting very weary, so that
they eagerly received any thing in the shape of reading. But some of them, I trust, read them for the
sake of the benefit they hoped to receive from their
contents. It was a source of great satisfaction to behold so many persons engaged in themes of high im-

port to their soul's best interest. These seeds were
sown with a prayer for their success; and who can
tell what immortal plants may spring up in some of
their hearts, growing to a tree of life, and bearing
fruit to flourish in the garden of paradise. Let me
urge you never to travel without these, or other useful
books to distribute on your way—like the girl in the
fairy tale of our youth, shedding gems and treasures
in your path. There is no library in this boat as upon
our Hudson and Eastern steamboats, and we were
often amused with the alacrity with which our books
were snatched up when we laid them down for a strole,
or to look at some object upon the shores. When we
returned we were always sure to receive them again,
and felt no vexation, as we knew they meant no impo-
liteness, and would be willing to lend us their own in
return. My companion had never been used to such
socialisms in his country, and was quite amused at
this free and easy sort of thing. Our books were
some of them French, and upon one occasion we
found them in the hands of a simple hearted son of
the forest, to whom books were so rare a treasure he
could not resist examining them. He returned it with
a smile, and said, shaking his head, ' how you can
make any sense out of that I can't see, for I cannot
read a word of it.'

We lost sight of the Michigan shore at ten o'clock,
and stretched across the lake towards the Wisconsin
coast, which we first saw at four o'clock P. M., thus
being nearly all day out of the sight of land. This
may give you an idea of the vastness of these lakes.
Wisconsin, or Ouisconsin, or Wiskonsan, here presents a high bank, called ' red banks,' from the color

of the soil, covered with forests, and showing no trace
of man, except at the mouth of the river Sheboygan,
two hundred and twenty miles from Mackinaw, where
is a small settlement called by the name of the river.

Fifty miles from Sheboygan we stopped at the town
of Milwaukie, towards which the tide of emigration
has been rapidly flowing. As the bay is crossed by a
bar, our large boat could not enter, and a small steamboat took from us much of our merchandise and most
of our emigrants. We did not go on shore, but contented ourselves with seeing the town from the boat.
It looked neat, with some comfortable dwellings,
several shops, hotel, court house, &c. It stands upon
the Milwaukie river Its population is 1,000. Several
rail-roads and canals are in contemplation from this
place across the territory, as rail-roads to Winnebago
lake; from Belmont to Dubuque; from Bellmont to
Dodgeville in the mine district; a canal from Milwaukie to the Black river, and another through the
Fox and Wisconsin to the Mississippi. Wisconsin
will be soon covered with a dense population, as it is
now a favorite point for emigration. The soil is very
rich, from one to ten feet deep, the surface undulating
prairie and woodland, consisting of 100,000 square
miles of fertile land. The grassy plains make fine
pasture lands, and the lakes and rivers produce abundance of fish, and give great manufacturing power.
Lakes Superior and Michigan, and the river Mississippi surround three sides, thus enabling them to send
their produce to market. Flour, rye, corn, barley,
white-fish, and many other articles have been exported
this year. Their lead mines are very rich, and their
valuable forests of pine trees will be another source of

wealth. These growing to the height of one hundred and eighty or two hundred feet, crown the heights of the northern region of the country, which is mountainous, containing several waterfalls, one of which is two hundred and fifty feet in height. The scenery is very picturesque. Madison, the capital, is a pretty, thriving town, surrounded by four transparent lakes, upon the shore of one of which it is situated; it sometimes goes by the poetical appellation of 'city of the four lakes.' When the roads and canals are formed, Wisconsin will soon become a thoroughfare to the Mississippi and the vast regions beyond; and those who have 'the world before them,' cannot make a better choice than this. Here we left our Buffalo hunters. Racine is a town twenty-two miles below Milwaukie. The houses looked new, and were arranged in rows upon the high green bank. The court-house was quite showy, having a portico in front, with pillars reaching to the roof, which was painted red, surmounted by a tin cupola. It stands at the mouth of Root river. We were now again in sight of Michigan, as the lake grows narrower towards the end. We have passed completely around this state, it being in the shape of a triangle. It is destined to be a great and flourishing State, surrounded as it is by the lakes, crossed by rivers canals, and railroads, and covered by a rich soil. It is two hundred and eighty miles long by one hundred and eighty, and covers 40,000 square miles. It has only been admitted into the Union as a State in 1837, and now possesses a population of 211,705. The country is level, except a table land in the center from which the rivers flow into lakes St. Clair, Huron, and Michigan. The remainder is covered with grassy

prairie land, with transparent lakes, and tracts of woodland.   Here grows the valuable maple from which
they obtain their sugar; the white birch, whose bark
is used for making canoes, roofing houses, or even
when split fine, in writing letters by the early settlers;
the oak, the beech, the hickory, sassafras, and various
other valuable trees.   Its energetic inhabitants are
busily engaged laying out canals and rail-roads to
intersect it in every direction, as means of conveying
their produce to its market.   One hundred and thirty-
one miles of rail-road has been contracted for, but
only forty-four miles finished, from Detroit to Ann
Arbor.   Over this 41,896 barrels of flour were conveyed this year to Detroit.   Three years since the
inhabitants of this state sent to Ohio for their flour,
and now they export 125,000 barrels of flour this year.
Education is not neglected; the legislature have appropriated 1,200,000 acres of land as a school fund,
which, as the land is rapidly rising, will be of great
value.   The celebrated Schoolcraft tells us, it was
deemed so inaccessible from swamps, that in 1818, it
was not thought fit for the soldiers bounty lands.
This was, however, soon discovered to be a mistake.
He further informs us, the soil is an argillaceous soil,
mellowed with sands and pebbles, underlaid with
schistose and calcareous rocks, clothed with an open
growth of oaks and hickories, the ridges covered with
walnut, ash, beech, and maple, while the valleys are
first rate corn land, diversified with limpid lakes,
grassy prairies and pebbly bottomed brooks.

July 6th.—When approaching Chicago, the 'haven
where we would be,' I did not so much watch for the

appearance of that famed town, as look back with regret at the beautiful lake I was leaving, for I was well assured 'I ne'er should look upon its like again.' Two days and two nights I had been sailing over it, never tired of gazing at its varied shores, or beauteous waters. Those who have never beheld these masses of pellucid, brilliant, green waters, can never imagine the extraordinary loveliness of the scene. They cover a surface of 150,000 square miles, and contain nearly half the fresh water upon the surface of the globe. That the water is fresh, is of great importance to those who dwell upon their shores, as it can be of more use for household purposes, and machinery. The valley in which the lakes repose, is said to have been hewed out by the deluge, leaving the deep chasms in which the waters lie; this is called the valley of the St. Lawrence, and very properly; but I must object to this immense chain of lakes, four and five hundred miles long, and nine hundred deep, being called the 'river St. Lawrence,' as some fashionable tourists have of late. The St. Lawrence river is an outlet, but is no more entitled to this designation, than is Niagara or St. Clair river. These lakes all lie in a valley which interposes between the primitive and secondary formations. The northern shores are granite rocks, sterile, and scarcely inhabited; while the southern is rich alluvion, covering sandstone and limestone.

The bustle of arrival aroused me from these reflections, and we were soon seated in the parlor of the Lake Hotel, in the famous state of Illinois, and town of Chicago. The rapid growth of this place you have heard of: in 1833 it could only count three frame dwellings and two hundred and fifty inhabitants; and now enumerates six churches, one hundred shops, several hotels, dwelling houses, and ware-houses, and between six and seven thousand inhabitants. Chicago, or Tshicawgo, as the inhabitants and Indians call it, is divided by a river of the same name into two parts, between which is a free ferry and a bridge. The shops are upon one side, and the dwellings upon the other. These last are in the style of country residences, enclosed with white palings, surrounded by piazzas and gardens; some of brick, but many of wood and neatly painted. Every thing looks quite new, as indeed it might; for where now the town stands, was, as late as 1833, a fort, before which was encamped seven thousand Indians. Fort Dearborn was erected for the purpose of protecting the frontier. It was attacked in 1812 by the Indian tribes, and their allies, and those who escaped massacre, sought protection in fort Wayne. Another fort was built in 1818, but is now deserted and let out for tenements. There are houses of worship here for several denominations; among them the Presbyterian church is most conspicuous. It is of brick and neatly finished. Part of the money required for its erection, was acquired by the ladies in a Fair. The Lake House is a very good hotel, situated among the dwelling houses. It is built of brick, painted white, which, with its green blinds, gives it a pleasant appearance; every thing within was comfortable and good of its kind. According to our usual practice, we ascended to the cupola of the hotel, where is a lovely view of the cottages and gardens at our feet, the broad prairies beyond, and the bright waters of Michigan behind us. This town

11

is beautifully situated upon the borders of the lake, through which it holds constant communication with Buffalo and the east. The other route I mentioned, from Detroit continues over the rail-road at that city, and by cross roads to St. Joseph's upon the lake, from which place steamboats are continually plying to Chicago. It is a shorter road, and gives the traveller a view of the interior of Michigan. The Illinois and Michigan canal commences here, which is to be carried to Peru on the Illinois river, a distance of one hundred miles, thus opening a communication with the Mississippi and the Gulf of Mexico. It is six feet deep and sixty feet wide, and is nearly finished. The climate here is variable. In the summer the wind will one day blow over the surface of the prairies, and the weather will become very hot; but the next day, perhaps, it will come from the lake and cool it again. In consequence of the vicinity of the lake there is not much snow, and it is not very cold.

We spent here one day only, but were able to see every thing in and about the town, and in conversation with those friends residing here, obtained every information. We intended making a longer stay, but learned that the regular line of stages left town that evening, which obliged us to go on or to stay longer than our time would admit. Before reaching here, it was our intention to go to Michigan City, which is in Indiana, upon the shores of the lake, and from thence cross Indiana to Madison, upon the Ohio, through a fine succession of rail and Macadamized roads. Our friends here, however, seemed to think it so monstrous a thing to return without beholding the celebrated Mississippi, when within a few hundred miles

only, that we determined to alter our course and go
down the Illinois river.

At nine o'clock at night we entered a commodious
stage drawn by four good horses, which was to take us
to Peoria, upon the Illinois, one hundred and fifty-seven
miles distant, for which we were to pay twenty-two
dollars, eleven each, bed and board included. Beside
us were two other passengers. Crossing the bridge,
we took up the mail at the post office, and then drove
through a long range of cheerfully lighted shops until
we found ourselves out of town. Here the road crossed
the *wet prairie*, as it is called, which, in some seasons,
when the lake is high, is overflown. Through this
wet land we went splash, splash, nearly half the night.
A rail-road is proposed here, which will render travelling more pleasant. Hour after hour passed away,
my companions all dozing while I sought sleep in vain.
The vast plain over which we were moving, seen
through the dusk of a cloudy night, seemed a fitting
place for dark deeds—a fine Hounslow heath, or Indian lurking place. But there are no bandits here,
and the Indians were all over the Mississippi, and I
was bidding such idle fears avaunt, when suddenly a
low plaintive wail sounded over the waste, startling
my companions from their slumbers. 'What was that
unearthly cry?' I asked. 'Only a prairie wolf madam.'
'Dear me!' exclaimed the other passenger, a youth.
'I hope there are not many of them, for sometimes
wolves attack horses.' 'Not in these prairies, sir,'
replied the other passenger, 'they are rather shy, and
afraid of us.' 'I am glad, at least, to see a light,'
returned the youth, 'there must be a house yonder.'
'Yes, a bower in the rushes, nothing else,' replied the

other man. 'If you follow that light it will lead you a pretty chase through the marshes ; it is a jack-o'lantern.' The hour, seen by the light of the coach lamp, proved to be twelve, and each settled in his corner for another doze. A sudden halt of the stage awakened us. The coachman took down a lamp and began to search for something on the ground. 'Halo, driver, what have you lost?' asked the youth. 'Only my road sir,' he replied. 'Lost your road!' exclaimed the youth in dismay ; 'Lost in these lonely moors among wolverines and jack-o'lanterns ! Here's a pretty fix!' 'Driver you ought to keep the skin off your eyes in such a dark night, I guess,' said the other passenger. I only wondered he could ever keep his road, as there was no house or tree to mark his course even in the day, and one might easily pass over the worn pathway in these grassy plains. The driver soon resumed his seat, having discovered his path ; and gave us the agreeable intelligence, he had gone three miles out of his way. A few hours after this, a huge body suddenly appeared before the window—it turned out to be a tree, a sign we were approaching a river. Soon after we found ourselves before the door of a small house, upon the banks of a narrow but deep and placid stream fringed with trees. This was the Des Plaines, a river which rises so near lake Michigan, that in times of its overflow, boats have passed from one to another. This interlocking of waters which flow different ways, Darby considers 'an astonishing hydrographical anomaly.' All the waters we had passed, have fallen into the Atlantic, while those we were now following find their way into the gulf of Mexico. The Des Plaines is called a branch of the

Illinois, which joins with the Kankakee, and afterwards the Fox, and the united streams take the name
of the Illinois. Many modern writers consider this
as the Illinois, and drop the name of Des Plaines,
which I should judge a proper arrangement. We
awakened the drowsy owner of the house, procured
some refreshment, and with fresh horses resumed our
journey.

July 7th.—I fell asleep, and when I was awakened
at dawn this morning, by my companion, that I might
not lose the scene, I started with surprise and delight.
I was in the midst of a prairie! A world of grass and
flowers stretched around me, rising and falling in gentle undulations, as if an enchanter had struck the
ocean swell, and it was at rest forever. Acres of wild
flowers of every hue glowed around me, and the sun
arising from the earth where it touched the horizon,
was 'kissing with golden face the meadows green.'
What a new and wonderous world of beauty! What
a magnificent sight! Those glorious ranks of flowers!
Oh that you could have ' one glance at their array!'
How shall I convey to you an idea of a prairie. I
despair, for never yet hath pen brought the scene before my mind. Imagine yourself in the centre of an
immense circle of velvet herbage, the sky for its
boundary upon every side; the whole clothed with a
radiant efflorescence of every brilliant hue. We rode
thus through a perfect wilderness of sweets, sending
forth perfume, and animated with myriads of glittering
birds and butterflies :—

> " A populous solitude of bees and birds,
> And fairy formed, and many colored things."

11*

It was, in fact, a vast garden, over whose perfumed
paths, covered with soil as hard as gravel, our carriage rolled through the whole of that summer day.
You will scarcely credit the profusion of flowers upon
these praries. We passed whole acres of blossoms
all bearing one hue, as purple, perhaps, or masses of
yellow or rose ; and then again a carpet of every
color intermixed, or narrow bands, as if a rainbow had
fallen upon the verdant slopes.   When the sun flooded
this Mosaic floor with light, and the summer breeze
stirred among their leaves, the irredescent glow was
beautiful and wonderous beyond any thing I had ever
conceived. I think this must have been the place
where Armida planted her garden, for she surely could
not have chosen a fairer spot.   Here are

> ' Gorgeous flowrets in the sun light shining,
> Blossoms flaunting in the eye of day ;
> Tremulous leaves, with soft and silver lining
> Buds that open only to decay.'

The gentle undulating surface of these prairies, prevent sameness, and add variety to its lights and shades.
Occasionally, when a swell is rather higher than the
rest, it gives you an extended view over the country,
and you may mark a dark green waving line of trees
near the distant horizon, which are shading some
gentle stream from the sun's absorbing rays, and thus,
' Betraying the secret of their silent course.'   Oak
openings also occur, green groves, arranged with the
regularity of art, making shady, alleys, for the heated
traveller.   What a tender benevolent Father have we,
to form for us so bright a world !   How filled with
glory and beauty must that mind have been, who conceived so much loveliness !   If for his erring children
he has created so fair a dwelling place, how well

adorned with every goodly show, must be the celestial home reserved for his obedient people. Eye hath not seen it—ear hath not heard it—nor can it enter into our hearts to conceive it.

> Wondrous truths, and manifold as wondrous,
> God hath written in those stars above—
> But not less in the bright flowrets under us,
> Stands the revelation of his love.

1 observe in all fashionable tours, what is eaten and drank seems to be matter of immense importance, and perhaps you will be disappointed if I do not touch upon themes of such high import. We had been warned our fare upon these ' lonesome prairies' would be poor, and of course we did not expect the tables of a New York hotel. The scarcity of stone, and of wood—as there are no pine and cedar except in the northern parts of Wisconsin—forbids much elegance in the few houses scattered along the road, and the first post house at which we stopped for breakfast was a rude log cabin. Our detention during the night had prevented our arriving at the usual breakfast hour, and it was supposed we had taken our meal elsewhere, and of course we were obliged to wait. ' Breakfast! Breakfast!' was the cry of driver and passengers, as we alighted. ' Aye, aye!' returned the landlord—'I will scare you up as good a feed as you could find in Chicago.' The room we entered was plainly furnished, but I remarked a pile of books upon a bureau, among which were the life of Gen. Harrison—Rollins Ancient History—Vicar of Wakefield, and several religious works. I regretted I could only place a few tracts among them. When I travel again in such lonely parts, I will endeavor to find a corner in my trunks for a few good books to leave among this reading peo-

ple. The mistress and her daughter were very busy scaring up our breakfast, of which, I should think the chickens were the most scared. They soon placed upon the table cloth, some fine smoking potatoes from their garden—nice indian meal cakes, eggs, milk, cheese, cucumbers, butter, bread, and 'chicken fixens.' Every thing, being native produce, was very nice, but the coffee being a foreign article, was not as good as I have seen before, I must confess. The landlady's method of preparing it was so novel, that I will write off the recipe for your edification. I had retreated to the kitchen fire, as I *slept rather cold* last night, it being misty, and there observed her process. She placed some coffee grains in an iron pot, which, being *scared* about a little until somewhat brownish, were laid upon the kitchen table, and pounded with a rolling pin. Boiling water being poured upon it, the coffee was dished up. Every one drank it contentedly, and I, being thirsty drank it also. The driver who sat next to me, having lived much in Chicago and other refined places rather turned up his nose, saying it was not half as good as he got at the Lake House. My companion contented himself with milk. While waiting at the door for the stage, our hosts, son galloped up, dismounted and tied his horse to the fence. The animal looked as untamed as if just caught, his wild bright eyes flashed from beneath his shaggy uncut mane, and he pawed the ground, snorted and struggled, as if determined to break away and scour the free plains again. 'Your horse loves not restraint,' said I, 'he wishes to be free.' 'Aye, aye! the critter snuffs a wolf and wants to be after him.' 'A wolf!' 'Yes—he is my wolf hunter, and dearly does he love

a chase after them.   When he sees them, nothing can
stop him from chasing them—but they give him a
pretty tough run sometimes.   I have seen him follow
one for a mile ere he overtook him, and then, with
one stroke of his foot, the wolf is dead.'   I am sure
the horse understood his master—his eye was fixed
upon us while he spoke, and when he ended, tost his
mane with a triumphant expression and stamped
fiercely upon the ground, as if his enemy were beneath
his foot.

'All aboard!' cries the driver, and we were again
upon our course, our horses prancing gaily as if refreshed by their breakfast.   A tree appeared against
the horizon, looking exactly like a sail in the distance—others followed it, and soon beautiful groups
of forest trees were sprinkled over the prairie in front.
This was a token of the vicinity of water, and in a short
time we found ourselves upon an elevated bank from
which we looked down upon a verdant valley through
the centre of which, ran a silver stream.   This was
the valley of the Des Plaines—having every appearance of being the bed of a broad and deep river.   Many
geologists, among them, Prof. Sheppard, thinks this
and the valley of the Illinois, have been scooped out,
by a vast torrent pouring from lake Michigan.   Upon
the opposite shore of the river and in this vale, at
the foot of the ancient bank, stands the pretty town of
Joliet, improperly spelt Juliet.   The whole scene, was
one of great beauty.   We descended the bank. which
is nearly one hundred feet high, and is composed of
yellow water-worn pebbles.   Winding down the road,
upon the high bank opposite, was a long train of covered waggons, filled with a household upon its way to

'a new home' upon the prairies. After fording the
stream, now rendered shallow by the summer heats,
passing over the green sward we found ourselves before the door of the principal hotel in the town. Joliet takes its name from the old French traveller,
father Joliet, who came here as a missionary in 1673,
and stands at the mouth of a little stream of the same
name. This is growing into a place of some importance, as the Michigan canal crosses the river here,
and all travellers to the Illinois pass through it. It
has a fine water power, for the descent of this river
to the rapids at Ottowa, is great—the lockage of the
canal being 142 feet The population is over 600.
There is here a court house, houses of worship, mills,
taverns, and several shops. We remained here only
long enough to change horses. While standing upon
the steps, the covered waggons arrived, from which,
looked forth men, women, children, dogs and cats,
while pots, and kettles, and chairs, were dangling below. A group of sturdy looking men stood around
the door. After our American fashion of asking
questions, I addressed one of them who stood near
me, and asked from what country he had travelled
'From St. Thomas, in Canada ma'am,' he replied.
'We are sixty families,' said another, 'and have left
there because we want more freedom. We would
live where we can say what we choose, and do what
we choose. There our tongues are fettered!' I learnt
they were going to Rock river, a very fashionable place
of emigration now. This is a beautiful stream, running through the north west part of Illinois into the
Mississippi. The land is prairie upon its borders,
which will well repay the agriculturist's labors, while

its rapids place a great amount of manufacturing power at the disposal of the settlers. The lead region is also in its vicinity. At the mouth of Rock river, in the Mississippi, is a pretty island of limestone, three miles long. which is occupied by fort Armstrong, garrisoned by United States troops. Dixonville on this river is a growing town. This I learned from my emigrants, and afterwards saw confirmed in a Gazeteer, So you see what a nice plan it is while travelling to extract information from all you meet. I am never bashful at asking. I bade adieu to the emigrants, hoping they would have their full of chat from which it seems they were debarred, and let the prairies ' prate of their whereabouts.' We re-crossed the river where we found the newer part of Joliet built in a solid manner, of the yellow limestone which is quarried here. The sides of the canal, and viaduct were also formed of this pretty stone, which gives quite a gay look to the place. It is said by Professor Shephard to be magnesian limestone, which occurs also at Chicago, abounding in orthrocera, turbo, terebratula, caryophillia, &c., and extends he thinks through the lakes. It is taken out here in stratified layers ; and at Chicago, where it has a slaty structure, it is used for flagging. A few miles from Joliet, we passed an object, to me of the greatest interest—it was an Indian mound. This was a perfect gem—as regular, as smooth, and as green as if cut out of an emerald—being an oblong of fifty rods high, and seventy or eighty long. Although centuries have passed since it was formed, it is as perfect in shape, as if just moulded. A beautiful, solitary thing it is, telling of nations and events now lost in the mists of time. We saw afterwards, several others, bearing upon their summits ancient oaks, plain indication of their great antiquity. Flowers again in untold numbers, were covering the prairies. and here are many of our garden flowers growing wild, as blue bells, flox, bouncing bet, sweet william, roses, cocoris, beliotrope, astre, &c., beside wild flowers as fringed gentean, solidago, orchis, yellow golden rod, scarlet lilly, wild indigo, superb pink moccasin flower, and scarlet lobelia. There were many I had never seen—among them was a species of teazle, having a tall stem, purple head, surrounded by a fringe of long pink leaves—I called it the Indian fairy, for as its dark head bobbed about, and its pink mantle flowed around it, it looked like a tiny Indian. In fact, flowers

" rich as morning sunrise hue,
And gorgeous as the gemmed midnight,'

were smiling and blooming in every direction. What a nice place for some hortuculturist to transport himself and cottage. Rural Howett would enjoy the scene—and Miller who loves to ' babble o' green fields' and flowers, would find fitting subject here for his blossoming pen.

I welcome every flower I see with tender pleasure as if the gift of a friend—for I know they were planted among us to add to our enjoyment. Their culture has soothed many a mourning heart, and their blossoming is as eagerly looked for in the spring, as if their own loved one was returning from the earth. There is nothing that can so soon transport us to scenes and friends long gone, and awaken buried memories of former joy as these brilliant creations. Earth would look dim without them—the bride would

want a grace—the bier would seem more gloomy—
while the sculptor, the artist, and the embroiderer,
would lose their prettiest model of adornment.

A line of trees proclaimed a river near, and we soon
dashed through the Au Sable, the horses dancing with
joy, as the clear cool waters curled about their feet.
The sight of a house upon the opposite bank, seemed
quite a novelty, as we had not seen one since leaving
Joliet, at nine o'clock, and it was now one. The
house was of boards painted white, and a hanging
sign proclaimed it one of entertainment. Here we
dined and changed horses. The meats were very
good, the pies and custards tolerable, but the vegetables were the finest we had ever tasted. Peas, beans,
potatoes all were very excellent. Every thing we saw
was from the landlords farm, which extended over the
prairie some distance from his house. He and his
men, came in from the corn fields when the conch,
sounded for dinner, and without their coats—their
shirt sleeves rolled up, they placed themselves beside
us—one does not dress for dinner upon the prairies.
While travelling in unsettled countries one must leave
all one's nicities at home. It took us some little time
to shut our eyes against soiled table covers, iron
knives and forks, &c.,—but once resolved to overlook
it, we succeeded, and ceased to notice it. When we
consider what a life these early settlers have led, we
should only wonder things are as decent as they are.
The man comes out here in his youth, with an axe,
upon his shoulder—hews him a space in the forest
and erects a log hut—here upon the floor, spread with
the skin of a beast perhaps, he sleeps, his only companions, his dog, or an Indian—he gradually acquires

12

furniture of his own making, and when he came to eating from a table instead of a stone or a stump, he thinks himself very comfortable. A table cloth is such a luxury that he scarcely remarks when it gets soiled, as even then it is cleaner than his log table, and knives of the coarsest description are treasures to him. Our landlord spoke of his prairie land with the greatest enthusiasm. The ground is very hard to break, generally requiring several yoke of oxen, while beneath that the mould is several feet in thickness without stones, requiring no manuring and apparently inexhaustible. Some of the old settlemsɪuə, where farms had been worked for twelve years, it was still as fertile as ever—giving the tiller very little trouble, and yielding rich crops. The oasis, or ' oak openings,' upon the prairies are very beautiful. We passed through one this morning. It presented the appearance of a lawn, or park around some gentleman's seat. The trees are generally oak, arranged in pretty clumps or clusters upon the smooth grass—or in long avenues, as if planted thus by man. From their limbs hang pretty vines, as the pea vine—lonicera flava, honey-suckle—-and white convolvulus. While our carriage wound among these clumps, or through the avenues, it was almost impossible to dispel the illusion that we were not driving through the domain of some rich proprietor, and we almost expected to draw up before the door of some lordly mansion. Our afternoon drive from the Au Sable to Ottawa was through a treeless prairie, looking very much like a vast lake or ocean. So much is this appearance acknowledged by the country people that they call the stage coach, a prairie schooner. When the sun shines brightly over the landscape, its yellow light gives the prairie an azure hue, so that one can scarcely see where the earth ends, and the sky begins. The undulations are a very singular feature in the landscape. This is best seen at early morning or sunset light—the summit of every little swell is illumined, while the hollow between lies in shadow, thus making the ground a curious chequer work. We saw many prairie hens, or species of grouse this afternoon, but no wolves or deer, much to my regret. The road is so much travelled that they avoid it and retire to more sequestered places. Birds innumerable, were sporting in the sun's light among the flowers, and butterflies clad like Miltons angels, in 'purple beams, and azure wings, that up they fly so drest.'

And now you ask, to what is the prairie land owing; fire or water? Many are the theories upon this subject. The Indian name for prairie, is scutay, (fire;) and they are in the custom of burning off the grass every fall. Some will tell you, to this must be traced the dearth of trees. As the mould is so deep—in some places twenty feet, and there are in it, except in one or two places, no trace of trees or the huge stumps they leave, this does not seem probable, at least the trees must have been burnt from ages. Others will tell you it is the sediment of an ocean which is spread over the land—or in some places large lakes. In Illinois it is said there was once as large a lake as Michigan, which, burst its barrier at the grand tower rocks upon the Mississippi. A chain of lakes it is said have once stood upon the western land which have left these basins of deep alluvion covered with herbage. These water theorists, one of whom is Schoolcraft,

point to the bowlder's of granite and gneiss which are
scattered over the country from the northern ocean
to the gulf of Mexico, lost rocks, as they are called,
as traces of this flood. Why not join the two theories?
The land has no doubt been covered with water; this
is proved by the 'lost rocks,' by the hard packed soil
like the bottom of a lake; by its inky blackness,
when wet, as we see in marshes, and, by the marsh
grasses, and water plants which are seen growing
upon it. This land, when dry was occupied by the
Indians, who kindled a fire at the edges of a circle,
among the rushes, which drove the animals in the
centre where they were caught. The roots of the
prairie grass is not destroyed by fire, and it therefore
could not so completely eradicate the roots of those
enormous trees which grow upon the western land.
There is nothing in a prairie land to prevent the
growth of trees, as wherever the fire is checked they
immediately spring up. The rivers also protect their
trees from fire.

Prairie land occupies two thirds of the State of
Illinois; the dearth of water, and wood, and stone,
will prevent them from being settled very thickly,
except in the vicinity of the rivers; so that these
beautiful plains will long remain undisturbed to gratify
the traveller's eye. The prairies would of course be
underlain with coal, as this great mass of vegetation
which has been destroyed by the floods which have
stood upon them, pressed beneath the incumbent
strata and exposed to heat, moisture, and pressure,
will produce fermentation, and afterwards hardened
strata; accordingly it is found that coal is universal
every where in the west. Why should we stop at

second causes in considering the origin of prairies; why speak of Indian fires, or rushing floods? The Almighty mind who hath conceived this admirable globe, and who, with such infinite taste, hath formed and beautified it, decking it with flowers and every other delight, has spread out this fair western world with lakes immense, and stately forests, wondrous cataracts, smiling prairies, and broad rolling rivers, to decorate the abode of His loved, although erring sons. He, in his wisdom, foresaw the time would come, when the exhausted soil, and crumbling institutions, and crowded homes of the old world, would require a new field for its overgrown population, and held this world perdu beneath the ocean caves until the fitting moment. When the hour had come, it arose fresh and blossoming from the sea, adorned with a goodly variety of mountain, lake, fair plain, and noble river, to compensate the lonely wanderer for the home he has been forced to leave. Now is not that a pretty theory? That this continent was much longer submerged beneath the diluvial flood, and is indeed a new world, is, I believe, generally conceded by geologists. There is something delightful to look upon the earth, as we do here, in its pristine glory and virgin freshness. The waters may have lingered longer upon the broad valley which lies between the Alleghany and Rocky mountains, depositing that rich alluvion which lies so deep upon the land, and when departing, ploughed its way through those great valleys where now the western rivers flow. It was then, perhaps before the deluge, the abode of that monstrous saurian race, some sixty feet in length, whose bones are now dug up in Texas, and

12*

must be under the soil. When their 'days were fulfilled,' they were destroyed and sank beneath the floods to harden in the limestone; and when the land had become dry, the mastodon arose and stalked over the western plains; for since he has been discovered buried in the soil of Missouri, with Indian arrows sticking in his flesh, he is proved not to be antediluvial. When his career was over, the Indian tribes were admitted into the new born world; and whatever interest we may take in their fate—however we may pity them, we must all agree they have misused their gift. Their *talent was hid*, the fields were untilled, the stores of marbles and metals, and materials choice and rare, which were placed there that man might rear him a comfortable habitation, and lordly temples for his God, remained unknown in their secret deposites. The Indian was doomed to share the fate of the mammoth: the barrier which concealed this world from the older part was loosed, and the waves of human population that rolled over it, has pushed back the Indians, step by step, and thinned their ranks, and will thin them, until their race also lies under the soil whose riches they knew not how to use.

It is a singular and interesting thing to stand, as I do now, upon the confines of the earth, as it were, 'at the green earth's end,' and gaze back through the vista of time, over Europe, and Africa, and Asia, upon the nations that have risen and flourished, and become extinct, each in its turn, like those animal races, whose story is sculptured, geologists tell us, upon the ribs and arches of the earth beneath us. There we look upon the decline and fall of nations—here upon their blossoming spring-time. And it is a curious

thing to look on here and see the machinery of *world
making* at work—to behold the progress of society
going on under your eyes, from its infancy to its
maturity. As in a panorama we behold the wigwam
of the savage pass away to give place to a log hut;
that disappears and a goodly farm appears; then a
settlement, a village, a town in succession, until at
last, an imposing city filled with institutions for all
arts and sciences; with temples, academies, and all
appliances of society in its state of culture and maturity. While thus watching nations rising and setting;
moved and transported upon the earth's surface as the
pieces of a chess-board, a guiding hand is as distinctly
visible, as upon the walls of Beltshazzer's palace. To
the poor Indian the hand-writing again appears: 'thou
art weighed in the balance and found wanting!' Be-
ware ye, who have inherited his land, that the sentence be not written up against you also!

A *ground swell*, rather higher than the rest, placed
us upon an elevation, from whence we looked down
upon the enchanting vale of Ottowa. A verdant plain
lay below us, over which two bright rivers were winding, the Fox and the Des Plaines, which meeting,
formed a broad and noble stream, which runs 220
miles from this spot to the Mississippi. The Illinois,
first takes that name here. The plain was bounded
in the distance by groves of stately trees, and by the
bluffs of the Illinois. In the centre of this fair valley,
just where the 'bright waters meet,' is the little town
of Ottowa. It is youngling, just come out, and contains only 1,006 inhabitants, but is rapidly increasing.
A gentle descent of about a mile, brought us to the
banks of the Fox, beneath the shadow of the shrub-

bery which fringed its shores we drove some time, following its windings and gazing at the bright sheen of its waters glittering through the foliage. We forded it twice while crossing the valley, and so pure and transparent was the stream, that the pebbles which lay upon the sandstone floor, could be seen as distinctly as in the hand. The canal passes here, and the workmen were building a handsome viaduct, across the stream. The Fox river is here about 100 yards wide, but is low at this season. It rises in Wisconsin, and is navigable to within fifteen miles of lake Michigan near Milwaukie. Many parts of its shore are richly wooded. The rapids upon the stream afford a great amount of water power, serviceable for machinery. A short drive, after again crossing the Fox, brought us before the door of the principal hotel, called the Mansion House. The site of Ottowa only having been laid out in 1830, ten years since, you cannot expect many details of its fine streets and churches; I leave that for the next year's tourist. The buildings principally consist of shops, arranged in a square, upon one side of which is our hotel, and upon another side, a large brick court-house is in progress— this being a county town. The Ottawans are much disappointed that the canal did not terminate at their town, instead of Peru, fifteen miles lower down the Illinois. Notwithstanding this, the town must increase, and enjoys considerable trade, as it is surrounded by a good farming country, prairie and woodland, with abundance of limestone and sandstone in its vicinity. Its water power will in time render it another Rochester for the Genessee farmers, who will soon be raising their grain in the plains around. Beside this it is the centre of an extensive coal basin, which crops out in various places in the neighborhood. Chicago now receives supplies of that article here, which she once obtained from Ohio. When the Illinois is high, steamboats from St. Louis reach here, but at present they ascend no higher than Peru. They gave us a very nice supper here, which we partook in company with the boarders, travellers, and our driver. This last attacked the ham and broiled chickens right manfully, declaring he was as hungry as a prairie wolf. Pray do not expect a bill of fare at every place—suffice every thing was as good as could be expected—nay better, for who would look for such city dainties as orange sweetmeats and iced cakes in this young wilderness settlement. Every thing desirable can be obtained, by the steamboats here, except good cooking, and style at table—these will come in time, and their absence affords *variety* in our wanderings.

A peep at the 'Ottowa Republican,' and several neighboring papers, amused us until the stage horn sounded—we entered our stage—the leaders were touched, and we bade adieu to Ottowa I fear forever. I shall not soon forget that lovely purple evening, which threw such a charm over the scenery as we drove from Ottowa to Peru, a distance of fifteen miles. Our road lay beside the bright Illinois, upon prairie or bottom land, which lines each side of the river throughout its whole length, making a valley from one to five miles broad, skirted with high limestone and sandstone bluffs. The ground was gay with flowers, and as the twilight threw its purple haze over the opposite shore, it became alive with hundreds of brilliant fire flies, larger and more luminous than any I had ever seen. Many a time have you and I sat in our early days upon the banks of the Passaic, watching these brilliant creatures as they starred the black robe of night, but we never beheld them so large, and dazzling as these western lights. The river was as smooth as a mirror, upon which was reflected the trees and rocks with perfect distinctness, but it had a darker hue than those bright waters we had passed, being tinted with a brownish topaz. I remarked this to my companion, who attributed its dark shade to the alluvion and black mould through which it flowed. 'It cannot be wholesome,' I said, 'I should not like to drink it.' 'I guess if you had been on top of that rock three hundred years ago,' said an old man who sat opposite me, peering out the stage at the opposite bluffs, 'you'd been glad to drink it ever so muddy or unhealthy.' I opened my eyes and stared enquiringly at him. 'That's the rock where the Ingins were starved to death,' he said in answer to my look. 'Indeed!' I exclaimed, ' Is that *starved rock?*' Our heads were out the window, and we looked with much interest upon the scene of that Indian tragedy. A high cliff of alternate sandstone and limestone layers, stands out like a turret from the rocky bluffs one hundred and forty feet above the river—it was spotted with moss, and fringed with trees, which the sun's last rays had tinged with gold, and amber, and rose. 'Yes, ma'am, that's the rock,' continued our fellow traveller. 'Down to the river they sunk their kettles with bark ropes, in hopes of getting water, but the cruel Pottawattamies cut the strings, and so they died.' And *so they died!* What images of anguish, sorrow, rage and despair, does that short sentence convey to our minds!

The fate of the unhappy band of Illini, who dwelt in the fair land which has taken their name, has been related by Schoolcraft and Flint; but as I think you have not seen their works, I will tell it you. The Illini were defeated in battle by the Pottowattamies, and retreated to the top of this rock, which by a narrow ledge joins the land. This spot they defended some time, but at length their provisions and water failed. They scorned to surrender, but one by one lay down in dignified composure, and, like Cæsar, drawing their mantles over them, died in silence. The last one who had defended the rock at length expired, and the enemy seeing no one appear, entered the strong-hold to find them all at rest. Their bones repose there now. The rock is passed, and upon the prairie at our right we behold the brazen glare of a fire lighting up a dozen dark figures which are flitting around it. This is an emigrant bivouac. Some of their wagons taken from their wheels shelter the center where the men repose; the women and children remain in the other vehicles. A fire in the midst keeps off the moschetoes, and perhaps a prairie wolf, thus affording under the mild sky a comfortable place of repose without the expense of a hotel. The prairie grass forms a soft bed for the men, and food for the cattle.

'I reckon the Ottowa folks are pretty considerably nettled,' said our old traveller, in a voice which rendered 'night hideous' with its harshness. 'They thought the canal would end there, and they would git all the trade.' 'The Ottowa folks don't depend on no canals, 1 guess,' replied another passenger, apparently a neighboring farmer, taking up the cudgels for his favorite town. 'Ottawa's a great and increasing place, which will beat *Chicorgo* yet. Wait a while and you'll see rows of factories and mills upon the Fox, and you'll see the rapids scooped out below, so that the steamboats can come up at all times, and then I would'nt give a cent for your Peru. Ottawa folks keep their eyes skinned I tell you!' 'Oh! you prairie chickens crow loud; you are always laying out for mills to grind the grain what you mean to raise. You'd better come and open a shop now, or a bank, at Peru; things will rise when old Tippecanoe comes to the white house.' 'Tip me none of your old ginerals, if you please, said his opponent. Van's the man for me. Give me Van Buren for President and things will rise enough.' The gurgling of water, as we forded the Little Vermillion, drowned the noise of these village politicians much to my comfort. Soon after we found ourselves in the midst of a group of Irish shantees, occupied by the canal laborers, flanked by a row of low wooden tenements, upon the bank of the moon-illumined Illinois. 'This, ladies and gen- tlemen,' said the farmer, in a tone of derision, 'is the grand town of Peru!' 'Yes, and bigger than Ottawa was, when it was as newly settled as Peru,' answered the Peruvian disdainfully. As I looked around me, I thought of Tinkerville and its public square in the forest; but every thing must have a beginning. The steamboat frontier was waiting to receive us, and we were soon, with our luggage, translated to her deck. Fatigued as we were we could not leave the deck for some time, for the *night sun*, as the Indians call the moon, was shining brightly down upon the smooth sur face of the Illinois, lighting up her forest glades as we

passed, and throwing fantastic shadows over the silver
water.   However, a night and a day in a stage coach
has beaten all romance out of us, and we at length
retreated to our snug state-room.   The mosquitoe
nets were drawn over us, and we soon bid to nature
and to you a fair good-night.

LETTER VII.

My dear E.—We were detained during the night by a heavy fog, and instead of reaching Peoria at six, found at breakfast we were many miles this side of it. Breakfast over, I have seated myself upon the guards, a sort of balcony which runs around the outside of the steamboat, and with note-book in hand am prepared to give you a faithful picture of all I see. The river is still and bright, reflecting every little twig and leaf. There is no villa, or ruins, or lordly mansion to embellish the scenery, but it is indebted to its wild forests alone for its loveliness. It flows and bends in a very graceful manner around the soft green islets, or low points fringed with trees of new and unknown form and beauty. Frowning above the trees in the back ground are the cliffs, waterworn as if once the river's ancient bound. Occasionally our track lay close to the shore, and we gazed into the forest's deep recesses; now a dark jungle is before us, haunt of the wolf and the panther; and again, a noble grove of witch elms, or long vistas through which the early morning sun was streaming, or a patch of brilliant smooth sward surrounded by a circle of trees, the papaw, or the silvery barked white maple, its bright green leaves turning up their silver lining to the breeze. Sometimes a little bay appeared between two promontories, covered with yellow and white water lillies, and the perfumed nymphea odorata, the home of the swan or the wild fowl. The willow here occurs frequently, dipping its leaves in the stream; sometimes the shining willow with its long and slender brilliant leaves. The locust is frequent; many varieties of oak, the red bud, cotton wood, and many other trees festooned with vines of every tint and variety.

I wished much to see a prairie wolf, and looked out eagerly among the forests in vain. Just now a man who was looking to the shore exclaimed 'There's a wolf!' he pointed to the spot, where some dark animal was cowering under a log. My companion declared it was a pig, and some one else a dog, whatever it was, it soon run away into the forest. I declared it should be a wolf, and to please me, it was unanimously voted a prairie wolf. A deer I looked for in vain; the noise made by our puffing high pressure engine, being sufficient to scare every animal away from our path. We passed Hennepin during the night, and this morning Lacon and Rome, both small places, situated upon those elevated banks or plateaus, which alternate with the woodlands along the river. The two first are both in Putman county containing two hundred and fifty-two square miles, and a population of two thousand one hundred and

thirty-one. The stream which had become narrower,
about a quarter of a mile in width ; now swelled
out in an expanse two miles broad and twenty long,
called Peoria lake, by the indians Pin-a-ta-wee. It
abounds with fish we were told, as sturgeon, buffalo,
perch, pickerel, and cat fish and the alligator, garr,
seven feet long, covered with scales, the former we
had often seen during the morning, spring from the
water, and plunge back again leaving a silvery circle
growing wider and wider upon the polished surface
of the river. The water was now unruffled by a rip-
ple, the shore at our left covered with forests throwing
their shadows over the water while upon a high bank
at our right, was the pretty town of Peoria, It was
a very sweet and tranquil picture. This has ever
been a favorite haunt of the Indians and French.
In 1779 a village stood here called La Ville de Mail-
let, inhabited by French courier des bois, Indian hunters, and fur traders, a stopping place for the French
upon the lakes and their settlements on the Mississipi.
Subsequently Fort Clarke was erected here for the
United States troops, and now a pretty town with six
houses of worship, several acadamies, market houses
shops, hotels, breweries, mills, and dwellings and a
handsome court-house with pillared portico and tin
covered cupola have arisen upon the bank. The shore is
composed of pebbles, about twenty feet high, extending back one quarter of a mile, where another step of
six or ten feet brings you to a fine prairie, leading to
the bluffs. A row of buildings surmounted the banks
principally shops, but among them we observed
several small taverns, as the Napoleon Coffee House,
Union Hotel, and Washington Hall. Upon a brick

house farther in town my companion espied the sign
of the Clinton Hotel, which being the house to which
he had been recommended, he accepted the services
of the porters of that establishment, who with those
of the other houses had been soliciting his custom.
How to land, was the next consideration, for upon
rivers which have so great a rise and fall, it is difficult
to construct wharves.   After grounding, backing
fastening a stake in the mud for a rope, which immediately came out again, we were at last stationary. A
plank was then projected to the shore, down which we
were all trundled. We had now reached the end of our
journey, one hundred and seventy miles from Chicago,
and took leave of the Chicago line, being left to our
own devices to wander farther. We found the Clinton hotel a good house, and charges low, being only
one dollar and twenty-five cents a day each.   The
host is a very gentlemanly person, and the ladies of
the family well educated and agreeable. We partook
of a very good dinner of native produce, even to the
wild raspberry tarts, which appeared at desert. I like
this much more than being fed upon foreign dainties
which one can procure any where.   There was a picture in our dining room which was a complete *sign of
the times*; upon it was painted a cider barrel, from
which a man was drawing 'hard cider,' bearing the
motto, 'Old Tip's claims to the White House cannot be
jumped.' This had been borne as a banner by the
Peoria delegation at the whig convention of Fort
Meigs. If one might judge by what one sees, Gen.
Harrison will have the votes of all the west, as he
seems to be very popular as far as we have been.
Upon returning to the parlor we found a centre table
13*

containing annuals, and several excellent volumes of
the best authors, bearing the names of the young
ladies of the house.   While I looked over these, my
companion took up the Peoria Democrat, and expressed his surprise to see such a paper in so new a place,
and in it such proofs of the trade of the place.   The
type and paper were as good as any in our city, and
contained advertisements of goods, drugs, wines,
fruits, and other articles, which makes one wonder
how such things could find their way there.   Another
column explains this, where are notices of steamboats which ply between this place and St. Louis, but
three or four days voyage to New Orleans; consequently, one may command any thing here.   In three
years the Michigan canal will be finished, which will
open a communication with the Atlantic through the
lakes and the New York canals.   Peoria cannot fail of
being a place of much business, for besides the above
named advantages, the land around it is rich prairie,
interspersed with wood land, or timber, as they call it
here, crossed by several mill streams.   It is but
seventy miles from Springfield, the capitol of Illinois,
a large and handsome town, doing a great deal of
business, and situated in the celebrated county of Sangamon.

Over the level country around Peoria good roads
are laid out in every direction.   A railroad is in contemplation from hence to the Mississippi at Warsaw,
while another, the Bloomington and Peoria railroad,
is soon to be laid down from this to the Mackinaw
river, forty miles.   It is on the high road from the
gulf of Mexico to the north, and already travellers
are taking this rout to the eastern States.   We found

here a young lady and her father who had come from Mobile. They left there in a steamboat for New Orleans, from thence other steamboats brought them up the Mississipp to Quincy, from whence they rode in a stage to Peoria. They were on their way to New York, and had taken this rout from its novelty. In the afternoon we rambled down to the shores, where I found some very pretty pieces of agate, jasper, and other pretty pebbles, and gathered several singular shells and flowers. The shells were principally large muscle, lined with pearl, some of them beautifully irredescent. A neat cottage on the bank with its door open looked so inviting that we ventured to enter and ask for a glass of water. The woman willingly filled a pitcher from a cool spring near, and invited us to sit down. She looked ill, and the children around her were thin and pale. I asked her the cause, and heard a sad story of fever and ague sickness. They had removed from Pennsylvania, and had all been ill as soon as they arrived, but had hopes of being after a while acclimated. The cause of their sickness was as usual, their exposure to the heavy fogs which arise from this river at night, which strangers should avoid for a year at least—and probably other imprudence. Her husband was a carpenter, who had sufficient employment where they had lived, and there they were well and happy. To my question of the cause of their removal she answered. ‘Oh, he had heard of the west, where every one is sure to get rich, and so he came.’ Most of the emigrants we have met with could give us no better reason for removing hither than this woman. They hear the west spoken of as a great, rich, and rising country;

pull up their household by the roots, and, 'westward hold their way.' I believe no one but our people can thus readily leave their homes, and the graves of their fathers to seek a residence in new and untried regions. Among the emigrants, we were often surprised to see so many from the neighboring States. Hoffman met a man during his 'winter in the west,' who had removed his household from one end of the State of Michigan to the other, merely because, the mould was a foot richer at Kalamazoo—his own being eighteen inches. A man removes from the eastern border to the west of Pennsylvania. Perhaps he there erects a house and in a few years sees a good farm around him; another wishing to remove west, offers him a sum for it, so much larger than his original outlay, that he is tempted to sell, and emigrate farther west. He with this money purchases a place of a man in Ohio, who sells in the same way and passes on. In a few years the Pensylvanian again sells, and again removes, so that there is a constant stream going step by step to fill up the immense plains and valleys which here abound. Fashions for emigration prevail; a place becomes popular; every one is excited by the accounts of this new *Dorado*, and westward ho! is the cry. Boon's, Lick in Missouri, Salt river, Platte river, Oregon, Rock river, Wisconsin, Michigan, and Iowa, each have had its run, and its partisans. But there is 'more than meets the ear,' in this; fortunately their destinies are not left to the guidance of their own variable fancies. There is an overruling Power, at whose command their steps are hither bent. When I see them on their march; people from every nation, men, women, and little ones, and cattle winding down

the road in their wagons, filling the steamboats,
and crowding the stages, all pressing in large bodies
towards the land of milk and honey, they remind me of
the Hebrews plucked up from an over-grown country,
and led with an Almighty hand, to the land of promise.
May these travellers, study the eventful journey of the
Palestine emigrants, and shun those errors by which
they were driven forth from its fair fields. The Hebrews were told, if they would obey their heavenly
leader, ' the land shall yield her increase, and the trees
of the field shall yield their fruit'—and ' ye shall eat
your bread to the full and dwell in the land safely,' and
' ye shall lie down and none shall make you afraid' ;
' I will be your God and ye shall be my people.' *
What magnificent promises! And how powerful the
promiser!   Oh that these people would lay these
words to their heart, and consider well the Hebrew's
fate! They were also promised to be made ' high
above all nations which He hath made, in praise, in
name, and in honor.' † There be those who predict
this for our country ; let these read the conditions by
which this may be obtained, and dread curses ‖ which
await a failure! We continued our stroll, back of
the town across the prairie, or *steppe* upon which it is
built, to another about twelve or fifteen feet above it.
From thence is a fine plateau which reaches to the
bluffs. As we sat upon this eminence the view was
very pretty. The sun had been long gone, but a
delicate amber shaded with purple tinted every thing.
Below us, was the green prairie crossed with dark
purple paths over which the ' lowing herds' were
winding slowly, as if loth to leave their free pastures

* Lev. xxvi, 4, 12.   † Deut. xxvi, 19.   ‖ Deut. xxviii, 16.

for the confinement of a barn yard.   The cattle
raised upon prairie grass are very fat, and the Illinois
beef commands a ready sale in the New Orleans
markets.   The butter and milk we met with here was
uncommonly rich, equal to our first rate Goshen
butter.   Beyond the prairie is the town, beneath
which, flows the quiet Illinois, bounded by dark forests and elevated bluffs.   While we were thus sitting
enjoying the ' coming on of grateful evening mild,' the
deep silence was broken by the sweet sound of a
church bell, echoing over the river and the still forests.   At once these words of Milton so very appropriate to our situation sprang to our lips;

> " On a plat of rising ground
> I hear the far off Curfew sound,
> Over some wide watered shore,
> Swinging slow with solem roar."

There was apparently an evening meeting about to
be held, and we rejoiced we should be enabled to enter the courts of the Lord, a privilege we had been
denied for some time.   Our path to the town lay past
several very pretty cottage residences, ornamented
with shrubbery and flowers—thence, following the
sound of the bell we found ourselves before a small
meeting house.   It happened fortunately to be the
meeting which enjoyed the administration of the Rev.
Mr. S——g, of the presbyterian persuasion, whom we
found to be a very pleasing, intelligent, and pious
man.   We were very much gratified with his discourse,
which we found very appropriate.   He spoke of man
as a traveller, the end of whose journey must certainly one day approach, and earnestly bade us to take
thought for that event, as there were many there
who ' before the frost is spread over our prairie, may

be lying under its sod.' He reminded us much of Amos, the herdsman of Tekoa, for his similies were all drawn from rural objects—the sun, the clouds, the prairie, the river, and the scenery around him. We no longer wondered at the accounts we had receiv- ed of the high religious and moral standing of the place, and the great amount of good done in it. This last year, twenty-three thousand dollars were contribu- ted by the people of Peoria towards charitable and religious institutions. We walked home under a bright moon, our hearts much refreshed by all we had heard, and we were rejoiced the Lord had placed such a faithful servant in these fair prairies, to uphold his name.

July 9th.—While wandering along the shore this morning, we descried the smoke of our expected steamboat, and hastened back to the hotel to pack our trunks. It was the Home, from Peru to St. Louis, and we were to take passage in her for Alton, on the Mississippi. We bade adieu to sweet Peoria with re- gret. The remembrance of it will long 'perfume our minds,' as old Izaak Walton says. Its situation, its excellent society, and religious privileges, and its good schools, must certainly make it a desirable place of residence, or of trade. It is two hundred miles from St. Louis, and one hundred and seventy from Chicago. When in the saloon of the Home we were pre- sented with a book in which to write our names, place of residence, whither bound, and *our politics*. While leaving this, our eyes fell upon a piece of pink satin, framed, which hung against the wall, upon which was printed the rules of the boat. Among other things it forbid 'any gentleman to go to table without his

coat, or any other garb to disturb the company. No
gentleman must pencil-work or otherwise injure the
furniture ; (I suppose whittling was meant. Upon our
lake boat we saw the boxes of merchandize and barrels on deck, fast disappearing under the whittling
knife. A piece a foot long and two inches wide would
be torn from the box and cut to pieces by a restless
passenger.) Beside these, we were told ' no gentleman was to lie down in a berth with his boots on, and
none enter the ladies' saloon without permission from
them.' We found in this boat, three indications of
being near the south, liquors upon the table, gambling
in the gentlemen's cabin, and a black chambermaid
slave to the captain. Among the passengers, were a
man with his wife and sons, unlike the most I had met,
going west, but making a retrogade motion to the
east. They were driven away they said by the fever
and ague, from which they had been suffering ever
since their removal west. Their yellow gaunt appearance fully testified to the truth of this. He had
been a shop keeper in the State of New York, who ex-
periencing some reverses, was persuaded to remove
to this golden region by his wife, who was now no
longer able to lead the village fashions. He bought a
lot, and mill privilege, in an embryo town—their house
was situated under the boughs of a forest impenetrable to the sunbeams, surrounded by decaying leaves,
moist new soil, and a mill pond. The town's people
were too busily occupied in building banks and hotels,
to dig wells, and drinking out of the marshy springs,
of course all fell ill by turns. Their boy, they said,
had been at ' death's door,' and now, although better,
was afflicted with an *ague cake*, which they wished me

to feel in his side. I am convinced a little prudence
and knowledge, will keep many 'healthy, wealthy, and
wise,' who, without it are easily discouraged, fall into
difficulties, and wish to try a new place. We have
met many upon the road, who have nearly equalled
the old woman on the prairie, who had begun the
world seven times.

The other female passenger was a young girl who
had come down the river in the boat, her home being
on the prairie, back of Peru. She was a pretty inno-
cent country lassie about sixteen, travelling alone, on
a visit to a brother living on the river, whose wife
was ill and required her services. Her travelling
dress was a muslin striped with pink; and her hat one
of that description we call Dutch bonnets, made of
pasteboard covered with pink glazed gingham. She
was rejoiced to examine my wardrobe, and cut new
patterns, as she lives far from the haunts of men and
mantua-makers. My Mosaic brooch pleased her much,
and she asked me if I had bought it of the pedlar who
she heard had lately arrived in that part of the country
with a lot of new goods, and whom she was eager to
see. I was obliged to say I had not purchased it from
that fashionable depositary. She then proposed to
show me her clothes; mine being new to her, she
supposed her's must be new and desirable to me. At
her request the chamber-maid drew from the state-
room a huge chest of black walnut, which she opened,
and, among other things, displayed a pretty straw
bonnet trimmed with gay ribbons and flowers. That
was her Sunday bonnet. She also drew forth a topaz
pin which had reached here in a pedlar's cart, and was
a present to her by her brother. 'This pin has lasted
14

wonderfully,' she said, 'considering how much it has
been borrowed.   At every dance or party when I do
not go, some of the girls borrow and wear it.   It has
been lent for ten miles around.'   This young lady had
been brought when quite young, by her family, from
Ohio, whence they emigrated here.   They had all
suffered much from the fever and ague, but were now
acclimated, or rather had corrected the causes of their
agues, and she had become fat and rosy.   I have remarked in several instances, that the children born
here, or brought here young, grow up strong and
ruddy, and their parents suffer the most.   It is only
the first generation who lose their health, as the land
improves and diseases vanish about their homes by
the time their children are grown.   This family live
upon a large and productive farm which yields, among
other things, according to her account, four hundred
bushels of peaches.   In the season of this delicious
fruit her mother gives a peach feast, inviting all their
friends and acquaintances, who, after eating as much
as they like, carry away each a basket full.   Her
family sell several barrels of dried peaches every
year.

Twelve miles below Peoria we stopped at the town
of Pekin, built upon a bank elevated fifteen feet above
the water during high tide; but now, all these places
are much higher.   The captain told us he should be
here some time taking in merchandize, and we employed the interval in seeing the lions of the town.   I
told the little country girl our intention.   'Lions!'
she said, 'I guess you mean wolves; there are no
lions in these parts.'

Pekin is a small place and only contains eight or

nine hundred inhabitants, and five or six streets. The shops seemed well filled with goods, and presented a goodly show of tin, iron-ware, dry-goods, crockery, provisions, etc. I purchased a green gauze veil here and several small articles, all of which I found much more expensive than in our Atlantic shops, freight being high on the Mississippi. In paying for them I found a new currency here, my shillings and sixpences being transformed into *bits* and *pics* or picayunes. The Pekin Express lay upon the counter which we amused ourselves looking over while waiting for change. The person who kept the shop turned out to be the oldest inhabitant of the place, that important personage who, in a storm, always determines if there has been ever a greater one or no. He might very well be the oldest, as the town is but ten years in existence. 'Pekin,' he said, 'would have been ere this far ahead of any town upon the river, were it not that there were two parties among the commissioners who were to lay it out; these pulling different ways the town was nearly lost between them. The rich country behind, and the river in front, had befriended them, and they soon expected to have their branch of the railroad finished to Mackinaw river, whose water power and timber bluffs were very valuable.' We remarked as we walked, a large hotel nearly finished; a presbyterian, methodist, and several other meeting-houses; office of the 'Tazewell Telegraph'; academy, and some dwellings. We lay here four hours with a hot sun reflecting from the sandy bank, impatiently watching the barrels of flour which seemed as they would never cease rolling from the large store-house upon the bank, down to our vessel. These barrels are from the steam flour mills, which turn out two hundred barrels a day. Beside these, we took in a hundred sacks of corn, and some other merchandize. The captain seemed well pleased with his morning's work, saying he had a *streak of luck* that day. Three miles below this he had another 'streak.' At the mouth of Mackinaw river scows were waiting him, loaded with bundles of laths and staves, and long dark boards, which I took for mahogany, but which proved to be black-walnut. The Mackinaw is a clear stream, having rich bottom land, bounded by bluffs covered with white oak and cedar. The prairies through which it flows, are rolling and tolerable land with several mill seats.

The Illinois looked beautiful this afternoon. Its glassy waters scarcely moved, and it seemed so content with its sweet resting place, and at the silent admiration of those stately trees, which were sending their cool flickering shadows over her and gazing down at loveliness, that it would fain linger upon its course, as some young languid beauty, conscious of a graceful position which is winning admiring glances from every beholder.

Among the trees, beside the usual elm, oak and maple, we observed several enormous wild cherry trees, nearly one hundred feet in height, and at least fifteen feet in circumference, and the paw paw, the coffee nut, the red ash, American nettle, a tall, slender tree, with pretty red berries, and many unknown to us, or to those around us. The islands in this river are small but covered with soft, luxurious herbage. The birds and wild fowl were out, enjoying themselves, chattering, pluming their wings, and visiting each other from tree to tree. Among the wild fowl, we observed teal and brant, and wild ducks, skimming over the water, or wheeling in flocks over our heads. One, apparently in a spirit of daring, would set out to cross our path—leaving his little cove, he would glide with the utmost rapidity over the river in front of us, leaving a silver line on the smooth surface of the stream, and after we had passed, glide back, bobbing up and down upon the waves in our wake. When he arrived at home, what a quacking and chattering and fluttering was heard! In one little cove, or bayou, was a little island, covered with rich grass, and shaded from the sun by the dense grove whose branches met over it—this seemed to be quite a colony of ducks, who were going and coming in rapid but graceful evolutions from the main land. A young man who stood near us named the place Quackville, and declared when he returned home he would publish a map, and sell off the lots. We passed several towns to day, as Liverpool, Havanna, Beardstown—the former a small settlement, but which its inhabitants intend to make larger, as they have already a railroad in contemplation across the Mississippi. Beardstown is a place of some importance. It is a county town, and its commerce greater than any upon the river. Mechanics of all descriptions are to be found here, as bakers, shoe makers, tailors, blacksmiths, cabinet makers, silver smiths, carpenters, joiners, coopers, painters &c, &c. see Peck. There are also here steam flour mills, saw mills, breweries, distilleries, &c. A canal is projected here, to connect the Illinois with the Wabash, (which divides the state of Illinois from Indiana,) by means of the Sangamon and Vermillion

14*

forks.   While passing these towns one is surprised at their rapid growth, for when Schoolcraft rowed his canoe up this river twenty years since, it was a wilderness only inhabited by Indians.   Opposite Havanna, the Spoon river enters the Illinois.   Its Indian name is Amequeon, which means *ladle*, and is much prettier than its present name.   It is one hundred and forty miles in length, navigable most of the way, and capable of being cleared further.   The soil is dry undulating prairie, with considerable timber—and some of it upon the forks of the Spoon is the richest in the state—its forks and tributaries affording good mill seats.   It is in the military bounty land, which commences just above it, and terminates at the junction of the Illinois with the Mississippi, making a triangle of five million three hundred and sixty thousand acres, about ninety miles along the Illinois, and the base of the triangle, ninety miles across to the Mississippi, near Quincy.   This is appropriated by Congress to the soldiers of the regular army in the war between the United States and Great Britain.   Two thirds of this land is prairie, and the rest timbered, crossed by a variety of rivers and creeks.   The soil is generally a black vegetable mould from fifteen to thirty inches deep.   Much of the best of this land has been bought up by a company who have opened an office at Quincy, where they sell it from three to ten dollars an acre, while other parts are sold at the price government established for its lands all over the States, one dollar and twenty-five cents an acre.   Government has given to the State of Illinois every other section.   Sangamon river comes gliding down over its pebbly floor, a pure transparent stream, between Liverpool and Havanna.   It runs through Sangamon county, of whose fertility, beautiful scenery, crowded population, rich prairies, numerous streams, and valuable timber groves, we have heard such flourishing accounts. By the way, I can never get reconciled to the western custom of calling woods timber, woodland, or groves, or forest, timberland. My young country girl, Maria, in relating an interesting romantic event which had occurred in her region of country, instead of speaking of a ramble in the woods said ' we had gone to walk in the timber.' In this famed county is Springfield, the capital of the State. The Sangamon river is one hundred and eighty miles long, and navigable nearly to the capitol, seventy-five miles, by small steamboats. With a small expense it can be cleared. We do not see the Illinois in all its grandeur, as the water is low. It falls, our captain says, one and a half inches a day, and has fallen eight feet since June. It will arise in the autumn, and when its present channel is full overflows the bottom land to the bluffs. This makes the river shore, unless very elevated, rather unhealthy, and consequently uninhabited. Soon after passing the Sangamon, we stopped to take in wood, and we embraced the opportunity to take a sunset stroll in the forest. A small cottage embowered among wood-piles, inhabited by a woodman and his family, were the only signs of human life we saw. These sylvan solitudes however, are not without their denizens, for the birds were skipping from bough to bough, the turtle were romantically reclining upon the logs beside the water, the wild fowls, and the paroquets were chattering in concert with the mocking bird. There the squirrel also

"Sits partly on a bough his brown nuts cracking,
And from the shell the sweet white kernel taking."

Here however in these pretty nooks he sits undisturbed, for no boys ' with crooks and bags' can molest his quiet haunts. We enjoyed the deep forest walk very much having been now so long cramped in a steamboat, and wandered along among the stately beech and graceful linden, the black walnut and locust, swung upon the festoons of the enormous vines which hung down from the trees, and breathed with much satisfaction the perfume from the dewy herbage, grape vine buds, and yellow jassamin which climbed the boughs around us. The steamboat bell recalled us to the shore in time to see a steamboat pass, being the second we had met this morning.

There is much travelling upon this river during the summer months. Our captain told us he had made fifty-eight trips last year from St. Louis to Peru, carrying ten thousand passengers. This seems a great number, but we are a travelling people, and with the emigrants going west, it may be true. I am chary of repeating things heard upon the road as I know my country people delight in quizzing travellers. I have had some awful examples of this lately, sufficient to make me cautious, in regard to certain tourists from abroad to this country; and when told any thing dubious, remember the *three miles of roast pig ;* the *drunken ladies of Boston ;* the *piano with pantalets* upon its legs ; the canvass bags to hold specie in times of bank troubles, etc. etc. Pretty Maria's travelling bonnet, which I described to you, also reminds me of the misconceptions to which travellers are liable, who take a hasty glance and go not to the best sources for information. As proof of the poverty of the country, low style of dress and manners, an European traveller tells his readers the richest ladies wear hats of their own manufacture, made of pasteboard covered with calico or gingham. And so they do ; but only to run in the garden, or to a neighbor in the connty, for you know we all, when in the county, use these as garden hats, as they shelter the face so well from the sun. I wish you could transport yourself here at this moment, and seat yourself by me upon the huricane deck, and see how perfectly the forest shore is reflected upon the quiet polished Illinois. This stream cannot be called a flowing one for it has scarcely any current, but reposes in its bed with the tranquility of a lake. Now it lies in evening's deep shadow, while, as we look above, the topmost plumage is tipt with gold—this gradually disappears,—darkness succeeds, except where one struggling moon-beam, from the Indians Tibic geezis, *night sun*, streams down the long forest vista, and lies like a silver ribbon across the river. I always go to bed with the chickens while on board a steamboat, as a light attracts mosquetoes, and here river fog forbids us to sit out of doors—so good night.

July 10.—Off Meredosia. This is a thriving town, built upon one of those elevated terraces which occur frequently along the river as if on purpose to raise the settlements above the damp alluvion, and to give them a pretty effect. It is in a good situation to rise, as it is a sort of business port to Jacksoville, to which a railroad of twenty-three miles is in operation ; and Morgan county, upon which it is situated, is a thickly peopled district, having good timbered lands, mill streams, quarries of lime and free stone ; and is wa-

tered by many streams.   Jacksonville is a large town
where there are several churches, a court house, mills
and shops.   The Quincy and Danville railroad passes
through Meredosia, to the Wabash river, two hundred
and twenty miles.   Through this river, communication is held with the lakes.   Their exports are between two and three hundred thousand dollars, and
imports five hundred thousand dollars.   Here we took
in several passengers.   Six miles below Meredosia is
Naples, a small collection of shops and dwellings,
situated upon a high bank.   Upon one house, larger
than the rest, I read the name 'Napoleon Coffee
House.'   I looked around for Vesuvius, but saw it
not, nor any other Neopolitan traces.   The names upon
this river are very ludicrous, and striking monuments
of the want of taste in those who bestowed them.
One would imagine, from reading my last letter, I had
been travelling in seven league boats, or in a balloon,
as I have touched at Peru, Pekin, Havanna, Liverpool, Naples, Brussels, Rome, (part in the night,)
&c.   While the Indian names are so pretty, why are
they neglected for such worn out European designations. Peoria, and Illinois, and Ottawa are very pretty ;
Hennipen is very well, as given in honor of one of the
early discoverers of this county from France, and it
might be thought a debt of gratitude, but every
pioneer has not so good a name, and if this custom is
followed, it saddles us with such names as already
abound, viz : Jo Davies' County, Pike, Cook, Higgon-
bottom, Hancock, Buggsville, Toddtown, Dodgeville.
Moreover, the Indians were the first explorers, and if
any, they are entitled to this honor.   To obviate this
it has been proposed to take something local, but un-

less persons of taste are consulted, we shall hear
of more Bigbonelicks, Bloodyruns, Mud Lakes or
Crab Orchard's.   I wish Congress would take the matter in hand, and form a committee of nomanclature to
name every new settlement.

We are constantly passing steamboats.   In 1836, at
Beardstown, there were four hundred and fifty arri-
vals and departures, and at Naples their account was
the first year, 1828, nine; from March to June, 1832,
one hundred and eight, and now, of course all these
figures must be doubled.   Among our passengers we
have an old Kentucky woman, who has been living
several years upon this river.   She was so rejoiced to
see a slave again, that soon she and Violette, our
chambermaid, became quite intimate friends.   She frequently borrowed her pipe to have a comfortable
smoke out upon the guards, where, with Violette beside
her, she would smoke and chat for hours.   A lady on
board, who had lately become a convert to temperance
cause, was extremely offended at the sight of spirits
upon the dining table.   Her husband argued for their
use upon the ground of frequent impure water, and
fever and ague, from which the stomach is fortified.
The wife, however, was not convinced; when, in the
midst of a high argument, our old woman put her
head in at the door, and taking out her pipe, after
slowly puffing off her smoke, uttered this oracular
sentence: 'For my part, I think there are lots of gnats
strained at, and lots of camels swallowed,'—and disappeared.   The husband left the argument for the
card table, whence he arose sometime after, grumbling
at his losses, and galled by the discovery that the
winner was a well known black legg, whose practice

was to live in steamboats during summer, to fleece such silly sheep as himself. In the winter he returned upon his laurels, to New Orleans or St. Louis, to revel upon his winnings.

This morning we passed one of those machines employed by government, during low water for the purpose of clearing away the sandbars. It is a large wooden ark, worked by steam. A great shovel takes up the mud, brings it up, and throws it into the scow at the other side which is emptied upon the shores. The State has appropriated $100,000 to improvements upon this river. There are several sandbars, and below Ottowa ledges of sandstone which, if removed, would render the navigation unimpeded at all seasons of the year quite to Ottowa, two hundred and ten miles above the mouth of the river. We stopped so often to take in freight and passengers, that we began to be fearful we should not reach the mouth of the river and behold its junction with the stately Mississippi before dark—however, 'we came a good jog' this morning, to use our old Kentucky lady's phrase, and now after tea we are sitting upon the guards watching for it. We are continually passing streams which run into this river—Crooked creek, comes down about one hundred miles through a very fertile region of country with a soil of argillaceous mould from one to four feet deep. * Its banks are lined with oak, maple, hickory, black walnut and much other valuable timber. Bituminous coal, and free stone quarries are also found there. Apple creek, at whose mouth is a small settlement; Macoupin creek, its name taken from the Indian Maquapin, a water plant,

* Becks Gaz., of Ill.

whose smooth leaf floats upon the bayous and lakes in this region; its esculent root, after being baked under heated stones is a favorite food with the native tribes. There is a settlement upon this last named stream commenced in eighteen hundred and sixteen, which then was the most northern white settlement of Illinois. The population of the State four years after, in eighteen hundred and twenty, was fifty-five thousand two hundred and eleven, and now, eighteen hundred and forty, it is four hundred and twenty three thousand nine hundred and thirty four, a great increase in twenty years. We have now upon each hand, the two last counties which border the Illinois. Green, on the east, contains excellent land, well settled by eastern families, many from Vermont. It is one of the richest portions of land in the State, traversed by fine water courses and bounded by two large rivers,— containing beautiful prairies, and excellent timber. In the cliffs which border the Mississippi on this county, bituminous coal is found among the sandstone and limestone strata, and crystal springs flow from their sides. Calhoun county on our right is the southern point of the triangle containing the military bounty lands. The point where the Mississippi and Illinois meet is low prairie subjected to inundation and consequently unhealthy; coal has been found here, and the large trees are famous for their honey. As we were near the mouth of the river, and my little fellow voyager, Maria, had not yet landed, I asked her how far we were from her brother's residence. She said she had been looking out for it, but every place had a different name from that of her brother. I recommended her to ask the captain; he sent her word we

15

had passed it twenty miles back.   Poor Maria seemed overwhelmed with consternation.   The town, we found upon enquiry, was in the interior, the passengers landing at an old tree upon the shore and we all now remembered a plain country-man, upon the bank who made numerous signs to the steamboat, flourishing his arms frantically.   Maria with the rest supposed he was in jest, or a madman, but now remembered he was like her brother, who must have seen her and motioned her to stop.   Maria had expected a town, and did not imagine that her stopping place.   As our boat was so uncertain in its movements the poor man must have spent the day upon the shore, and was now doubtless very anxious about his young sister.   There was nothing for her to do now but stop in the steamboat at St Louis until its return trip.   I felt sorry for the poor girl, only fifteen, and thus left to the tender mercy of the world.   We spoke to the captain and chambermaid, who both promised to take charge of her and land her at her brothers when he returned next week.   The afternoon is beautiful; we are peeping up the forest glades, as the channel runs near the shore, or inhaling the rich perfume which the summer breeze shakes out from the trees.   Suddenly the forest is passed and we gaze over the low prairie which lies between the two rivers, bounded by a line of round green hills which range across the country. 'The bluffs of the Mississippi!' exclaimed my companion, 'and we soon shall see its famous waters.' We hastened up to the hurricane deck, and placed ourselves in a good situation for beholding the scenery; a little excited at the thought of looking upon the grand and celebrated stream.   The Illinois

flowed as straight and still as a canal, about four hundred yards wide, we glided over its waters and soon
found ourselves in a broad majestic stream which
came rolling down between a range of bluffs; here,
a mile broad, upon whose bosom some lonely islands
stretched across from the mouth of the Illinois.   The
view was delightful upon each side ; the fair plains of
Missouri at our right, and upon the Illinois side, bold
beautiful cliffs, or green cone like hills, covered with
a soft carpet of verdure, sinking down upon the east
side into lovely green dells. This style of hill is
called by the French, Mamelle. In one of these
pretty nooks, nestled at the foot of a bluff, is the
town of Grafton, from whose balconies the inhabitants
obtain a fine view up the Mississippi. This town is
only a few years old, but expects soon to rival Alton,
as most of the travelling from the interior to the Missouri towns opposite, is through it. It has already
laid out upon paper a railroad to Springfield, the capitol.   The rapid tide of the 'father of waters,' presented a great contrast to the languid Illinois.   The
color is brown, but of a different tint from the Illinois,
being a dark coffee brown, but clear and sparkling.
We looked a last farewell to the fair Illinois, upon
whose banks, or on whose water we had travelled
for four days and four nights, a distance of nearly
four hundred and fifty miles, if we include the Des
Plaines. The loveliness of the scenery all this distance merits the encomiums made upon it by the early
French writers. This was a favorite river with the
French, and La Salle, Charlevoix, and Marquette, describe the beauty of its shores in glowing terms.
   The bluffs upon the Illinois shore, as we descend the

Mississippi, become more bare and precipitous, and have a waterworn appearance as if the water had once flowed along their summits. The regular stratification of the sandstone and limestone of these cliffs, present the appearance of mason work, crowning the heights with castellated resemblances, so that we might imagine we were passing beneath some mountain fastness, with its frowning walls, dungon keep, and warder's tower. Occasionally masses of white limestone are strewed along the shore, or grouped upon the green sloping bank, as if some large city had there arisen upon the river's side. Turning a sharp angle of one of those bluffs we found ourselves before a large imposing looking town, built upon the bank of the river, which came sloping down from the bluffs behind. This we learned was Alton. While our crew were mooring our boat upon the steep bank, we gazed with great curiosity and interest upon this place, larger than any we had seen since leaving Detroit fourteen hundred miles behind. To the left the rocks were crowned by a large solid looking building which we were told was the penitentiary. In front was a row of high ware-houses made of limestone, filled with goods and men; while a mass of houses and steeples at our right were brightly reflecting the rays of the sinking sun. The shore presented a busy scene; men and carts and horses were transporting goods or luggage, or busily employed Macadamizing the bank—a great improvement upon the wharves we had passed. A large brick building at our right hand, with a white porch and steps, bearing the sign of 'Alton House,' being our place of destination, we directed our course towards it. The keeper of the house being absent, and it being no one's business to take care of us, we spent some time wandering about the well furnished parlors, and staring at the waiters who were washing up the tea things in the dining-room, ere we could find any one to listen to our wants. We had left behind us the land where a living is only to be obtained by effort, and where the landlord and porters are on the alert in order to catch the stranger and take him in. Here, the cool American manner obtains; and although to the hungry, tired traveller rather annoying, yet, when we reflect upon the peace, and independence, and plenty, which produces this indifference, he will do as we did, throw himself upon a sofa, keep cool, and quietly await the arrival of somebody.

While amusing ourselves looking around at the furniture, we observed a portrait of, as we afterwards learned, the master of the house. As much as we had heard of the wild independence, the *devil-me-care* manners of our western brethren, we were here taken by surprise. He was without his coat—actually painted in his shirt sleeves—having upon his head an old straw hat! It was probably a warm day, or he was in too much of a hurry to put on his coat when he went to sit; and besides, it was nobody's business but his own how he was dressed, or if he were dressed at all, and I suppose we may be thankful he retained his white robe ' any way.' Luxury, refinement, and conventual forms may be carried to excess; but I am not prepared to say the other extreme is better. A boarder in the house happening to stray in, we told our wants, and he kindly sent a waiter for the master of the house. He came instantly and with the greatest

15*

alacrity and wish to oblige, took us up stairs. All the
rooms proving full or engaged, except one too small,
we were directed to another house, which, after a
short moonlight walk, we reached. The Eagle tavern,
a favorite name for hotels, I think, in our country, was
a comfortable house, although not pretending to the
style and fashion of the Alton House. And now
having finished these last few lines, while our supper
was preparing, I hasten to bid you good-night.

LETTER VIII.

My dear E.—Harassed by no compunctious visitings for the enormous package which I dismissed to you this morning through the Alton post-office, I have seated myself deliberately before my little desk to prepare you another. We have spent a delightful day among our friends here, and are very much pleased with the towns of Alton, for there are two of them. We are now, four o'clock, waiting for the steamboat to take us to St. Louis, and I employ the time in making a few sketches of the place for you. Alton is built as I told you, upon a sloping bank. This ground is very uneven, and upon some of the elevated portions are the public buildings. The churches here are well built and numerous, I think seven or eight; the streets wide and airy; places reserved for public squares, and several handsome private dwellings. The town has arisen rapidly, and from a small town in 1832, it has now fine streets, and houses, two hundred being built last year; merchants who transact business to the amount of several hundred thousand dollars, and even half a million in some instances. Eight or ten steamboats are owned here, and two railroads in contemplation, and the great national road it is thought will be conducted through this place. There are several religious societies here, each having houses of worship; among them the baptist church is spoken of as being nicely fitted up in the interior; it is built of stone. Every convenience and comfort of life is at hand; coal in profusion in the vicinity of the town, which is sold very cheap; limestone, freestone, and water lime, besides other mineral productions abound. The markets are stored with wild game—deer, partridges, prairie hen, and water-fowl; fruits both wild and cultivated; various sorts of fish; corn, beef, pork, and vegetables of the finest order. Madison county, in which it stands, is one of the richest in the State, being most of it upon the American bottom. It contains seven hundred and ninety square miles, and the value of its productions, exclusive of capital invested, and cost of buildings, amounts to two millions three hundred and sixty-nine thousand one hundred and fifty-one dollars and eighty cents. Of bushels of wheat, they have raised one hundred and sixty-five thousand five hundred and twenty. Corn one million three hundred and four thousand three hundred and thirty-five bushels. Tobacco, eleven thousand two hundred and eighty ponnds. Capital invested in manufactures, two hundred and ten thousand four hundred and thirty five dollars. But I suppose you do not care for these details. If I should come here again in a few years, I expect to see Alton three times its size, for although it may not rival St. Louis, as the inhabitants imagine, it must be the most considerable place after it, west of Cincinnati. The Illinois brings to it the produce of the northern lakes and States—the Mississippi waft to its doors the exports of the west, and takes it over to the Ohio, and to the gulf of Mexico, from which last it is only four or five days distant. The interests of religion and education employ the benevolent inhabitants to a remarkable degree and many thousands are expended every year for the furtherance of these objects. Among these rre Shurtliff College, Alton Theological Seminary, Alton Female Seminary. But enough of statistics, you will say, and I hasten to our own personal adventures. We ordered a carriage to-day to take us to Upper Alton, to visit our friends there, and were quite pleased to see as nice a coach and pair of horses as we could see in our own Broadway. After leaving the town we drove through some rich prairie land, interspersed with trees, through which we obtained fine views of the swift rolling Mississippi, and across it the verdant plains of Missouri, with green swelling hills beyond. A drive of two miles brought us to Upper Alton, a pretty small looking village, with spires and neat dwellings peeping through the trees. This place is very pleasantly situated upon an elevated plateau of ground about two miles from the lower town. Families here enjoy great advantages, in regard to the education of their children, as colleges and schools abound in its neighborhood. The society of this place is very superior, and its situation healthy.

We found our friends in a large picturesque house in the cottage style, surrounded by piazzas, whose pillars were wreathed with the clustering Michigan

rose, and shaded by the graceful cotton wood, and
pretty red bud and locust. Here indeed was a western
paradise! upon the Mississippi banks we found realized,
those visions so many have sighed after, a lodge
in the vast wilderness, a secluded retreat from the
haunts of men, where the confusions and follies of the
world are only remembered as a troubled dream. A
charming young family, and a well selected library,
render this retirement most delightful. A seminary upon a new plan had been lately erected near their abode,
and with a view of showing us every thing of interest
around them, our friends drove us in their carriage
through a pleasant road in an oak forest, to the Monticello Female Seminary. The building is of limestone
of that region, four stories in height. It stands within
a lawn ornamented with groups of trees, and a fine
garden is laid out in the rear. This extensive establishment was founded by Benjamin Godfrey, Esq., a
gentleman of Alton, who, to this benevolent purpose
devoted a large share of his property. While a resi-
dent of the west, many examples had come before his
eyes, of the miseries arising from the imperfect education of the young women who settle here. The
dearth of servants rendered it necessary for the young
wives around him to superintend, if not assist in
household labor, and he saw how much better it was
they should come prepared for these duties, and quite
able to perform them, instead of wearing themselves
out, and pining away over tasks, which, by being new,
appear much more arduous than they are in reality. As
the evil lay in a defective system of education, this generous individual at once saw how great a desideratum
an institution would be, uniting useful with ornamental

accomplishments. With a public spirit to be much
applauded, Mr. Godfrey erected this spacious building,
for educating 'wives for the west.' Eighty young ladies is the limited number, all to be over fourteen years
of age. With the course of scientific study usual in
female seminaries, the pupils are taught music, in-
structed in religion, and in various *household duties*.
Among other lessons, they are taught to set a table,
arrange their rooms, even sweep and scrub them;
wash, starch and iron all their clothes. Some young
ladies, who had been bred in idleness, or who had
come from the indulgent homes of Alton, or luxurious
mansions of St. Louis, where slaves await their nod,
were very reluctant at first to undertake these menial
employments; but the advantage which so good a
school presented in its other departments, rendered
their mothers deaf to their complaints. They were
soon, however, broken in, and sing as merrily over
their wash tubs, as the other pupils. As gain is not
the object of its generous founder, the price of admission is placed low, still there are some, whose means
are too straightened for even this, and these are allowed
to pay for their instruction, by labor in the house.
The eagerness to get admittance for young persons, is
very great, and many thus receive instruction who are
of high respectability, and are enabled to attend to
the younger branches of the family, or even, if required, teach others. Some of these young persons
are beneficiaries of a benevolent society, called the
'Ladies' Association for Educating Females.' The
object of this society is to 'encourage and assist
young females to qualify themselves for teaching,
and to aid in supporting teachers in those places

where they cannot otherwise be sustained.' Young
females of all ages are selected from poor families
and placed in schools, where they are watched over
by these benevolent ladies, their tuition paid, and to
each, every year, is addressed a circular letter of ad-
vice, with the donation of an appropriate, instructive
book. When prepared, they are placed in situations
where they can support themselves. Several have
become missionaries, and at this school are two of
the Cherokee tribe who are preparing to be teachers
among their people. The great amount of good performed by these ladies entitle them to the hearty
wishes of the benevolent and patriotic. The Rev. J.
Spalding, in his address before the seventh annual
meeting at Jacksonville, says: 'Since its commencement it has aided one hundred and forty-seven young
ladies in their preparation for usefulness and heaven,
thirty-one of whom are professed followers of the
Lamb. Now that 1 have thoroughly described the institution, we will leave the carriage and enter the
house. We were shown into a neatly furnished parlor, where we were soon joined by the principal of
Monticello, the Rev. Theron Baldwin, a gentleman of
great information and piety. He kindly explained to
us the principle upon which the seminary was conducted, and then offered to show us the house. Every
thing was arranged with the greatest order and neat
ness. The dining, school, and recitation rooms, were
large, clean and airy, and the bed rooms commodious.
Upon the ground floor was a chapel fitted up with the
beautiful black walnut of their woods; here divine
service is performed, by the Rev. Mr. Baldwin, to the
school and people of the neighborhood, who assemble

there every Sunday.   You see the Illinois people are
determined their people shall enjoy the blessings of
education ; and when we reflect how much the destiny
of our nation depends upon the next generation, we
cannot devote our time or our money to a better purpose, than furthering such institutions.   We left the
seminary, pleased with its arrangements, and wishing
all success to the generous individual who originated
the establishment.   It is delightful to see wealth so
well employed, to behold the ' just steward' thus ably
disposing of his master's property.   Such disinterestedness shone out in bold relief from the selfish and
reckless waste of fortune which we had beheld in
our pilgrimage, like one of his own ' oak islands,'
upon a sunny and treeless prairie.

Once more we experienced the pains of parting,
and were forced to leave our friends that afternoon.
We returned to our hotel where we are awaiting the
arrival of our steamboat which is to take us to St.
Louis.   When I look around in this interesting country,
and upon such towns as Alton, I wonder why our Atlantic cities are so full of people.   How many young
men do I know there, and indeed, whole families, who
are struggling for a living, and denying themselves
every comfort that their spare income may suffice, to
give them a showy appearance in public ; crammed
into crowded boarding houses, narrow, hot, dusty
streets, when there is here in this wide beautiful
land, room, fresh air, fine scenery, employment, everything to be enjoyed, at half the expense they are forced
to lay out among so many discomforts.   The steamboat
bell warns me to put up my note book, and I will re-
sume when aboard.

We found ourselves in a small steam-boat, which makes regular trips between this town and St Louis, twenty-five miles. Alton looked very pretty when we turned to bid a sorrowful adieu, and we regretted our time would not allow us to remain in this interesting place. We are now all eagerly looking out, for the giant Missouri, whose junction with the Mississippi is but two miles below Alton. At length the point is in view, all gather upon the guards, and bend our eyes towards the right shore,—we are now before the mouth and behold an extraordinary scene. The Missouri does not, as travellers tell us, come rushing, and bounding, and dashing along, striking the Mississippi with such a concussion that volumes of mist arise in the air,—we beheld nothing so wonderful—a broad stream rolled down between its verdant banks, rapidly, and very like a torrent, but in quite a decent and proper manner. Its color— alas, for our pellucid lakes—is a tint not often recognized by artists, but generally called gruel or soap-suds hue. It holds in solution such an extraordinary quantity of clay, that one wonders how the steamboat can force its way through it. Its rapid current is distinguished by the curls and little whirlpools among the mud. Where it meets the Mississippi is a small ridge of clay, and thick masses push themselves under the clear brown water, coloring it more and more with its impurity, until at last, the unhappy Mississippi, after struggling for some time, is completely lost in the clayey stream, as some pure young heart, striving against temptation, but lost at last. The streams continue separate for some miles below St. Louis, and there the river takes the Missouri character. I looked up the vista of this grand stream, as we passed its mouth, with sentiments of awe. A mighty mass of water—it came rolling down nearly four thousand miles from its source in the wild recesses of the Rocky Mountains, bearing upon its bosom, not a fleet of Argosies, but materials for their construction in whole forests of gigantic trees.

Such an admirer of water as you know I am, you may be sure I regretted the soiling of my bright brunette Mississippi. To watch the foam of our vessel had been a favorite pastime, but alas, what a change from the diamond and emerald of our lakes, the topaz of the Illinois, the Zircon of the Mississippi to the soapsuds of the Missouri. I have called the Mississippi coffee color; it is now coffee-au-lait, and indignant must the father of waters be under so great an oppression. Several green islands adorn the stream, and the shores are spotted with a few houses, and now chimney, and roof, and tower, piled up against each other, proclaim a city, and we are soon in sight of the city of St. Louis. An old castellated Spanish mansion is the first relic we have seen of that brave Castilian race which once reigned over these broad lands. It is, I think, their *ultima thula*, their most northern point. The appearance of St. Louis, from the water, is very much like Albany, as it is built upon rising ground, consisting of two plateaus of land, the last elevated several feet above the other, but its water craft gave it quite a different character. We are used in our cities to behold the water in front, bristling with masts, but here we saw steamboats alone, there being about seventy moored at the wharves, which gave a novel and western appearance, to the scene.

The flat boat, is fast disappearing, and steamboats, are the only style of boat, with few exceptions, which we see ; of these, five hundred and eighty eight have been built upon the western waters.*   The city of St Louis stretches a mile along the elevated shore, and nearly the same distance back. We almost fancied ourselves in New York again, so great was the stir upon the wharf. The ware-houses, of brick or limestone, made of the rock upon which they stand, appeared filled with goods and customers, boxes and bales, carts and barrows were floating about, and every one seemed active except the negro slaves who were plodding about their work with the usual nonchalant gait of this merry but indolent nation. We missed our good wharves at home, and even the paved bank of Alton, for a shower had rendered the shore muddy. Surely some Yankee might contrive a more commodious landing ; something that might rise and fall with the river, or a long pier. We drove to the Missouri House, where we arrived in time for tea, and at night were lulled to sleep by a Spanish guitar, and chattering of French voices from the shops and *cafes* in our neighborhood.

* Hall.

LETTER IX,

My dear E.—The days we have spent here, we have been very busy, except Sunday, in examining every thing in and about this place. It is a very nice city, and one of much importance, has increased much lately, and will continue to increase. Its population is twenty-four thousand five hundred and fifty-five. In 1825 it was only six thousand. There are several good churches here, some of which, we attended to-day, it being Sunday. There is a pretty episcopal of the Gothic form, a baptist church, of brick, having a neat white porch in front—an unitarian, of plaster—a methodist, and a large cathedral belonging to the catholics. This is an odd picturesque building, and is one hundred and thirty-six feet by eighty-four broad, built of grey stone. You enter by a porch supported by four Doric columns. The body of the church is divided by columns, lighted by elegant chandaliers; the sacristy and altar are very handsome; the windows of painted glass; and their is in the church a fine

16*

painting of St. Louis, presented by Louis XVIII. The bells are from Normandy. We had penetrated two thousand miles in the wilderness of the west, and were glad to find we had not yet ' travelled beyond the Sabbath.'

What nice resting spells these Sabbaths are! When whirled upon the stream of life, our attention occupied in avoiding the snags and sawyers and cross currents in our channel, how refreshing, how necessary is it for us to anchor for a little while, and look about, and consider our future course. The Sabbath is a precious anchor to the soul, giving it time to meditate upon its future career, and consult those charts which a kind heaven has sent to direct its route. The Sabbath is necessary to man, and was given in mercy. Physicians tell us rest is required for the machinery of man; that the brain and nerves, while forever upon the stretch will decay much sooner than if sometimes relaxed. It was the opinion of the great Wilberforce, that the suicide of Lord Londonderry and that of Sir Samuel Romilly was owing to their neglect of this day of rest. Speaking of the death of the former he says, ' he was certainly deranged—the effect probably of continued wear and tear of the mind. But the strong impression of my mind is, that it is the effect of the *non-observance of the Sabbath*, both as abstracting from politics, from the continual recurrence of the same reflections, and as correcting the false views of worldly things, and bringing them down to their own indistinctness. He really was the last man in the world who appeared likely to be carried away into the commission of such an act, so cool, so self possessed! It is very curious to hear the newspapers speaking of incessant application to business, forgetting that by a weekly admission of a day of rest, which our Maker has graciously enjoined, our faculties would be preserved from the effects of this constant strain. I am strongly impressed with the recollection of your endeavors to prevail upon the lawyers to give up Sunday consultations in which poor Romilly would not concur. If he had suffered his m.nd to enjoy such occasional relaxations it is highly probable the strings would never have snapped, as they did, from over extension.'

July 13*th*.—This morning we took a coach and drove about to every thing worth seeing in the city. In the French part of the town, the streets are narrow and present quite a foreign and antique appearance. Here are several neat, white-washed steep roofed dwellings surrounded by piazzas, and occupied by the French part of the community. Main street, which corresponds with our Pearl street, runs parallel with the river, about a mile. It appears a very busy street and here one may obtain goods from all quarters of the world brought up from New Orleans,—and domestic wares from the country around. As you ascend from the river the streets are wider and better built, and the upper end of the city is laid out in wide streets fast filling up with handsome buildings, public and private, some of these last, surrounded by courts and adorned by trees. Here many eastern people dwell. A gentleman of the place, told us there had been nine hundred houses put up in the city this year, and from appearances I should think this a true estimate. There is a medical college in progress, and a large hotel

nearly finished, which is said to be the largest hotel in
the States. It is of red brick ornamented with white
marble, and is altogether a handsome building. It is
to be called the 'St. Louis House.' Several institutions are conducted by catholics, as the Convent of
the Sacred Heart, and the University of St Louis. In
the library of the latter are nearly seven thousand
volumes. The court house is of brick, with a circular
portico supported by white colums. It stands in a
large court in the centre of the city surrounded by an
iron railing. We entered the hall, and ascending to
the cupola, beheld a very delightful scene. The city
is laid out as in a map below us—behind stretch the
verdant prairies, in front the swift rolling Mississippi,
and beyond it, the rich fields of the American bottoms
in Illinois, and the white buildings of Illinois town
opposite. While leaving the court house we were
attracted by some advertisements upon the door, for
the sale of slaves. We noticed one for the sale of
'Theresa, a likely negro girl about twelve years of
age.' This was our first intimation we were in a land
of slavery. You must not expect a dissertation upon
slavery, for whatever my opinions are I shall keep them
to myself, as I cannot mend or alter the state of things
by my advise, nor is it a woman's province to meddle
in such high matters of State. However I might
think, I certainly shall never speak in public upon the
subject, as I have a good old friend, called St Paul,
and he in one of his letters says 'It is a shame for a
woman to speak in public,' and 'women should be
keepers at home.' It is true I am not a keeper at
home just now, but I am travelling for health, and not
to enlighten the people with my wisdom. The num-

ber of slaves in Missouri is forty eight thousand nine hundred and forty-one—its entire population is five hundred thousand. We visited a museum here, celebrated for its collection of organic remains, and we were surprised at the number and good preservation of these 'medals of creation.' The owner and keeper of this museum is Mr. Koch, a man of great enthusiasm upon the subject of paleantology. He had just returned from an expedition to the interior of Missouri from whence he had procured ninety weight of bones. Seeing our interest in these things he admitted us into an interior room which had the appearance of a charnel house, filled with bones and skeletons, which his servant was covering with preparation to preserve them from the effects of the air. Among them were gigantic remains of the mastodon and other huge animals, with teeth in excellent preservation. This museum contained many well preserved specimens, the most important of all was a huge animal with tusks, which he called missourium. He found also a head of an unknown animal which is certainly the largest quadruped whose remains have been discovered, having two horns each ten feet long, extending out horizontally on each side, making with the head, a length of twenty-five feet from the tip of one tusk to that of the other. The missourium, so called from the State in which it was found, was an animal much larger than the elephant, having tusks measuring four and a half feet in length, and one and a half in circumference near the head. These animals, with the antediluvial rein-deer, and horse of a large size, and myriads of broken bones, were found by Mr. Koch last May, near the sulphur springs, at Little

Rock creek, twenty-two miles south of St. Louis.
They were in a valley surrounded by high cliffs; this
great deposite of bones forming an 'osseous brescia,
such as is found upon the east coast of the Meditterra-
nean sea.' 'The lower strata upon whose surface these
bones were deposited,' says Mr. Koch in his written
description which he gave us, 'consists of a bluish
sand resembling that which is often found upon the
bottom of the Mississippi.' These bones were cemented in a layer of gravel one and a half feet in
thickness. The cement is calcareous, of a yellow
grey color, containing saltpeter. It combines the
bones and gravel together, so that it is with the
greatest difficulty they can be separated; this layer
is covered with a crust of chrystalization. The next
strata is composed of small pieces of rock, and bones,
broken, and in some instances ground to powder;
these rocks are limestone, some of them weighing
several tons. The next strata is blue clay from two
to four feet in thickness, containing few bones; this
clay is covered with broken rocks again, above which
is the soil covered with trees. The whole mass
makes a hill, sloping down from the rocky bluff, of
thirty or forty feet, to the creek. Mr. Koch is of
opinion these animals herded together, and sought
shelter under these cliffs during some great convul-
sion of nature, and here met their death by being
crushed by crumbling rocks, and covered with debris.
Here we saw also the remains of that animal which
I mentioned in one of my former letters as having
been killed by human hands. Beneath it had been
built a fire of wood, and around it were Indian axes,
and large pieces of stone which had been thrown at it

as if for the purpose of killing it. The animal had
evidently been mired and killed by the inhabitants,
This is a discovery of great importance, proving the
mastodon, according to Indian tradition, had lived
since the deluge. He showed us the elephant fish, or
spoonbill, taken from a lake in Illinois, which was
saturated with oil, although it had been cleaned and
dried several years; also some live specimens of
prairie animals—the wolverine, the prairie wolf, and
the marmot or prairie dog, a small grey animal,
famous for dwelling in the same nest with the prairie
owl. You have heard of this prairie dog, whose
villages extend over many acres in the prairies; they
burrow under the ground, having, over the entrance
to their hole, a small mound about two feet high and
eighteen inches wide. Charles Lucien Bonaparte says
of them, ' It is a very odd circumstance that this owl
and dog should share the same habitation, but so it is;
and they present an example of unity which is quite
pleasing.' Another striking feature in the case of
these animals is, they make the same cry, *cheh, cheh,*
pronounced several times in rapid succession.

In the afternoon we strolled out to the suburbs of
the town to see the Indian mounds, several of which
are grouped together near the river bank, in the environs of the city. One of them is enclosed within the
grounds of General Ashley, an ornament as rare as it
is beautiful. Upon another is built the city water-
works. Upon one, about twenty feet high, a truncated
cone, covered with soft grass, we seated ourselves,
enjoying the silence, and watching the Mississippi's
flood rolling below us, while we mused upon the fate
and fortunes of these ancient ' mound builders.' The

thermometer had stood at ninety-six all day, and we
were glad to escape the heat and dust of the city.
The sun had disappeared, but had left a soft amber
radiance upon shore and river, and a purple haze upon
the tops of the distant bluffs of Illinois. While gazing
upon these monuments, and looking at the relics of a
lost race which they contain, we try in vain to pierce
the mists of time and answer the 'who were they?'
which we ask ourselves. The vast valley between
the Alleghany mountains, and the Rocky or Chippewayan chain, is studded with these antique mounds,
from three feet to two hundred feet in height. They
are generally in the form of a parallelogram except
in the north-west where they take the shape of a cone,
and by a late discovery, in Wisconsin, they are seen
taking the figure of men and animals. There is a
human effigy which is one hundred and twenty-five
feet long; the others are rude resemblances to the
buffalo, birds, alligator, etc.; these are all lying down
upon the surface of the earth. Our Indian tribes each
take the name of an animal, as fox, beaver, buffalo,
etc., which custom might have also prevailed with the
effigy builders. There are several grouped together
here, around the one upon which we are sitting, and
several upon the Illinois shore opposite. These last
consist of small ones surrounding a larger one, which
has a circumference of six hundred yards at the base,
and is ninety feet in height; half way down the side
is a step, or platform, cut into the hill about fifteen
feet wide. It is called Monk's hill, from the circumstance of its having been the residence of some monks
of La Trappe, who, during the troubles of the revolution, fled to this country and built a house upon this

mound. Here they kept a garden and supported themselves selling its produce at St. Louis, and by repair-
ing clocks and watches. Their penances were very
severe. What an illustration of Shakspeare, ' patience
on a monument,' were these old men while meditating
upon a tumulus in a howling wilderness. In vain we
puzzle our brain as to the cause of these structures,
and ask are they erected for mausoleums, watch
towers, or temples? Those which have been opened
contain human remains, ancient pottery, instruments
of war, and are evidently places of sepulchre. Some
of them contain rude earthen vases which had been
filled with food for the use of the deceased. In
vases discovered in an Indian sepulchre, near Steu-
benville, upon the Mingo Bottom, were bones of tur-
kies, oppossums, &c., which had been placed there,
that their friends might not want food upon their journey to the land of spirits. Stone pipes are also found,
cut out of their sacred red clay of St. Peters, or stea-
tite greenstone and limestone, some bearing resemblances to eagle's or other bird's heads. Arrow heads
of flint or quartz, are also found with the former article, with idols, silver and copper rings, and rosaries.
You have heard, I suppose, of the circle of mounds
around which is built the town of Circleville, upon
the Scioto river, of Ohio. Here was an ancient city,
enclosed by a double wall of earth, with a ditch between the walls. The walls and ditch occupy nearly
seventy feet, which gives thirty feet as the base of
each wall, and ten for the width of the ditch. This
circular town, or it may be fortification, was three
hundred and fifty yards across. A square fort is near
this, the walls of which were twenty feet wide, without

17

any ditch. The fort is three hundred yards across, and is an exact square. The present town is laid out on these ancient and venerable works; the court house, built in the form of an octagon, stands in the centre of the circular fort, and occupies the spot once covered by a large and beautiful mound, but which was levelled to make room for the building. This forms the nucleus, around which runs a *circular street*, with a spacious common between the court house and street; on this street the principal taverns and stores are erected, and most of the business done. Four other streets run out of the circle, like radii from a centre. On the south side of this circle stands a conical hill, crowned with an artificial mound ; a street has lately been opened across the mound, and in removing the earth, many skeletons were found in good preservation. A cranium of one of them was in my possession, and is a noble specimen of the race which once occupied these ancient walls. It has a high forehead, large and bold features, with all the phrenological marks of daring and bravery. Poor fellow, he died overwhelmed by numbers, as the fracture of the right parietal bone by a battle-axe, and five large stone arrows sticking in and about his bones still bear testimony.'*

We must regret the destruction of these mounds, but in consideration of those which are allowed to remain undisturbed, and of the taste and fancy displayed by the citizens of Circleville, in laying out their town among them, we may forgive them. There is an ancient fortification near the junction of the

* Am. Jour. of Scien. vol, 25.

river Wisconsin with the Mississippi, in the angles of
which mounds are erected.   Upon the plantation of
Walter Irvin, Esq., about ten miles from Natchez, and
seven from the Mississippi, is another very singular
group of fortifications and tumuli.   If you desire my
opinion, I should decidedly say they were erected
over the slain in battle.   Sometimes they contain but
one body, perhaps of some great chieftain, whom the
enemy's archers have stricken; others are erected
over several bodies, laid in layers, who, as fast as they
have fallen, have been laid upon the mound, the earth
placed over them, to receive another layer, until
the tumulus is finished.   Where they are grouped together, and where fortifications remain, the spot may
have been the field of some great battle, whose slaugh-
tered ranks required many mounds to cover them.
We know it was the custom of eastern nations to erect
mounds over the dead.   The army of Alexander
erected over the body of Demeratus a monument of
earth eight cubits high and of vast circumference.
Semiramis raised a mound to the memory of Ninus.
We read of their erection by the Babylonians in their
trenches, during seiges.   Who were the people
that erected these tumuli is wrapped in mystery which
I shall not endeavor to penetrate, but refer you to
Delafield's Antiquities of America, who seems to have
discovered much in the Mexican records, which
throws light upon the subject.   It is his opinion they
were Sycthians who crossed to this country over
Behring's Straits, and these people were once the
builders of the tower of Babel, and dwelt upon the
plains of Shinar.   When dispersed by the confusion
of tongues, a portion of them wandered through Tar-

tary to the ocean, and there crossed, and gradually passed down the North American continent, to Mexico and Peru. He deduces his evidence from, 1st. Philology—as three-fifths of the American dialects resemble the language of northern Asia, two-fifths the Coptics, and others the Sycthian; which last he traces in the tribes of South American, and the others to the North American savages : 2nd, Anatomy, which proves 'there is much resemblance between the cranium of the race of the mounds and ancient Peru, with those of the modern Hindoos;' mythology and hieroglyphics, architecture, manners and customs. The pyramids of Mexico, Peru, our country and the Sycthian nations, are the same, with little variation; some of earth, and others of stone. Mr. Delafield gives a plan of a building used as a receptacle of the remains of the princess Tzapotee in Mexico, which much resembles some of the ruins in Ohio. This is called Mignitlan, the place of desolation. In the article upon manners and customs, he relates the discovery of some shells of the pyrula perversa in a tumulus, which are used in Asia at religious ceremonies, and only found upon the coasts of Hindostan. He traces these nations from the plains of Shinar to Tartary, where are numerous mounds, some in groups as they are found here, all containing bodies, with idols and implements of war, provisions, &c. In his interesting book, he exhibits the celebrated Aztec map, upon which by hieroglyphical figures their course is traced from Behring's Straits to Mexico and Peru. Among other figures we see there a boat, rowed by a man, meaning crossing the water; a large tree, indicating their arrival from the icy regions to a fertile land; a rushing river, telling of the Mississippi; and lastly, a Mexican plant, denotes their arrival in that land. Surrounding, and between these figures, are hiero glyphics signifying battles, towns built, sacrifices, councils, feasts, &c., and the number of years that the tribe remained in one place. He has sustained his hypothesis very ably, and yet we may say, with Schoolcraft, this is a race ' whose origin, whose history and whose annihilation live only in conjecture.' It is to be hoped the citizens of St. Louis are aware of the treasures enclosed within the city and will take measures for their preservation—the place would be capable of much ornament as a public garden. As our country becomes settled these interesting reliques will be destroyed if care be not taken to prevent it. Their number may give us an idea of the myriads who once roved over these plains, and we may say, while passing through the regions of the west, we are travelling over a 'buried world.' Beside these races, the Spanish, French, English, and Americans have lived and died here.

The city of St Louis which is now so filled with Americans that it is rapidly assuming an American appearance, was once inhabited by French alone. The founder M. Auguste Choteau was alive when La Fayette visited here, but very aged. When young, enterprising, and ardent, he led the expedition which in seventeen hundred and sixty four ascended the river to found a city. He selected the site and with his own axe struck down the first tree; houses soon arose, and the limestone rocks around, as if by magic, were transformed into ware houses. As the French influence in the country was lost, the town stood still

17*

until the American emigrants flowed in, and since then it has rapidly arisen to its present flourishing state, doing a business of six millions of dollars annually. St Louis is the capitol of the far west, and must continue to increase. It is the central point of the great valley of the Mississippi which extends two thousand five hundred miles in width from the Alleghany or Apalachian mountains to the Chipewayan; and three thousand miles in length. It is seated upon a noble river, by which it is only three days voyage to the Mexican gulf,—only eighteen miles from the mouth of the grand Missouri, thirty six from the great artery of Illinois and two hundred from the Ohio, through whose waters it has access to every portion of the States. Behind it is a noble region of land watered by magnificent rivers, abounding in metals, coal and stone quarries, covered by a rich soil, and blessed with a mild climate.

July 14*th*.—The morning being fine we were advised to take some of the fashionable drives, and accordingly sat out for the Prairie House. The citizens could not choose a pleasanter place to enjoy fresh air and verdure. As we left the city, we passed several handsome country seats, and then found ourselves in the prairie, which is of the species of land called ' barren,' covered with dwarf oak, crab apple, hazel bushes and prairie plums. The road wound through copses, and tufts of shrubery for three miles when we arrived at the Prairie House, which is a pretty building, surrounded by shade trees and gardens. After cooling ourselves with ice creams, we re-entered the carriage and drove three miles further

to the Sulpher Springs. Leaving the coach at the
door of a large house, we descended a deep dell,
shaded by weeping elms, immense oaks, and beeches,
among which ran a brook 'that to the sleepy woods
all night singeth a quiet tune.' The water was bright
and sparkling, but very nauseous, and tasted to my
companion like the Harrowgate waters. The walks
around this stream are very pleasant, and must be
quite refreshing to the tired and heated citizen.
There is much company here during the summer.
We took another road home, and passed through a fine
prairie the commencment of the celebrated Florisante
prairie which stretches from St Louis to the Missouri.
Although trees were grouped upon the plains, we
passed several spots,

> "All paved with daisies and delicate bells,
> As fair as the fabulous Asphodels."

In returning we passed a load of fine looking coal,
which, we were told, came from Manchester, a small
town a few miles distant.

At two o'clock we went on board the steamboat
Monsoon, in which we were to go to Cincinnati.
Every minute we expected to go, but hour after hour
passed away and still we did not move. To our questions the captain gave several reasons for the delay
which seemed very vexatious to him. We endured
the day, as hot as it was, by amusing ourselves with
reading, writing, looking at the opposite shores, which
we should have visited by means of the steam ferry
boats which were crossing continually to Illinois
town, had we not imagined we were soon to depart—
and in watching the busy crowds upon the wharf,
among whom was an old negro before an auction

store attracting customers by ringing a bell instead of using a red flag as with us—but when night came, and we were obliged to pass it in our hot narrow berths, among mosquetoes which no net would keep off—listening to the noise and profane converse of the crew of the boats around, and imbibing the perfume of a dock, we became very much vexed and very impatient to be on our way.

July 15*th.* It was ten o'clock this morning before we started, and then discovered it was the arrival of a large party of St Louis fashionables which had kept us stationary, and who, instead of coming as expected, chose to remain to attend a party that night.

We, who had been used to the punctuality of our eastern cities, where the captain stands, watch in hand, to give the signal for moving at the appointed moment, were extremely annoyed at such proceedings; but before we grumble too much it may be as well to look upon the other side of the question. The steamers upon these rivers make long voyages, and require much freight, and passengers, to pay their expenses.

From St. Louis to Cincinnati is eight-hundred miles, for which we were to pay twelve dollars each, and finding only a few passengers engaged, the captain waited for this party, hoping in the meanwhile, some of the upper steam-boats would arrive, and bring him some more freight, or passengers. The only thing we could reasonably complain of was his bad faith, if he had openly told us, the state of the case, we should have quietly remained in our hotel, awaiting his summons; instead of placing the delay to the broken machinery, some hands missing, provisions not arrived, &c., off at last amids the shouted adieu from the motley crew of Negro, French, Spaniard, and Yankee, which lined the guards of the long range of steam-boats, lying along the front of the city. There are one hundred and sixty steam-boats plying between this city and other ports. The city and its spires now fades away; and we station ourselves, in a favorable position for beholding this famous country. The Illinois shore is low, covered with forest, and is the rich part of the State, which was called by the Spaniards, American bottom, bottom land being the alluvion which is found upon the river shores between the water and the bluffs, and which is usually overflowed at high water. A feature peculiar to the county is, the land nearest the river is highest owing to the constant deposit, and when the water retires lakes are left along the low land, which gradually dry away. This bottom extends from the Kaskaskiah river to the mouth of the Missouri, two miles from Alton, eighty miles—and from one half to two miles in length to the bluffs which bound it, containing two hundred and eighty-eight thousand square acres. The soil is of inexhaustible fertility, averaging from twenty to twenty-five feet. Coal is abundant in this alluvion, and in the bluffs. This is carried to St. Louis in great quantities, over the railroad, to Illinois town. The Missouri side rises into high limestone bluffs, upon which is built near the city, Jefferson barracks, a fine quadrangular building, containing fifteen hundred United States troops, and a few miles farther Herculaneum, having at the edge of the cliff a high shot tower. Near this tower is a bowlder of vermiculae limestone fifty feet by three hundred. Through a cleft in the rocks comes rushing down the clear bright Maramec. It takes rise among hills covered with pine trees, so valuable in this region. Its banks are rich with lead, iron and salt, and has formerly been a favorite haunt of the Indian tribes from the quantity of pottery, bones, and arrow heads found there. Behind these cliffs commences the celebrated lead region, where such quantities are exported. The mineral region of Missouri, Iowa, and Wisconsin, are stated by Dr. Owen, the State geologists, to be capable of producing more of this article than the whole of Europe. Missouri sends some to China, and has exported this year, to that country, five hundred pigs of lead, to be used for lining tea chests. The rocks appear broken up in odd fantastic shapes, taking the name of devil's tea table, backbone oven, grand tower, etc. This last in a tall solitary rock, about one hundred feet high, covered by a tuft of cedars, its stratification as distinct as if it was a stone tower. The cornice rocks are a ledge which runs along the top of the bluffs for nearly ten miles. These rocks are said by geologists, to have been once the barrier of a large lake or inland sea, over them poured another niagara, which, wearing through them, caused their jagged appearance. When it burst through, it carried with it and deposited that enormous mass of alluvion which extends an hundred miles into the gulf of Mexico. The rock along this shore is mostly a blue compact limestone, thought by Schoolcraft to be the muscle kalck of the Germans; sometimes it occurs fœtid. Near the city of St. Louis, in this limestone, were found the impressions of two human feet, as if the person had stood upon it while soft. The impressions were perfect, and were not sculptured in the rock. This slab was cut out and taken to New Harmony, upon the Wabash.

The scenery I am attempting to describe is very beautiful and varied. The broad river, about a mile wide carries us rapidly along from promontory to point, crowned by a village, ever showing us new beauties. The high wall at our right hand is not a mere line of rocks, but supports the land which commences from their summits, as if the river once flowing at that height had gradually worn its way down. This, however is not the case, the deep bed having been scooped out by diluvial torrents. An amateur of geology at Alton, has another theory, and attributes the location and course of their rivers to fissures in the coal measures. One side of the fractured strata is raised and the other depressed, so that perpendicular rocks do not appear upon both sides of the rivers. Whether this be the cause of their direction I know not; but that the cliffs occur upon but one side of the stream, I observed upon the Illinois and Mississippi. St. Genevieve, which we passed this afternoon, is one of those old French towns, which were built during the sway of France over these fertile regions. We stopped at the landing where are a few houses, while the village is a short distance up the Gabouri creek, upon which it is built. We could see the steep slate roofed French houses, neatly white-washed; the court house and catholic church, whose cross glittered in the afternoon sun. Beside the river is a fertile portion of land which was allowed to the town by the Spaniards as *common land* upon which was raised the produce for town consumption. The town once stood here beside the Mississippi, but as the bank began to crumble away they removed farther inland. About thirty miles in the interior are the celebrated iron mountains, formed of micaceous iron ore. The pilot knob is three hundred and one feet high, with a base of a mile in circumference. The iron occurs here in masses of several tons weight. The other hill is three hundred and fifty feet high, both ores yielding eighty per cent. Near the town is a quarry of fine white marble, and a deposite of dazzling white sand which is sent to Pittsburgh and sold to the glass factories. This is one of the ports from which the iron and lead is shipped.

Kaskaskia is another French town nearly opposite this place, but being built four miles up the Kaskaskia river, we could only see its landing. It was settled by La Salle in 1683, and was supported by the Indian fur trade, and afterwards by flour, exporting in 1746, eight hundred weight to New Orleans. There is here a catholic nunnery. The Kaskaskia river is a fine stream which runs into the Mississippi, a short distance above St. Genevieve upon the Illinois shore. It is four hundred miles long, but navigable not quite a hundred, owing to obstructions which could, with small expense, be cleared away. Some of the best land in the State is upon its banks.

Chester is a small town a few miles beyond it, seated at the foot of a high range of cliffs. Although small in appearance it carries on a brisk trade, its exports by steamboat being, in 1836, one hundred and fifty thousand dollars. Among other manufactories is one for making castor oil. Near this is fort Chartres, built by the French in 1720, to defend themselves against the Spaniards.   It was a fine specimen of the style of Vaubon, and built in the most solid manner, but now lies in ruins, having large trees growing upon its prostrate walls.

At the mouth of Big Muddy river, forty miles below Kaskaskia, we stopped to take in wood, and we went on shore to take an evening stroll.   The French named this stream *riviere au vase*, from a vase of earthen ware discovered upon its banks.   There is much good coal upon its shores.   We wandered through the ' the forest's leafy labyrinth,' wondering at the great size, and luxuriant foliage of the trees. The locust here grows to the height of eighty or ninety feet; the beeches, oaks, and sycamores, are enormous.   The parsimon grows larger here than with us.   We also observed the Chickasaw plum, the pawpaw, and cotton tree.   We seated ourselves upon the bank of the river, and looked upon it with wonder as it came rushing wildly past, much like a stream which has just plunged over some high ledge of rocks. Upon its bosom it bears a forest of trees, some old and water-worn, shorn of their honors, and some torn away in all the glory and beauty of their youth.   The water comes with such velocity that it tears away the earth from one side of the river carrying it to the other, thus constantly changing the shape of the shores, and varies its channel so that the navigator is often puzzled to find his course.

I am glad I have looked upon the Mississippi.   To read of it and to see it are two different things.   All these wondrous works of the Creator give us clearer ideas of his power and his goodness.   It is indeed an extraordinary sight—a river over three thousand miles

18

long, and from a mile to one and a half miles wide,
traversing eighteen degrees of latitude through various climates, from the arctic to the equator, over
'more degrees of latitude than any other river in the
world.' Some writers call this river the Miss Sipi,
'father of waters,' while others tell us its name is
Namæsi Sipu, Tish river. It flows from Itasca lake,
a transparent cool reservoir of water, fifteen hundred
feet above the gulf of Mexico, a clear beautiful
stream; plunges over the falls of St. Anthony, and
then, a broad river one mile and a half wide, it sweeps
in long regular bends through a wide valley adorned
with varied scenery, until it enters the gulf of Mexico. Sometimes it is lined with bluffs from one hundred to four hundred feet high, or a soft green prairie,
sloping banks, impenetrable marshes, large cities, and
pretty villages. The clay which the Missouri brings
with it is heaped upon the shores, or in a pile at the
bottom of the river, upon which a snag, a long trunk
of a tree is flung, which, standing upright, pierces the
bottoms of vessels; or as a sawyer, rises and falls, to
strike the unfortunate bark which happens to pass
over it. The danger from these is, however, much
diminished by the ingenuity of Captain Henry M.
Shreve, who has contrived a machine worked by
steam, by means of which, when the water is low, he
raises the snags and sawyers from the river. We
were told he this year extracted fifteen hundred,
besides tearing away from the banks many thousands
which were 'topling to a fall.' It seems a hopeless
task to pull away the hanging trees from the wooded
shores of a river three thousand one hundred and
sixty miles long, whose banks are constantly under-

mined by the waters; besides the Ohio which runs
twelve hundred miles; and when these are cleared
the mad Missouri coming down over three thousand
miles through a forest clad country, continually sends
down fresh victims which it has wrenched from their
homes, to consign in all the 'pride of life' to destruction. As if not content with the mischief, the Mississippi sometimes takes a fancy to make a *cut off*; instead
of following the curve or bend which it has made into
the country for perhaps twenty miles, it dashes with
fury against the earth in front until it cuts its way
through and reaches its former channel, tearing away
with it houses, lands, and whatever had stood in its
path. This malicious conduct the Indians impute to
its enmity to the white man, and fills up its channel,
plants snags and sawyers to vex and to wreck him.
The earthquake in the year 1811, the year in which
Fulton launched the first boat upon the western
waters, they say was caused by their Manitou, to
frighten the white man away from his country. The
earthquake was felt in many places slightly, but at
New Madrid, upon the Mississippi, it was very severe.
Houses and chimneys were thrown down; land raised
for some distance down the river, and in many places
it cracked apart vomiting up fire and red hot sand.
Lakes were formed of miles in length which still
remain. The introduction of steam is fast conquering
all obstacles. Before its introduction three or four
months were employed in voyages where now it is
done in so many weeks. The flat-boat floated upon
the tide, or pushed along with poles; and when a
point was to be cleared the crew landed, and fastening
ropes to the trees drew their bark along; this process

was called *cordelling*. There are now upon these
waters four hundred and thirty-seven steamboats,
from thirty to seven hundred and eighty-five tons, besides flat and keel boats, but no sloops or sail boats,
except an occasional sail put up by the keel boats.
These boats are very different from those used upon
our eastern waters. Our cabins and saloon you know
are upon the same deck with the machinery, and
dining rooms below, while above is a fine long prome-
nade deck. When you enter one of these boats you
step upon the lowest deck, having the machinery in
the centre, while the ends are covered with freight,
or deck passengers who cannot pay the cabin fare.
Ascending a stair-way you find yourself upon the
guards, a walk extending all around the boat like a
narrow piazza, from which several doors open into
the rooms. The whole deck here is thrown into three
apartments; the ladies cabin at the stern having state-
rooms around it, opening upon the deck or into the
cabin; from this folding doors lead into the dining-
room surrounded with gentlemen's berths; beyond is
the bar-room, from which you pass into an open space
where, around two smoke pipes, the male passengers
assemble to smoke and chat. The ladies cabin is
handsomely furnished with every convenience, and in
some instances with a piano. Above this is yet
another deck called the hurricane deck. This is the
best situation for viewing the scenery, were it not for
the steam-pipe which, as these are high pressure
boats, sends out the steam with a loud burst, like a
person short of breath.

July 16*th*.—I arose with the dawn, to obtain a peep

at the junction of the Ohio with the Mississippi. We turned from the wide Mississippi and its turbid waters, into the glassy Ohio, around a point of land upon which is built the town of Cairo. The land is low here, and subject to inundations, but it is expected the art of man will overcome this, and Cairo, at the junction of these two great rivers, will become a large city. The central railroad is to commence here, which will cross Illinois to Galena, from thence to the Mississippi river, a distance of four hundred and fifty-seven and a half miles. There are several other towns upon, and near this point, as America, Unity, Trinity, and Fulton, where a statue to the great steamboat projector will be erected. A little farther on is another village, called Caledonia.

Our passengers consist of a party of fashionables, on a jaunt of pleasure to the Sulphur Springs, of Virginia; some travelling merchants, and several persons visiting the towns upon the river. A state room was observed to be constantly closed, and a young man about twenty, who occasionally came from it, squeezed himself in, as if afraid his companion would be seen from without. The curiosity of the young ladies was soon excited, and by means of the chambermaid they ascertained it was the young man's wife, a young girl, apparently about fourteen, who was thus carefully secluded. A run-away match was immediately whispered about; the young people became quite in a fever to obtain a glimpse of the fair heorine. It was a long time ere their wish was gratified, as she never left her room, taking even her meals there. Our mornings on board are generally very social, the ladies sitting with the gentlemen of their party upon the guards, or gath-

ering in groups with their work, while the male passengers are smoking, talking politics, or gambling.
The negro banjo, and merry laugh, or joke, of some
son of Erin, echoes up from the lower deck; but in
the afternoon the siesta is the fashion, and every one
turns in his berth to take a nap. I did not follow this
custom, as I was unwilling to lose any of the scenery,
so that I usually stole out of my state room, like a
mouse from its hole, and after a long look up and
down the river, stole in again, the heat being too great
to allow of a long stay. Yesterday afternoon, op-
pressed with thirst and with heat, for the thermometer
on board stood at ninety-six, I went into the ladies'
cabin in search of water, a jar of which filled with
lumps of ice, was placed upon a marble table in one
corner of the cabin. The ladies were all in their
berths except two, who were using every ' means and
appliance,' to keep themselves cool. They were each
in a rocking chair kept in motion, their feet upon an
ottoman, made a table for their books, while a large
feather fan in one hand, and a lump of ice in another,
were tolerable arms against the fire king. Miss Mar-
tineau expatiates upon the indifference of our females
to the scenery of nature, and I dare say, she would
place these two upon her list of nil admirari ladies,
but travellers are very apt to look upon the surface
of things; these ladies, and indeed almost all we
meet in steamboats, have been so often over the
scene, that they know it by heart, and need not brave
heat and storms to see it, as a stranger would. Our
people are a restless body, and men, women and children are always upon the move. As thirsty as I was,
I hesitated to drink the thick muddy water, for while

standing in our tumblers, a sediment is precipitated of
half an inch. Oh how I longed for a draught of cool
spring water, or a lump of Rockland lake ice! While
drinking, one of the ladies advanced for the same purpose. 'Dear me! what insipid water!' she said, 'it
has been standing too long. I like it right thick.' I
looked at her in surprise, 'Do you prefer it muddy,
to clear?' I asked. 'Certainly I do,' she replied, 'I
like the sweet clayey taste, and when it settles it is
insipid. Here Juno!' calling to the black chambermaid who was busy ironing, get me some water
fresh out of the river, with the true Mississippi
relish.' Every one's back is indeed fitted to his bur-
den. This person had lived upon the banks of the
Mississippi, had drank its waters all her days, and
now it required to be muddy ere it was palateable.
The chambermaid descended to the lower deck, where
a gallant black beau drew a bucket from the river, and
after satisfying the lady, she resumed her ironing.
Against this practice of ironing in the ladies cabin I
must uplift my voice. I suffered from this annoyance
upon the Illinois, Mississippi and Ohio. Constantly
there was a woman washing upon the lower deck,
where the water thrown from the wheel, falls upon
the deck in a pretty cascade, and another is ironing
above. All the ironing of the boat, and crew, and often
of the passengers, is done in the ladies small sitting
room, the steam and perfume of the wet clothes, charcoal furnace and of the ironer is extremely disagreeable. In one instance I knew this to be the case all
night, the girls taking it by turns; and I never travelled
one day without this addition to the heat and other
discomforts of a steamboat. In such long voyages it

may be necessary to wash for the captain and crew, but surely bed and table linen enough might be provided to reach Cincinnati, where they stop long enough to have them washed. If not, why may there not be a room in some other part of the deck. The captain in some instances reaps the profits, as the chambermaids are his by hire or purchase, and if they charge all as they did us, one dollar and fifty cents a dozen, the profit must be considerable. It is sometimes, as in our case, a great convenience to travellers, but another place should be provided. But to go on with my afternoon adventures. I left the cabin and walked out upon the shady side of the guards. All was still except the booming steampipe; every one was asleep or reading. I leaned over the railing and found the banjo player and his audience all in slumbering attitudes, or swinging in their hammocks, and every thing denoted silence and repose. Suddenly a terrific and astounding bang, clang and clatter, as if the boat had been cracked to atoms, the wheel house was broken in pieces, the boards flew over me, and a torrent of water flowing from it nearly washed me from the deck. In a moment every one tumbled out and rushed upon the deck exclaiming, 'what's the matter?' 'are we snagged'—'has the boiler burst'—'is it a sawyer.' The old Kentucky lady who had stepped out first, took her pipe from her mouth and said quietly, 'It's only a log;' 'Oh, only a log;' 'nothing but a log,' echoed from every mouth, and returning to their cabins they all stepped into their berths again. I looked around me in amazement. 'Only a log!' said I to myself and what is a log. The steamboat is broken and stops, all is confusion and crash, and I am told it is nothing but a log. 'Madam,' said I, turning to the Kentucky woman, 'will you have the goodness to tell me what a log is.' 'There they are,' she said, pointing with her pipe to the river. Floating along like so many alligators, were long branchless trunks, which had been wafted along thousands of miles from the Rocky Mountains perhaps. 'But, pardon me madam, how are these logs able to create such a disturbance?' 'You seem a *stranger* child,' she replied; 'as these are floating along, and we are riding among them, what more natural than that they should get in the water wheel, break it, and stop the boat. But see, the carpenters are already at work, and I dare say they will have it repaired in the course of two or three hours.' So saying she knocked the ashes out of her pipe, took off her cap, and passed into her state room, to sleep away the hours we were doomed to pass under a July southern sun inactive. The most remarkable event connected with this accident, was the discovery of the fair unknown of the closed state-room. When the noise was first heard, the young man rushed out, bearing a plump rosy young girl in his arms who, as soon as he put her down, began to tell the beads of a long rosary which hung from her neck. One glance sufficed to tell him the nature of the accident, and he left her to walk towards the wheel house just as the Kentucky lady disappeared. Seeing the poor thing's agitation, I turned towards her and endeavored to sooth her. 'I thank the Virgin Mary it is no worse,' she said kissing her cross, 'but something dreadful will come to punish my wickedness. Oh how could I leave my dear mother Abbess and the sisters!' Stopping suddenly she gazed around her in affright, for she had unconsciously said more than she intended. 'Oh dear, what am I saying!' she exclaimed 'where is Edward, why did he leave me!' I soon succeeded in soothing her, and when I related my conversation with the old woman, she laughed merrily at my ignorance. Her young husband returned, and was so delighted to see her cheerful, that he immediately drew chairs, we all sat down and were soon as social as old friends. I was much amused with the surprise of my companion who had come in search of me, when he saw me upon such familiar terms with this mysterious couple. The little creature seemed delighted to escape from her confined quarters, and relished a little chat so much that she this morning came to my room, and sat some time with me. We passed this morning several islands, one of them containing ten thousand acres, which, with the rocky shores of Illinois, make the scenery very pleasing. Paducah, upon the Kentucky side at the mouth of the Tennessee, is a small town seemingly solidly built of brick, but chiefly interesting from the romantic story attached to it. It takes its name from an Indian heroine, who was here sacrificed in revenge by a party of Pawnees. Fort Massac is a few miles below it which was taken from the French by an Indian stratagem. The Indians dressed in bear skins, made their appearance in the vicinity of the fort, which enticed the Frenchmen out for a chase, when another band rushed into the fort and took it. All were massacred. From thence to the mouth of the Cumberland river the shores seem uncultivated, as the settlements are back from the river, but we were compensated by a glorious show of trees vines and foliage of every hue. The sycamore here grows to enormous height, sixty or seventy feet, full of branches; these great branches stretch up eighty feet higher and spread out all around it. The white of its trunk and limbs has a very pretty effect among the green forests. The white maple is also a beautiful ornament to the groves, its leaves being a bright green, but every breeze stirring among them displays the brilliant white lining. Its trunk is silvery hue.

Upon the Kentucky side of the river we have the pretty yellow locust, the hackberry with its dark foliage, the mulberry, juneberry, with its red fruit, and leaves lined with silvery down, and above all the tall and graceful cotton wood tree, popular angulati, whose bright green foliage is very beautiful in contrast. The groves of this tree are very ornamental to a landscape. Among these trees upon both shores, we observed the brilliant bignonia radicans or Virginia creeper, which mounted to the tops of the highest trees, and swinging down, arranged itself in graceful festoons, adorned with its pretty scarlet, trumpet shaped flowers. The river is more placid than our last, but is not yet free from the defilement of the Mississippi, and takes a yellowish tinge. Golconda we passed about twelve o'clock, upon the Illinois side, a small town, remarkable for nothing but its fiery red brick court house, with a cupola. There is a small settlement at the mouth of the Cumberland river, before which was a row of steamboats, which were in waiting for the rise of the river, to ascend to Nashville, in Kentucky, which lies upon this river. Illinois, as if wishing to leave a good 'impression upon us at parting, rises in masses of limestone, presenting every variety of scene, overhanging cliffs, promontory, walls, and castellated appearances, being the foundation of the State, for at the summit the ground continues in a plain to the lakes. Sometimes our course lay so near these rocks, that we could distinguish the flowers spring from the crevices, and the chrystal rills which jumped from rock to rock. This destroyed the illusion of towers and turrets, but we were compensated by being able to examine the limestone which presented various shades from the yellow clay marl to the compact and blue limestone and light solite. A large cave runs under these rocks, the mouth of which is surrounded by a grove of graceful cypresses, which tree we have observed occasionally upon the shore, before and after this. The mouth of the cave is an arch about thirty feet high. This cave has in the time of the flat boats been a sort of tavern, where the crew and passengers have waited sometimes for days, in a storm. It was once also a robbers' haunt. Many persons, anxious to descend to posterity, have cut their names upon the rock, and taken from the wildness and seclusion of the scene by large black letters, but I shall not minister to their ambition by writing their names. Shawnee town, is a place of considerable importance in the southern part of Illinois. It stands upon a plain, elevated from the river, with a back ground of bluffs, and seems a considerable place. The situation is most beautiful, and it makes a pretty picture from the river. A band of Indians of the Shawnee tribe once lived upon this spot, but at the approach of the white men retired to the western plains beyond the Mississippi. At Shawnee town, commences the great saliferous formation which ex-

tends through the valley of the Ohio, to its head waters, and spreads away upon each side through Ohio
and Kentucky, and along the Alleghany mountains.
The strata of this formation consists of sandstone,
limestone, coal, argillaceous rocks, and slate stones,
but the peculiar rock from which the salt water is
drawn, is a white calcareous sand rock full of
cells and vacant places, once containing salt. There
is also an upper layer of white sand rock, from which
a small quantity is produced.* To procure this, the
boring is sometimes carried very deep, several hundred feet, as the strata generally lie below tide water,
in this valley, and some wells are sunk three hundred
feet below the present surface of the ocean. Where
they strike the flint rock strata it is very tedious, the
workmen not being able to bore more than two or
three inches in twenty-four hours. Carburetted Hy-
drogen gas rises in almost every place where the salt
is found, and wells are often sunk from this evidence
alone. Sometimes the gas comes up with such violence as to drive out the boring machine, or flows
with the water, and again, rushes up in sudden explo-
sions, at intervals of hours or days, springing up in
the air to a height of a hundred feet. This gas easily
takes fire. Petroleom, is also found accompanying
the salt, and is used by the inhabitants for bruises, or
to oil machinery. Filtered through charcoal, it is
burned in lamps. In the country upon the Muskingum
river are several deposites of salt rock, or Muriatife
rous rock. In Hockhocking valley, salt is reached by
boring to the depth of five hundred and fifty feet, and

* Dr. Hildreth.

19

at another place eight hundred feet. Here the water is very pure and strong, averaging fifteen per cent of muriate of soda, and runs in a constant stream of twelve thousand gallons in twenty-four hours. Salt is also found in the Monongahela valley. Upon the Kiskiminitas river, five hundred thousand bushels are exported annually; it is found upon the Guyandot, and in the northeastern parts of Kentucky, but the most extensive salines are upon the Kenawa river where the strata occupy an extent of twelve or fourteen miles upon the river. Fifty gallons of water, yield fifty pounds of salt of fine quality. In some places coarse salt, and in others fine table salt is made. This necessary article was first discovered by the animals who seem to be very fond of it. The mastodon, elk, buffalo, and other animals were in the habit of resorting for it to certain places which retain the name of Lick, as Buffalo Lick, Big Bone Lick, etc. At the lick upon the Kenawha, the paths worn by these animals are still visible. For many years salt was brought to the western valley with great labor over the Alleghany mountains, upon the backs of horses, and sold for two or three dollars a pound. Now it can be procured at the salines for half a cent. Around the salines are fragments of broken pottery and other Indian articles, showing the aborigines were in the habit of digging for it. Upon Salt creek, near Shawneetown, is a very ancient salt work, which was once resorted to by the Indians. Vessels of earthen-ware bearing the impression of a basket are found there, and one which was evidently used for evaporation is large enough to contain sixteen gallons. This great deposite of salt seems to be inexhaustible; for twenty four years it has been manufactured at Kenawha, and in these last years one million of bushels a year, and the supply has not diminished.   Two hundred bushels are made a day.   The process used is to convert the water by heat to brine, and afterwards evaporized.

Ten miles below Shawneetown we pass the mouth of the Wabash, the boundary line between Illinois and Indiana, a beautiful stream running six hundred miles through Indiana.   Upon the shores of the Ohio near it are groves of the Pecaun tree, *carya olivæfornis.* It is a beautiful straight tree, bearing a very pleasant nut.   Pecaun, according to Schoolcraft, is the Chippeway word for nut.   At sun down we stopped to take in wood and to procure milk.   As it was rather damp I did not land, but was much amused with the antics of men and boys, who delighted to have space, frolicked and jumped about the woods.   The southerners in their thin pink and purple or blue striped coats, added to the gaiety of the scene.   Our steward with his tin kettle entered a small cottage, or rather log cabin, near, and procured a supply of fresh milk, which we saw a young country lass draw from their cow she had just driven home.   While our husbands strolled together, my little catholic confided to me her history, after the fashion of travelling heorines you know. She was the daughter of a wealthy planter in Kentucky, who, although of the presbyterian faith, had sent his child to a catholic nunnery to be educated. She had, as is very common in such cases, become a convert to the catholic faith, and when her parents came to carry her home, declared it her intention to take the veil and never leave her convent.   Her parents intreaties and despair were of no use; stay she would, and did. A convent, however, was not to be her destiny, for she fell in love with a young gentleman, brother of a friend of her's at the same convent, who often came there to see his sister. The attachment being mutual, they had, with the assistance of the sister, contrived to elope. They were now on their way to New York, and she was so fearful of being recognized and brought back, that she would not at first leave her state-room. 'Were you not sorry to leave your mother?' I asked her. 'Oh dear yes, she and the sisters were always so kind to me .' 'I mean your mother and your father, not the mother abbess.' 'Alas! my parents are such sad heretics that I ought not to love them. I shall never see them in the next world, and it is better to be seperated here.' I was shocked at her answer, but thought the parents were well punished for the culpable step they had taken in placing their child where she was likely to embrace a religion different from their own. I wish to say nothing against the catholic religion, but if parents are unwilling their children should imbibe its tenets, they certainly do wrong to place them where they are taught. It is a custom too common in the west and south, and this is not the first instance I have known of division between parents and children in consequence.

July 17th.—We are now sailing along the coast of Indiana, having bid adieu to the beautiful State of Illinois, after having travelled through it and along its coast over eight hundred miles. This State seems to be endowed by nature with every requisite for the comfort or enjoyment of life. It is three hundred and

eighty miles long and two hundred and twenty broad.
Upon three sides it is bounded by the Mississippi,
Ohio, and Wabash, and upon the fourth by the great
lakes; it is crossed by streams, canals, and roads, and
thus is enabled to send its produce in any direction.
The soil which covers it is of inexhaustible fertility,
capable of producing the richest fruits, grains, and
vegetables, covered with woodland and prairie, and
abounding with coal, metals, and quarries. It presents a level plain, inclining gently to the Mississippi,
consisting of thirty-seven million nine hundred and
fifty-two thousand acres,*   The prairie land occupies
two thirds of the State; the rest is wooded or bottom
land.   These prairies were once covered with herds
of buffalo, wolves, and panthers; all now, except a
few wolves, are far away over the Mississippi.   These
grassy pastures are valuable for cattle, and the soil is
easily tilled, and produces trees where the fire is kept
off. All sorts of grain, neat cattle, swine, horses,
tobacco, cotton, and sugar, are raised with ease. The
amount of the productions of this State, according
to the tabular statement drawn up by the United States
Marshall, H. Wilton, Esq., is fifty-one million four
hundred and eleven thousand six hundred and six dollars.   Take this account, and the number of its population, four hundred and twenty-three thousand nine
hundred and thirty-four, and then turn to the state of
the country only twenty years since, when it was the
home of Indian tribes, with a few white men scattered
over it, and you will obtain some idea of the sudden
increase of the west.

The want of timber and water, as pine is scarce in

* Peck.
19*

Illinois, and upon the prairie there is but little of any kind, has prevented the settlement of the prairies. It is the opinion of all whom I heard speak upon the subject, they were the most eligible places of settlement, as water can be procured at the depth of fifteen or twenty feet, and timber easily brought over the smooth plains in wagons, while cutting down forests to clear the land is toilsome, and expensive. The centre of the prairies is always higher than the skirts, which if it renders them dry, makes them more healthy places of residence than the dank, humid ground of a forest. The tobacco, beef, and wheat of Illinois are superior to that of the neighboring States, and finds a ready sale in the market; the latter weighing sixty-eight pounds to a bushel.* Very good wine is made there from the sweet grapes which abound in every part of the State. Coal is found in abundance every where, and will be constantly discovered; iron and copper occur in some places, while the lead mines of this State, Wisconsin and Missouri, yield more than the whole of Europe including England. It is generally a foliated glittering sulphuret found in cubical crystals, yielding fifty per cent. in log furnaces, and sixteen more after further process. The masses occur in clay and veins in the rocks. This rich mineral was so near the surface that the Indians frequently dug it up, and men in want of money were in the habit of procuring it, sure of a ready sale at St Louis. The people of Illinois obtained their nickname of suckers from the practice of going up the Mississippi when the spring opened for lead, which was the period of the annual voyage up the river of the Succar fish.

* Judge Hall.

Thirty-three million lbs., was produced in all the lead region last year. The scenery of the mineral region is very beautiful and is watered by the Mississippi, Wisconsin, and other rivers. The interests of religion and education are not neglected; the State has laid aside in lands and money, three millions for the latter object. Colleges are being erected, churches are building, and every thing for the comfort and refinement of life is here in progress. So if you have a mind to emigrate come to Illinois. We have to day passed several villages upon each side of the river, possessing little of interest to write you, except Hoarsville upon the Kentucky shore, where we stopped a little while. There is a coal mine in its vicinity. The Indiana shore presents an elevated bank upon which we continually saw farms and cottages, but the opposite shore is low and subject to inundation, which gives it a lonely appearance. Both sides however are adorned with beautiful trees. Here beside giant beech, walnut and various oaks, were the pretty red bud, cercis canadensis, the Ulmus Americana, red maple, sassafras, cornus florida; upon the Kentucky bank, besides extensive groves of cotton wood, were the basswood, or American lime with its yellow tassels, the gum, American nettle with its red berries, June berry and an endless variety of others, beautiful and rare. Fairy isles are occasionally passed, covered with pretty shrubs and flowers and fringed with the soft bushy willow called here *tow*. Indiana shows many pretty villages, embowered among her trees, or scattered along her sloping banks, and we have to day passed Troy, Evansville, Rockport, Rome, Fredonia, Manchport, while the other side, Westport is quite a conspicuous and pleasing town, situated upon a high bluff, its houses perched like eagles nests, upon the high points of the cliff, while the brick court-house stands upon the bank beneath. The river upon both sides had for many miles back, presented a succession of these bluffs, wild and rugged, but after leaving Rockport, the rocks become more like regular hills, rising gradually to a high summit, cone shaped, covered with lofty trees and a carpet of verdure. We here saw that singular feature of Ohio shore scenery, the hills upon one shore faced with a level plain upon the opposite shore. Each shore presents a succession of hill and valley, the hills on one side being opposed to the valley of the other. As if, while the river ran from east to west, the strata crossed it N E. and S W., a rupture in these would leave room for the river. This agrees with the theory of our Alton friend, that the location and course of this river was caused by a rupture in the coal measures. The boys upon the Ohio have imitated the Illinois ducks in their pastime, of which I wrote you; when our boat has passed, they push off the shore into the agitated water of our wake, and seem to take much pleasure in bobbing up and down. We sailed under cliffs this afternoon of rough, rugged, jagged limestone, with precipices and romantic dells, quite sufficient to satisfy a whole boarding school of romantic misses. The setting sun cast his shadows far over the river, leaving us in shade, while far above the trees which fringed the cliffs were painted with gold. A ray piercing through a vista in the rocks, fell upon the windows of the pretty town of Evansville, tipping its spires with burnished gold, lighting up the windows, as if each house kept high festival. Tint after tint of all this glory has faded, and see, the river is white with mist now rising high above the trees. After the intense heat of the day this strikes you with a chill, and they who know its fatal effects hasten within—reluctantly I follow them and bid you good night.

July 18*th.*—We are now approaching the falls of the Ohio, which are rapids caused by a ledge of blue limestone rocks, which here cross the river, and impede the navigation except in very high water. To avoid this, a canal is cut across the bend of the river, two and a half miles in length to Louisville. This canal is excavated out of the compact limestone, and the cut is in some places ten feet deep. There are four locks. The amount of tolls received here from eighteen hundred and thirty-one to eighteen hundred and thirty-seven, was, according to Judge Hall, four hundred and seventy-five thousand twenty-five dollars and fourteen cents, and he gives a list of four hundred and seventeen steamboats which passed through the canal during the year eighteen hundred and thirty seven.

There is a small place called Shipping Port, at the mouth of the canal, where we observed several handsome carriages in waiting, for those who thus preferred it, to the slower operation of ascending twenty-two feet of lockage. Here were several steamboats moored. As we entered the second lock, the North Star, a fine boat, of one hundred and forty-eight tons came dashing into the lock we had left, and when we had both ascended, the Maine, which we had passed upon the river yesterday, entered the first lock, so that we had the novel spectacle of three large steamboats, filled with merchandize and passengers, all at one time rising and falling in several locks. The locks are large enough for first class boats, and the whole of the canal is finished in the most solid and beautiful manner. It is fifty feet wide at surface. No horses are used, we passed through by steam. The strata cut through at the canal presented, 1st. friable slate three inches; five feet of fetid limestone, containing petrifactions, water lime, blue limestone compact grey limestone, with nodules of quartz and limestone. The water lime was used by the workmen. Cedar trees were dug up, human bones and *fire places*. When we had left the canal, we beheld before us the sloping bank, covered with houses, manufactories, churches, &c. This was Louisville, the capital of Kentucky, seated upon a gradually rising bank, commanding a fine view of the river and the Indiana shore opposite. We landed, and as we had but two hours to remain here, we immediately entered a coach, and directed the man to drive us through all the streets, past every remarkable building, and in fact show us all the lions. My head was out the window a dozen times, calling 'Driver what building is that?' The streets are wide and straight, containing many handsome buildings. Main street is the principal business street, and is lined with rows of shops upon each side, for, it seemed to me a mile, and in the suburbs, iron and cotton factories, steam mills, &c. The private houses are handsome, and some of the new ones, built of the native limestone, threaten to rival any in the State. The hotels seemed calculated to accommodate a large number of travellers. The court house which is now building, is very large, and when finished will be quite an ornament to the city. It is an oolite limestone found in Indiana. We passed a high school, seminary, twelve churches, a theatre, three markets, and a large building with wings, having a portico in front, supported with marble columns, which is, we were told, the Marine Hospital. This city carries on a brisk trade. There are twenty-five steamboats, over a hundred tons burthen, which ply between this port and Cincinnati, and New Orleans. Louisville is five hundred and thirty-four miles from St. Louis, and we have one hundred and thirty-two more to go to Cincinnati. If we are to believe one of their papers, the cause of education flourishes, as there has been published, this year, by one firm, one hundred and thirteen thousand volumes of school books, they having in these and other works expended sixteen thousand dollars worth of paper. Our driver stopped at the gate of a public garden, which he said was a fashionable resort. We peeped in, but were more anxious to behold works of art than nature, and soon re-entered the carriage, and finding our time expired, returned to the vessel. Here we were obliged to wait some time, and in the meanwhile amused ourselves, in examining the shore. Corn Island, with the rapids glittering in the morning sun, was upon one side, and upon the other, the town of Jeffersonville, is situated upon an elevated bank, on the Indiana shore. The buildings are very showy, being of red brick, and some of them pretty. Steam ferry boats are constantly passing between this place and Louisville. Corn Island, is said by the Indians to have been the last stand of the last of the mound build-

ers, who, they say, were driven away from the country
by their ancestors.   I forgot to mention New Albany,
which we passed a few miles beyond Louisville.   It
is a considerable place, doing much business, and
having several churches, lyceum, schools, and other
public institutions.   The heat drove me into the
ladies' cabin, which being empty, I sat down to put
down a few notes.   I had scarcely seated myself,
when the young catholic runaway, I mentioned before,
rushed in, and throwing herself beside me, hid her
head in my lap exclaiming, ' Oh, they are here, my
mother, my father! they will separate me from Edward forever!'   I looked towards the door with much
anxiety, for I had heard the southern planters were a
gouging, raw head and bloody bones sort of people,
who whipped a slave to death once a week, and I feared
for the fate of the poor young wife.   My information
however, had been taken from foreign tourists, and I
found this idea like many others I had imbibed from
them, was far from truth.   Imagine my surprise, when
a pleasant, good humored looking man entered the
room, and seating himself in a chair, gave way to a
hearty fit of laughter.   His wife, a tall, slender, lady-
like looking personage, walked directly up to her
daughter, and folded her in her arms, while gentle
tears flowed over her cheeks.   I looked at the father
in perplexity, wondering at his extraordinary merriment, and at Edward who stood beside him, having,
I thought, a most unbecoming smirk upon his countenance.   The lady looked up to her husband reproach-
fully, but said nothing.   ' My dear madam,' he said at
last to me, ' I understand you have taken a kind interest in my little girl's concerns, and I owe it to you

to explain the circumstances of the case. Anxious to give my daughter the best of education, I sent her to a convent not far from my estate, where there were some very accomplished ladies from Europe, who could teach her all I wished her to know. But when I went to take her home, my lady fancied herself a catholic, and renounced her home and friends forever. I returned home in despair, and while revolving my future proceedings in this disagreeable affair, Edward, the son of a dear friend, who several years since had removed to New York came to make us a visit. In telling him my difficulties, I added how glad I should have been, had this not occurred, to give her and my plantation to him. 'I will scale the convent and carry her off,' he said, in a jest. The idea struck me as a good one, I pressed it upon him, and you see here they are, and have my hearty blessing.' The bride, as her father spoke, had gradually dried her tears, and raised her head a little. When she began to understand the denouement, she first blushed deeply with mortification, then pouted, and at last burst suddenly into a merry laugh, and ran like a fawn into her father's outspread arms, exclaiming, 'Oh, you naughty papa! you good for nothing papa!' The party soon after departed, and I received kind expressions and adieus from all, and a few tears from the bride. All pressed us to visit them, and the father said if we would only come to Big Bloody Bone Buffalo Lick, he would show us the finest blue grass fields, best corn and tobacco, and heartiest negroes in all old Kentuck. And if I wanted a nice young girl to wait upon me, I should have the pick of all his slaves. I was quite delighted to meet with such a romantic adventure, for I had been looking out

20

for something, as you must be very tired of hearing about nothing but trees, and rivers, and towns. Pray do not think I made this out of my fertile brain, I assure you it is true.

After leaving Louisville the shores become more cultivated upon each side than they have been. Extensive cornfields, in Indiana, show they are as great 'corn-crackers' as their neighbors. The houses are better built, and always of brick or limestone, as pine is scarce upon the Ohio. The Kentucky river empties into the Ohio, about sixty miles above Louisville; it is a beautiful stream coming down from the Cumberland mountain, running through high limestone cliffs, and a rich country, containing salt, coal, and iron, in abundance. It is three hundred and twenty-five miles long, and upon it stands Frankfort. At its mouth is a town called Port William, a small place. Kentucky shore, now becomes more cultivated and its blue grass fields nod in concert to the maize of the opposite side. Nothing could be prettier than the Ohio as we sailed along its 'amber tide' this day. The yellow marl, which occurs so frequently along its banks gives it a yellowish tinge. The river looked as if it had been arranged by the hand of a landscape gardener, so prettily combined was the grand and beautiful. The trees are so many of them cultivated with us in our ornamented grounds, that it takes from the wildness of the scene. Here we saw the locust, the horse-chestnut, the willow, tulip and column like cotton tree. Among these the Virginia creeper, grape, and other vines are clustering and swinging in the summer breeze. Springing from spray to spray was the mocking bird, blue bird, and brilliant green and

red paroquet flashing in the mid-day sun. Among
these are pretty towns, farms, and cottages—the
whole having a back ground of jagged precipice, or
smooth swelling hills. Madison, upon the Indiana
shore, is the place where we were to strike the Ohio,
if we had journeyed through Indiana as we proposed at
first. A railroad leads from this town to Indianapolis,
ninety-five miles, and is completed to Vernon, twenty-
five miles. From Indianapolis to La Fayette is a
McAdamized road, and another rail-road will soon
be completed from the latter place to lake Michigan. That would have been our route, and we
should have seen some of the best towns in Indiana. Madison is a very pretty town, and larger than
any we had passed. It is built principally of brick,
and we counted six churches and a court house, besides banks, founderies, factories, mills and boat yards.
The streets are wide and McAdamized. It is situated
upon a sloping bank of the river, while behind it,
the hills which rose up to nearly three hundred feet,
were covered with farms, dotted with sheep and
cottages. Some handsome mansions were erected
among the hills in conspicuous situations and must
have commanded a fine view of the town beneath, and
the river winding away through bluffs and forests in
front of them. The population is about two thousand.
Madison is fifty-three miles from Louisville, and
twenty miles farther is Vevay, settled by a party of
emigrants from Switzerland. The river here stretches
away to the north, leaving a point which is the county
of Switzerland, bathed upon two sides by the Ohio,
and containing very fertile soil. Here the transplanted
Swiss have made a new home, and it is a very beauti-

ful one, occupying themselves in raising grapes. Their vineyards are very flourishing and they make much good wine. They cultivate the blue grape, Madiera grape, and the native county grape, which makes good wine. The hills here, no doubt, often resound with the songs of their father land from which they are so many miles distant. As we approach the State of Ohio we feel as if we were returning to a cultivated country, for farms and dwellings, of superior style, denoting wealth and prosperity, occur frequently upon the shores. One of them was quite elegant, built of brick, faced with marble, and adorned with a portico in front, of the same material. Our setting sun is obscured by dark frowning clouds, which threaten us with a storm. It comes in whirling spray and wind which makes our stout bark rock under us, and the terrific thunder out-roars our groaning steam-pipe. In the course of half an hour it was over, but hundreds of lofty trees had been swept from the banks and now were floating past us in all their leafy honors. A sudden stop in our boat's speed sent us all out to ascertain the cause. I asked if it were another log, but found the engine had met with some breakage, which would detain us a little while. The steamboat was laid by the shore, and took this opportunity to get a supply of wood. As the evening was mild we left the boat for a stroll, and to say we had been in Indiana. With some little effort we climbed the cliffs, and when there, found ourselves in front of a neat farm house surrounded by barns and orchards. The passengers spread themselves about in every direction, and we were very much provoked to see some of them wantonly pulling off the young green apples and throwing them to the hogs for amusement.   I do not know what kind of consciences these people had—I would as soon have stolen the farmer's pigs as his apples ; but I know men and boys are always rather lax in their morality towards apple orchards.   Prompted by a Yankee curiosity to see the inside of an Indiana cottage, I opened the gate, and after passing through a small court-yard adorned with flowers, we entered the open door and found ourselves in a neat apartment with comfortable carpets, chairs, etc.   This room opened again upon a long piazza at the side of the house, ornamented with a row of clean bright churns and milk pans.   The farmer and his wife now entered followed by a troop of children bearing pails loaded with foaming rich milk.   They were surprised to find strangers in their house and quite a crowd in front of it.   Soon understanding the case, they kindly invited us to be seated and offered us a choice of new milk or hard cider. They had emigrated here from New York State soon after their marriage, and having hewed themselves a home in the forest, had gradually, by industry and perseverance, brought every thing around them to its present flourishing condition.   They seemed happy and healthy.   From their door there was a lovely view of the winding river, and the plains of Kentucky opposite.   When we had descended to the shore we amused ourselves gathering specimens of the rocks. They were a hard dark brown limestone, and appeared a mass of organic remains, containing encrini, terabratula, and orthoceratites.   We searched the pebbles along the shore in hopes of finding some of the pretty silecious specimens which I had found upon the Illinois, but succeeded, however, in picking up

20*

only some small pieces of jasper and a few petrified shells. At a little distance a flat boat was drawn up to the shore and fastened to a tree; one of those long odd looking species of water craft which once was the only kind seen upon these rivers. A man came from it, and as he reached us, bade us politely good evening, and asked what we were searching for. Some persons would have found his conduct very improper, and his question impertinent, but I never mistake the frank, kind, independent manner of my countrymen for impertinence. We returned his salute and informed him of the object of our search. ' You'll find nothing here so pretty as is on the Mississippi and lake Superior. I've been pretty much over them regions and found some rale beauties—they are called cornelions, and red a'most as them what's used as watch seals. I found some geodes, I think they call 'em, also.' I said I had heard of those and hoped some might have been washed down upon these shores. ' My wife's got some in the boat which she'll show you ma'am if you walk there.' I looked up at the boat from whose windows several female heads were taking observations, and concluded to go there. We followed our new acquaintance into his ark, which I found was his house and shop, he being a floating pedlar, and had anchored, or rather tied his ark to the rocks here to avoid the storm. His boat was not the common flat boat, but was of the species called keel boats, and occasionally carried a sail. In addition to his sail he used oars and poles to propel it with. It was a rudely built affair, just high enough within for a man to stand, but every thing was comfortably arranged. His wife and his other woman were setting the supper table. At his request she readily displayed her stores, and would have pressed them upon me if I would have taken them. After we had returned to our boat we looked towards the shore and beheld the crew assembled for a jumping match. They were a motly assemblage of fire-men, covered with soot, pilots, stewards, etc. They formed a line—one of them placing himself in the centre, holding a stone in each hand, swayed himself backward and forward, and then sprang, some jumping eighteen, twenty and twenty-two feet, with the greatest ease. While crew and passengers were thus amusing themselves, we were aroused by the cry of 'The Ione is coming! away boys, away!' and bounding over the shore they were soon in the boat. We understood the meaning of this sudden **cry**, and were much amused with the amazement and terror depicted in the countenances of those who did not. 'What is coming?' they cried. 'Bears, wolves, sawyers, what!' It was soon all explained; the Ione was in view, which we had left behind us, and it was feared it would arrive at Cincinnati before us. The hands were working with all their might; the break- age was finished; the paddle threw up a whirl of foam; steam whizzed; pipes snorted; engineer's bell tingled, and away we went, hurry skurry, after our rivals who had passed us with a triumphant cheer. Straining every rope and piece of machinery we soon shot ahead of the presumptuous Ione, ringing our bell and shouting in our turn. She was determined not to be out done, and a regular race came on. We ladies all determined we would not go to bed, but would remain up, alarmed and uncomfortable; one went so far as to threaten to faint if the captain did not slacken his speed,

but we were laughed at by the gentlemen who enjoyed
the sport.   Hour after hour of the night passed away
while we rushed swiftly through the waters, with our
foe just in our rear.   'Hurra! fling on more wood!'
was the cry from below.   High blazed the furious fire,
illuminating the water around; the steam increased—
the engine worked madly—the boat strained and
groaned at every stroke, and seemed actually to spring
out of the water.   Behind us come our rival puffing,
panting, snorting, throwing out volumes of flame and
sparks like some fiery dragon of old, and as she came
near, we could see into her lower deck, where around
the fierce fire, shadowy forms were rushing, bounding,
carrying wood, heaping it on, shouting and cursing.
One strain too much—one upright snag in our path,
and we should all be strewed, some hundred souls,
upon the water, writhing, agonizing, dying—and all
for what? that we might arrive one hour the sooner
in the night, at Cincinnati, where we should be obliged
to lie still till morning; or perhaps it was the *honor*
of beating another boat,—honor here setting the steam
in motion as well as the sword.   Our rival, unable to
compete with us, abandoned the race, and was soon
left behind; our people satisfied with this wonderful
triumph relaxed in their speed; the ladies recovered
from their fears, and one by one crept into their berths.
We had here no such heroine as she who is going the
rounds in the newspapers, who in the excitement of
the race, finding the wood failing, directed her smoked
hams to be thrown on the fire.

Sixteen miles below Cincinnati is the residence of
Gen. Harrison, the candidate for the Presidency.   It is
said he lived in a log cabin, but it was a neat country

dwelling, which, however, I dimly saw by moonlight. To judge from what we have seen upon the road, Gen. H. will carry all the votes of the west, for every one seemed enthusiastic in his favor. Log cabins were erected in every town, and a small one of wickerwork stood upon nearly all the steamboats. At the wood-yards along the rivers, it was very common to see a sign bearing the words, 'Harrison wood'; 'whig wood,' or ' Tippicanoe wood,' he having gained a battle at a place of that name. The western States indeed, owe him a debt of gratitude, for he may be said to be the cause, under Providence, of their flourishing condition. He subdued the Indians, laid the land out in sections, thus opening a door for settlers, and in fact, deserves the name given him of ' Father of the west.'

We have now passed another State, Indiana, along whose borders by the winding of the river, we have come three hundred and fifty miles from the Wabash river. It is a fertile State, like its surrounding sister States, having but little hilly ground, most of it being undulating prairie. It is crossed by several fine rivers; has the Ohio for its southern, and lake Michigan for its northern border. It is two hundred and seventy-five miles long and one hundred and forty-five broad, containing thirty-eight thousand square miles. Except the sand hills of lake Michigan, and swamps of the Kankakee, its soil is of inexhaustible fertility. Canals to the aggregate length of two hundred and thirty miles have been completed, or are in a state of forwardness, and ninety-five of railroads. Indianapolis is the capitol, situated in Marion county, upon the White river, and in the centre of the State. This county is a very fertile one, having raised the last year, according to the marshal's report, nine hundred thousand bushels of corn ; sixty-seven thousand bushels of oats ; thirty thousand bushels of wheat, and twenty thousand head of hogs. Indianapolis is only twenty years old, having been, upon its site, a dense forest in 1820 ; now it has several public buildings, churches, schools, court-house, etc., and two thousand inhabitants.   The amount of tolls taken upon the canals and railroads of Indiana amount to twenty-eight thousand five hundred dollars.   Salt of a very fine kind is made in Fountain county.   Its population is six hundred and eighty-three thousand three hundred and fourteen.   At two o'clock at night we arrived at Cincinnati, and took up our position at the end of a long line of steamers, where we tried to sleep until morning.

LETTER X.

My dear E.—As much as we had heard of Cincinnati, we were astonished at its beauty and extent, and of the solidity of its buildings. It well merits the name bestowed upon it here,—*Queen of the west.* We have explored it thoroughly by riding and walking, and pronounce it a wonderful city. The hotel to which we were recommended, the Broadway House, was commodious and well conducted. The family is a very agreeable one, and well educated, but remain in their own private apartments. There are numerous other hotels of all descriptions, but none rival it, unless it may be the new one called the Henri House. Soon after breakfast we ordered a carriage, which we found to be quite as handsome as any we have in our city. We spent the morning slowly driving up and down each street, along the Miami canal, and in the environs of the city in every direction, and were quite astonished—not because we had never seen larger and finer cities, but that this should have arisen in what

was so lately a wilderness. Its date, you know, is
only thirty years back. The rows of stores and ware-
houses; the extensive and ornamented private dwellings; the thirty churches, many of them very handsome, and other public buildings, excited our surprise.
Main street is the principal business mart. While in
the centre of this street, we mark it for a mile ascending the slope upon which the town is built, and in
front it seems interminable, for the river being low,
we do not observe we are looking across it to the
street of the opposite city of Covington, until a steamboat passing, tells us where the city ends. Broadway
is another main artery of this city; not, however, devoted to business, but bounded upon each side by rows
of handsome dwellings. Third, Fourth, Seventh, Vine,
and many other streets, show private houses not sur-
passed by any city we had visited. They are generally extensive, and surrounded by gardens, and
almost concealed from view of the passers, by groves
of shade trees and ornamental shrubbery. An accidental opening among the trees shows you a glimpse
of a piazza or pavillion, where, among groves and
gardens, the air may be enjoyed by the children or
ladies of the family.

We visited a museum in hopes of seeing some
Indian relics or organic remains, but found these curiosities had met with the fate of all things in America,
destruction by fire. The owner of the museum had
been nineteen years collecting it, and it contained,
among other things, bones of mastodon, and mummies,
taken from a cave in Kentucky. The last, we were
informed by the wife of the proprietor, were in a sitting posture, wrapped in mantles, one having red hair,

the other black. She was now doing her best to collect another museum. Their house is a very nice
one, having three tiers of rooms, and is rented to
them for one thousand dollars. 'How did the fire
originate?' I asked of the lady of the museum. 'Why,
ma'am,' said she, 'you must know the cellar of this
house, unbeknown to me, was let out to a *yellow barber,* who had some powder for sale which blew up
to our garret one day, and set it on fire. I heard the
explosion, but thought it one of the steamboats at the
wharf——' 'Pardon me madam,' I said, 'but pray
how many times a week do your steamboats blow
up?' 'Why, I can't exactly tell——' 'Oh, well;
go on with your story.' 'That day I came into this
room before it was burnt, and says, George, says I,
to the man who is now playing on the organ just
as he was then, George, what is that which smells
so much like burnt paint? Why, missus, says he, it
is the back of this yere bench which was almost a
coal afore I put it out. Why, George, says I, how
did that happen? Why, the yaller barber's stove-
pipe was so hot, says he, it sot it afire. I ran to
the bench and found it had been, sure enough, burnt,
and the wall felt quite hot. George, what is that
crackling noise, says I. Why it's the yaller barber's
stove-pipe what's a cooling, says he. But I smelt
smoke, and I said to George, George, do run up *stars*
and see if there aint any fire anyhow. He went, but
soon came thumping down again, making as much
noise as if he had been a great mastydone. George,
says I, what's the matter? Matter! why, gorry,
massa missus! the roof's burnt and fell on the garret
floor, and the garret floor's afire and fell on the third

21

story floor—— Pshaw, George, you're poking fun
at me; but just then up runs my husband as wild as a
prairie wolf. Wife! Good God! the roof is all
afire! he cried and ran up stairs; when, just as he
reached the second flight, the third floor fell down
upon him, and he was enveloped in flames. He was
dug out, and you may be sure he was a show; burnt
to a mummy; his hat looking a bit of coke; his dress
hanging in scorched tatters, and blind with smoke, he
staggered about like a drunken nigger. He was six
weeks before he recovered from that burning.' 'Indeed; this fire has cost you much suffering.' 'I have
not told you all. There is a young girl, a distant rela-
tion living with me, to whom I am much attached; she
was up stairs, heard a noise, saw the fire, and went to
run down stairs, when behold the stairs was away—
burnt and fell down. She ran about like a wild Injun,
trying to escape, but could not, and at last sank down
at the place where the stairs had been, and expected
to die. Just at that moment, as if sent by Providence,
some men from a flat boat ran up to help us. 'Why,
mother, you're in a bad fix anyhow,' said one; 'what
is your greatest treasure here, and we will try to save
that first.' My greatest treasure, I said, is a young
girl, whom I dearly love, who is up stairs; but I am
afraid you cannot save her. He ran along and looked
up, when, just then, in a fit of despair, she flung herself down, thinking she might as well die so, as she
must die up stairs anyhow, and he being just under
caught her. She was very much bruised, and her
head is still much affected with heat and wounds.' I
truly sympathized with the unfortunate dillitante, as
the loss of a museum which one has been collecting

twenty years is a serious evil. I think it behooves
the citizens of Cincinnati to encourage her endeavors
to gather a new collection, by patronizing her museum.
From the upper balcony is a very beautiful view of the
opposite shores of Kentucky. The two towns of Covington and Newport line the bank with numerous
buildings, some of them very pretty; while behind
them arise a range of picturesque hills, covered with
luxuriant herbage. These two towns are separated
by the river Licking, whose bright waters, after flowing for two hundred miles through the fair plains of
Kentucky, enter the Ohio opposite Cincinnati. Beneath us we looked down upon the wharf, which was
a scene of mixed gaiety and business. A row of
steamboats lay along the shore, from and to which
flowed a constant current of men and goods. From
some of the largest, the music of the band which they
always carry sounded merrily, while broad, bright
flags floated out upon the summer breeze.

Re-entering our carriage, we drove down to Fulton,
a town about two miles from Cincinnati, but which
may be called a part of it, as the road is one long
street leading to it, containing iron founderies, water
works, lumber yards, &c. Omnibuses are constantly
passing and re-passing along this street. We observed
here several large steamboats upon the stocks, some of
which were copper bottomed, as a guard against snags.
Fulton looks pretty at a distance, seated at the foot,
of a round, soft green hill. After tea, we passed
through the city, to the river, along whose bank, is
a very pretty road. This is the fashionable evening
drive, and we passed several carriages, containing ladies and children, and young persons on horseback,

enjoying the bland evening air.   Although the heat
had been excessive during the day; it was now
perfectly cool, which is usually the case here.   Kentucky looked very lovely, as the setting sun tinged its
hill tops, and threw a rosy haze over its groves, and
fields and pretty cottages.   The broad river looked
placid and lustrous, as if rejoicing in the pretty reflections which lay upon its surface.   A small fort opposite, we were told was erected in honor of the hero
of Tippecanoe, Gen. Harrison, who is much beloved
here, and whom they expect to be the next President
of the United States.

July 20th.—I am happy to inform you the state of
religion and morals in this place, are such as would
please every lover of Jesus and of good order.   One
fact speaks for itself, there are here thirty churches.
There are also twelve public schools, and between two
and three thousand scholars, who are there educated,
What a blessed thing is it to see a city, instead of
lavishing its surplus wealth upon theatres and places
of dissipation, erecting schools, and such respectable.
nay, elegant houses of public worship as we see in
Cincinnati.   The consequences are seen in the circumstances and behaviour of the people.   Here is no
haunt of vice, no Faubourg St. Antoine, no *five points*,
the people keep the Sabbath, and are respectable and
happy.   Sunday morning we attended service at
Christ Church, where we heard the beautiful episcopal
service read by their pastor, the Rev. Mr. Brooks, who
afterwards gave us a very good discourse.   This is a
very handsome church, in the gothic form, abounding
in spires and abutments, it is a grey brick edged with

stone. The interior is very elegant. The pews are all lined and cushioned with blue, while the pulpit, and chancel, and reading desk, are a dazzling mass of bronze, and crimson, and gold; they are of bronze and gilt Gothic open work, lined with crimson velvet. Some antique chairs, and benches of oak, carved, lined and cushioned with velvet, stand here, while the whole is surrounded with a railing, and kneeling cushion of the same material and lining. The lamps and chandaliers are profuse and rich, and the organ beautifully built of bronze. In the same street is another episcopal church called St. Pauls, which is in the Grecian style, with a pediment in front, supported by columns. There are six presbyterian churches here, some of which we visited, and which are handsome and well attended.

In the evening we went to the church of the Rev. Mr. Lynde, a baptist clergyman, whose church is in a very flourishing condition, he having baptised five hundred new members last winter. This chapel is in Ninth street, and is a large brick building having a tall white spire. Every thing within is plain but neat. The seats are in the sofa style, edged with mahogany, lined and cushioned with horse hair, and having, several of them, the owner's name in brass plates upon the door, as in some of our churches. The lamps and chandaliers, as in the episcopal church, are more in number and richer than I have ever seen in our best churches. We were quite pleased with Mr. L. His manner had a dignity and firmness, as if thoroughly convinced of the truths he advanced; and his address to his people came with the power of one who spoke with authority. How pleasant it is to find this region,

21*

which so lately resounded with savage merriment or war cries, now echoing the truth as it is in Jesus.

July 21*st.*—We arose early, and walked out to see the markets. There are three, well built. The one on Broadway was filled with a profusion of meats, fruits and vegetables, which last were uncommonly fine. The streets around the market, were blocked up with wagons loaded with country produce. During our rambles through the streets I was struck by the sight of a building, the oddest I ever beheld. It was a huge ugly thing, being a strange mixture of styles, and an attempt at Gothic, Turkish, and Moorish. This was Mrs. Trollop's erection, built for a house of pleasure, and rooms were constructed for balls, refreshment, and dressing rooms, while below were to be shops. These balls were to be in the style of Almacks, quite exclusive. It is now a 'Mechanic Institute,' and when not using their rooms for the exhibitions, let them out to lecturers, exhibition of pictures, or a fair. The front is of brick adorned with Gothic arches, and the roof surmounted with Gothic ornaments. A square tower rises from the back of the building having a row of brick pillars in front, this contains a room having windows all around; on the top of this tower is another, a round one, having as I said, a sort of moorish top. We saw the time approach for leaving the 'Queen City,' with regret. We left it in the steamboat Agnes, a new and pretty boat, but small, 'calculated to run any where it was moist,' as the river is too low for the larger boats to ascend to Wheeling. The river's greatest rise here is sixty-three feet, and it then runs with a current of six miles an hour

When out in the river we looked sadly back at Cincinnati, which appears Queen like indeed, while majestically reposing upon her throne of stately hills, with the glorious river at her feet. Cincinnati is built upon two plains which rise in gentle slopes from the river. Fifty years ago, fort Washington stood here, and now there is a large city of forty-five thousand inhabitants, containing churches, lyceums, colleges, and doing a business of six million dollars. There are a great many manufactories, and forges, and the steel and iron business is carried on to a considerable amount, 'from ponderous beam of steam engine, cylenders and steam machinery, to household articles.' Its doings in the pork line you have heard of, several of the largest ware-houses were pointed out to us as 'pork ware-houses.' The Miami canal comes into the Ohio at Cincinnati, thus bringing to it the produce from lake Erie. The little Miami railroad is also to terminate here. A bend in the river, and the 'Queen of the West' is lost to our eyes. The river scenery is very beautiful to day, lined with thriving farms, dotted with pretty villas and towns, having a back ground of those peculiar green hills which occur upon this river called the Ohio hills. Among the towns we passed were New Richmond, twenty-one miles from Cincinnati, Moscow, Mechanicsville, Augusta &c. &c. Maysville is quite a large town in Kentucky which looked very gay as the sun, setting over the shadowy hills lighted up its scarlet brick houses and gave a brighter tint to the cotton wood groves with which they were surrounded.

July 21*st.*—When we left our state-room we found

ourselves near Portsmouth, the largest town we had seen since leaving Cincinnati. It is seated upon a platform elevated above the river at the foot of a group of pretty 'Ohio hills.' Every one looked very busy here, the shops displayed a goodly show of merchandise, two large hotels seemed full of people, drays were travelling about, water carts were being filled in the river, and little boys and girls were hastening down to come on board and sell their cakes and fruit. I did not go on shore, as we were to stay only a short time, but amused myself gazing about, and eating black and whortleberries which the little buckeye girls sold for 'a fip a quart.' This town is the southern termination of the Ohio canal whose northern outlet we had passed at Cleaveland upon lake Erie. The Scioto river also enters the Ohio here. It is a pretty stream 175 miles long. In the country through which it flows is much iron; and forges and founderies are established in many places around Portsmouth, which is a market for their produce. The hills opposite this place are of a grander character than any we had seen upon the Ohio, and now, with the lights and shades of early summer morning upon them, formed a charming picture for the inhabitants of Portsmouth. I remarked several pretty dwellings surrounded by shrubbery, which showed there were many here who were 'well to do in the world.' What delightful residences must these Ohio towns be, for persons of small fortune, or to tradesmen. All the comforts of life can be obtained with little expense, while good air, and good laws, shed health and peace around. Our passengers and freight exchanged for others, we turned our course from the shore, and followed the bends of La Belle riviere, (worthy of its name) as it wound through a well settled country, its shadowy hills now appearing more frequently, giving a more varied character to the scenery. The water grows purer as we ascend, and shallower, so that we can at times distinguish the sand and stones at the bottom. The Buckeye tree is seen in large groves, or pretty groups or copses, giving a very cultivated air to the shores, as we had been used to see it, ornamenting our streets, under the ugly name horse-chesnut. But although much alike in external appearance our tree is a transplanted one, originally from Asia, the Æsculus Hippocastinum, while this tree is a native of Ohio, designated by the botanist as the Æsculus Ohioensis There are here seven species of this tree, which from their deep green glossy leaves, and pretty flowers are a great ornament to the groves of Ohio. It is an useful tree, and from the softness of its wood is easy to cut. In the early days of Ohio, when the settlers were in want of many articles of household furniture, they resorted to the buckeye. After building their log cabins of its branches, they formed, according to Dr. Drake, cradles, tables, bowls, platters, spoons, and troughs for gathering maple sap. The covering of the nut can be used as soap, while starch and medicine are also procured from it. The nut being brown, with a round white spot upon it, is called buckeye; and in consequence of their frequent use, and constant praises of this tree, the people of Ohio received from their neighbors the soubriquet of Buckeyes. The western people are fond of these nicknames. I told you the Illinoisians were called Suckers, the Missourians are Pukes; the Kentuckians, Corncrackers;

Virginians, Tuckahoes; Indianians, Hoosiers; Michiganians, Wolverines, &c.

While sailing, or rather to use the customary phrase here, riding along these western rivers, one is struck with the destruction of trees. What magnificent forests we passed to-day, where the huge and towering sycamore, the dark green buckeye, the lighter cotton wood, the tall and graceful shaft of the sugar maple, the white elm, with its beautifully arranged branches and purple flowers, the silvery white maple, the oak, the beech, woven together by missletoe and other creepers, on the Ohio shore; and on the Kentucky bank, the blue ash, the coffee tree, stately tulip, yellow locust, dark leaved hackberry, basswood, and hundreds of others, make a mass of glorious forest scenery, such as I am sure earth cannot surpass. But the great rise and fall, and changes of this river, and its shores, destroy hundreds of these noble creations in a year. Countless numbers we saw along the banks, with all their roots exposed, holding but by one slight one, which any blast of wind might loosen, when it falls and is washed away. The shores were strewed with them in all stages; many struck down in youth, with their young foliage about them; others in the sere and yellow leaf, while others again stripped of leaf and bark, are piled in great 'wreck heaps,' where the current has hurled them, or floating down the stream, in time to become a snag and lie in wait to impale some unconscious vessel. While looking upon them in their innocence and beauty, I could not but pity their vampire fate, so soon to be transformed into malicious snags, to destroy the passing voyager. The quantity of yellow clay marl which occurs along the shores, contributes to their destruction, as it easily crumbles away. This also gives the peculiar rounded form to the Ohio hills, as the marl is washed down, giving the hills a smooth round shape.

At Sandy river, a stream which runs one hundred and sixty miles through Virginia, we bade adieu to old Kentuck. The rich and fertile plains of Kentucky were the favorite hunting grounds of the Aborigines of the surrounding regions, as there the buffalo, elk, deer, &c. roved in large herds. Extremely unwilling to surrender it to the white intruders, the Indians fought long and bravely for it, and so many severe battles took place there, that Kentucky acquired among the Indians the name of 'the dark and bloody ground.' The inhabitants have long been celebrated for their valor. Some of the scenery of Kentucky is the most beautiful in the States, and some of the land the most fertile. It is four hundred miles long, and contains twenty-six million acres. The wonderful caverns which occur in the limestone formations, you have heard of. Population, between six and seven hundred thousand. Virginia, the land of the cavaliers, and of Pocahontas, looked very inviting, as we sailed past it; her pretty hills lending beauty to every view. At Guyandot, we landed a party to visit the Sulphur Springs in Virginia, which are now quite fashionable. Our springs at Saratoga and Ballston, lose many southern and western visitors, since these, and so many others have been discovered in those regions.

July 22nd.—Off Gallipolis, a town settled by French people, who came here to avoid the excesses of the revolution. These persons, brought up in a delicate,

luxurious manner, were obliged to plunge at once into
all the hardships of a woodland life, and suffered
much ere their houses were erected, and all things in
order. Upon the opposite shore the Kenawha enters
the Ohio, after coming from the iron mountain
in North Carolina, through Kentucky three hundred
miles. It has dug for itself a deep bed in the limestone rocks, and upon its banks is the most rugged and
picturesque scenery in Kentucky. Coal, and salt
springs abound along its shores. The rapids of the
Ohio came in sight after this, and looked cool and
pretty, as the water curled and foamed over the ledges
of rocks and pebbles. The water was very clear and
we seemed sailing upon the bottom; but being so
unusually low, our boat, as small as she was, grounded
several times. In these extremities recourse was had
to *cordelling*. A rope was carried ahead by a small
boat, and fastened to a rock, or anchored; and a wind-
lass brought the boat up to the rock. After passing
the rapids, the river becomes shallower and more narrow; but as our boat only drew twenty inches, we
succeeded in going on, while some larger ones which
had accompanied us thus far, were left in the river, or
at some village. The islands are more frequent, and
some of them very lovely, mazes of beautiful forest trees
woven together in natural bowers by pea vines in blos-
som, scarlet creeper, and many other pretty and new
plants. The island of the unfortunate Blennarhasset,
is the largest and loveliest, containing seven hundred
acres. Through the circle of forest trees which border it, we caught glimpses of the centre which was
level, and once highly cultivated. Here he created a
paradise of lawns and groves, and gardens, surrounding

a dwelling, the residence of his charming family, to which were attached green and hot-houses, libraries and music rooms. Ambition has rendered this fair spot a desert; he never rose to the empire which he and his tempter, Burr, had hoped to create. After all, the saddest part of Herman Blennarhasset's fate is, that every tourist who passes the island, must mention his name and utter an effecting sentimentality about ambition; it seems like dragging him out of his resting place, to hear our taunts; if you travel this way, let me beg of you—

> "Breathe not his name, let it sleep in the dust,
> Where cold and unhonored his ashes are laid."

Parkersburgh at the mouth of the little Kenawha, is a quaint old fashioned town in Virginia; embosomed in hills. Here we intended to land and take the mail stage to Winchester, but it had just departed, and rather than remain there two days, until another stage, we concluded to go on in the Agnes to Wheeling. Accordingly we and our trunks were again on board, and we resumed our rambles. At sunset we stopped, at the town of Marietta, the first spot settled in Ohio. Its name was very prettily given in honor of the fair and unfortunate Maria Antoinette of France; in gratitude for the support she gave our cause. The town was laid out in 1788. The streets are wide, and adorned with forest trees, and parks. The houses are solidly built, having each its ornamented court and garden. The exchange, court-house, college, churches, and other public buildings are handsome structures. It is principally settled by New Englanders, whose love of good order and morality has not been left behind, for the motto

22

upon the town seal pledges their ' support of religion and learning.' Marietta is upon the Muskingum, which is between two and three hundred yards wide, and navigable for one hundred miles with large boats. It is a remarkably pure, healthy, bright stream, 'rolling its limpid waves over a sandy and pebbly bottom, variegated in summer months with the open valves of thousands of red and white shells scattered among the sand, rivalling in beauty the richest tessellated pavement of the Romans.' Upon its banks stands Zanesville, a large and handsome town, and in the county through which this river and its branches flow, are quantities of iron, coal, salt, limestone, and many other useful productions. There are also ancient mounds and fortifications upon its shores. Marietta appears beautifully as we approach, seated upon an elevated bank, at the foot of a range of the picturesque Ohio hills. These are about three hundred feet high, formed of ' argillacious earth, based upon sandstone.' The scenery this afternoon is of a grander cast than any we had yet seen upon the Ohio. The hills which have generally risen at some distance from the shore, now come close down to the water, so that, as we ride along we can look far up into their recesses. They have the same gracefully regular appearance, except that now and then a ledge of sandstone or limestone, breaks the smooth green side.

I have said very little about the cooking and victuals upon these western boats. The latter are very good, and finer beef, fish, bread, etc., cannot be found any where; the most fastidious palate might here be satisfied were it not for one thing—our western brethren are so fond of fat. Almost every dish of animal food is swiming in a greasy liquor. Doubtless I should

be used to it in time and like it as well as our young
southern friend who used to expatiate upon the delights of hominy and 'possum fat.' However, I cannot expect persons, wherever I may choose to travel,
to shape their table to please me, so I make a point of
taking things as quietly as if I had ordered every
thing. I generally succeeded, by declining gravey,
to obtain a piece tolerably dry, and this, with their
excellent vegetables, Indian bread, good butter, and
nice stewed dried peaches, the unfailing accompaniment to every meal, to secure a pleasant and healthful
repast. Tea and coffee we have met, of all shades
and varieties, but none so unique as the prairie coffee,
of which 1 wrote you. The accommodations are
comfortable, and in the ladies apartment, towels, basins,
and water enough, and leave to use your own brushes.
The gentlemen were confined to tin washbowls upon
deck, but if any one chose to ask, he might always
have a basin and towel in his cabin. We found nothing to complain of as serious annoyances, but received
every attention and politeness from captains and servants.

LETTER XI.

Although weary of the constant jar of these high pressure steamboats, and glad once more to step upon firm
land, yet, when told Wheeling was in sight, I felt regret
that I must now turn my back upon the beautiful Ohio
and the charming western land. I ought not to leave
the fair State of Ohio without saying a few words to
give yon an idea of its extent and condition—matters
which you may perhaps extract from Gazateers yourself, but this will save you the trouble. Gazateers and
tourists guides, however, are of little use in a region
which so rapidly changes its appearance, and increases
its population. Where you are directed to remark the
beauty of a grand forest, you find a large town, and
where, when the book was written, spread out a fair prairie, you find a country covered with farm houses, cornfields, fences and orchards. Along the coast of Ohio
we have sailed over an hundred miles on lake Erie,
and upon the Ohio river, four hundred miles. From Cincinnati here, which is all that distance, except twenty

or thirty miles we paid twelve dollars, six each; which, with board for three days, is not expensive travelling. The State of Ohio is nearly square, being two hundred and twenty-two miles long by two hundred broad, and with Indiana and Illinois, are parts of a great plain which inclines to the Mississippi, through which the rivers have cut their way into their deep beds. The geology of these States is very much the same, they being based upon that great secondary limestone formation which reaches from the eastern States to the Chippewayan mountains, and from the great lakes to the alluvion of the southern States. This is doubtless the deposite of the primitive ocean, as it occurs 'in layers of chrystaline and sedimentary, or in broken pieces cemented together.'* It is of all shades, from the dark brown ferruginous, to the light grey, the blue fœtid, the yellow silecious, and magnesian, the argillaceous, earthy, chrystaline oolitic, etc. In this limestone formation is a variety of fossil shells of many species, as the ammonites, spiriferi, encrini, producti, corallines, gryphea, madrepores, and various others. Its thickness is enormous, for it has been penetrated one thousand feet without reaching the primitive rocks.† Above this is the sandstone, and slate, and clay of the coal measures, and muriatiferous rocks. These sandstones are generally white ash color, or brown; a very little red has been discovered in this valley. One of our western friends, who has well studied the geology of that region, was of opinion that all the groups of fossiliferous secondary strata recognized and determined by European geologists have not been discovered here; but that

* Dr. Owen.   † Hildreth.

22*

they claim the upper new, red sandstone and oolites, that have not been subdivided; that above the oolites they have unconsolidated strata of great extent and thickness, which do not abound in fossils, and have not been sufficiently observed to justify and attempt to confer names upon them. Several of the groups of the European secondary are thought to be wanting here. The chalk group is certainly wanting; nor have any of the four received divisions of the supercretaceous, or tertiary, been identified in the western valley. The older pliocene, and it is thought the newer, have been observed in Alabama. The recent pliocene is here established; the accumulation of gigantic fossil remains; of mammalia at Big Bone Lick, Kentucky; at Bucyrus, Ohio; at Pomme de Terre, Missouri; and at Rocky Spring, near St. Louis, identify this group with certainty. The recent pliocene is not horizontal, it having been seen fifteen hundred feet or more above the level of the sea. Its remains of elephants, tetracaulidons, and other fossils identical with existing genera upon the earth demonstrates its geological era to be near us. There are several remarkable deposites in Ohio and the surrounding States— the sileceous, ferruginous, muriatiferous, and the coal. The sileceous deposite, sometimes called 'Flint ridge,' runs nearly through the State of Ohio, in a southwesterly direction from the Tuscarawas river, to the Sciota, near the Ohio. Its greatest width is four or five miles, being strewed over the ground in broken masses; beneath the soil; or, which is its most common situation, upon the tops of the hills; doubtless thrown up from the ocean in a fluid and heated state. This deposite occurs generally white, but is occasionally streaked with various hues, and is compact, cellular, and vermicular. The aboriginal inhabitants made great use of it for arrow heads; and the present settlers find it very valuable as whet-stones, hones, and mill-stones. The latter are thought equal to the French buhr stone, and are sold to the amount of twenty thousand dollars a year. Those from the deposite upon Raccoon creek, are very celebrated. In this silecious material occurs marine shells, beautiful and limpid quartz chrystals, veins of chalcedony, sulphate of barytes, flint, hornstone, and various other minerals.

The ferruginous deposite crosses the State from north-east to south-west, commencing at the division line between Ohio and Pennsylvania, upon lake Erie, to the mouth of the Sciota, and thence continues into Kentucky, to the Cumberland mountains, its average width being from fifteen to twenty miles. The iron occurs in several varieties, as a brown oxide, an argillaceous ore, pure, highly carbonated ore, etc. Its forms are also various; the ore occurring lamellated, disseminated in kidney shaped masses, columlar, stalactitic, cubic, in rhombic fragments, nodules, etc. It is extensively worked in many furnaces of Ohio and Kentucky. In this iron are marine shells and plants of a tropical climate.

I have spoken of the muriatiferous rocks, and I will now pass on to the coal measures. The quantity of coal found in these western States is wonderful. The valley of the Ohio, and it now appears the valley of the Mississippi are underlaid with coal. The Alleghany mountains are filled with it; at their bases it is heaped up in masses, probably of antediluvial vegetation, by the eddies of the currents. These moun-

tains seem to divide the anthracite from the bituminous coal. There is enough of this article in Ohio
to last thousands of years, twelve thousand square
miles being underlaid with it in one grand basin. In
Indiana, according to Dr. Owen, the coal formation
occupies seven thousand seven hundred and eighty
square miles; in Pennsylvania, the bituminous coal
embraces an area of twenty-one thousand square
miles; while in the States west of these, coal is found
in considerable quantities, but it has not been thoroughly examined. The richest deposit of coal in the
valley of the Ohio, is the basin through which runs
the Monongahela river; it is two hundred miles in
length and one hundred in breadth.* It occurs extensively in layers across the hills—that of Coal
hill at Pittsburg, supplies the city, which it uses in its
great manufactories. The coal consumed in this city
and its suburbs is estimated at 'seven millions six
hundred and sixty-five thousand bushels.' This useful article is easily procured throughout the west and
is consequently very cheap, being two, four, or eight
cents a bushel in different places. The iron and salt
furnaces, and manufactories of the west owe their
present flourishing trade to the abundance of this material. This coal is black bituminous generally ;
burns freely, and in some deposits, forms very good
coke which is used in the furnaces. In Licking Co.,
Ohio is a deposit of Canal coal, and another in
Guernsey Co. Beside these interesting minerals
there are numerous others in the Ohio valley which
are very valuable ; upon Wills creek Ohio is a deposit
of fine lias limestone—and there are in the State

* Hildreth.

various other stones suitable for building,—sandstones of fine quality used for architectural purposes,—gypsum, lead, copper &c. The coal measures abound in organic remains; some of them belonging to the tropical palms and ferns are very beautiful and perfect. When we see how important these articles are to the western land, and how profusely they are scattered and how easily obtained, one cannot think they are thus arranged by accidental convulsions of nature. We know that the greatest coal deposits are above the thirtieth degree of latitude, and is not this because the inhabitants below this degree do not so much require it, while the colder countries would be almost deserts without it, so good and beneficent is our great Father. You will say I am like the old woman who praised the goodness of God for making rivers flow by the side of cities. I think there is double enjoyment in every gift when we feel it is from His compassionate hand. Ohio is one of the finest agricultural countries in the world. Her productions are justly celebrated for their goodness and quantity. Her exports in flour last year is said to be seven million five hundred thousand dollars. The land belonging to the government sells here, as in the other States for one dollar and twenty-five cents an acre. Around large towns the owner of the lots asks of course more. We must bid Ohio now adieu and look around us a little. We were approaching Wheeling when I thus digressed. It appears very well from the water; you see a circle of swelling green hills with the bright river encircling a large island in the midst. The town runs in a long line across the slope of one of the hills, while a group of steamboats looking

wonderfully like a flock of geese were floating upon
the water beneath. People are busy taking out coal
from the hills, and trundling it down a wooden railway
into the vessels below. The hills are between two,
and three hundred feet high ; the coal stretches along
their face for fifteen miles and then dips into the
earth. It is a kind valuable for cooking, and some of
it is beautifully irridescent. The manufactories of
Wheeling are supplied with it and it is extensively
sold down the river, at the cost of three cents a bushel
when delivered to the boat. One million five hundred thousand bushels of coal are exported from
Wheeling every year. Wheeling is a second Pittsburg blackened with coal; while the smoke is rising
from forge, and furnace, and chimney, in every direction. Here we found the best landing of any town
upon the river, as the steep bank was walled up, and
we ascended by a long flight of steps. When upon
the top of the wharf we found ourselves before a
range of shops and hotels, while before us was the
' United States,' where we deposited ourselves and
luggage. After tea we set out for a stroll through
the town accompanied by a very agreeable party who
had left the boat with us, the remainder of our passengers going on to Pittsburg, about ninety miles
farther. We had been through so many new towns
that this looked quite antique, it being settled in
seventeen hundred and seventy by Col. Zane and his
brothers, who afterwards founded Zanesville. The
streets here run along the face of the hill, and contain many shops, manufactories, a large court-house,
hotels, banks and dwellings. Among the buildings
are seven churches, an academy, iron and brass foun-

deries, flint glass works, paper and saw mills, steam engine and machinery works, nail factory, cordage, wire floorcloth factories &c. Eight stages arrive and depart each day, Sundays excepted, and various steamboats stop here—so if you know of any mechanics or trades-people complaining of want of work in your crowded city tell them to wend their way hitherward. All kind of laborers will find business enough in the west. I think a society for exporting over the Alleghanies the poor European emigrants who are suffering in our large cities, would be of great service to them and to us. The population we were told nearly numbered ten thousand. Among the houses we observed one quite large and handsome; this we were told was built by Col. Zane, when the town was first settled and his descendants have resided there since. He was an active pioneer of the wilderness, and encountered many difficulties, and fought many battles with the Indians ere he was permanently settled in his beautiful abode. In these attacks the females of Wheeling showed much heroism and took an active part in the affray. The little settlement was once attacked by three hundred and eighty Indians when Col. Zane had with him but thirty-three men, but the women shouldered their rifles, joined in the battle and did much execution. Once, in despair, the garrison inclined to a surrender, but a young girl named Betsey Wheat, answered them in such an eloquent and indignant burst of irony that they rallied and defeated the enemy. In a second attack Elizabeth, the sister of Col. Zane, saved the fort by bringing into it a quantity of powder, braving, but passsing unhurt through the whizzing balls directed against her by the Indians.

Some of the buildings here are of the light sandstone of the country.

July 24th.—We were aroused early by the trampling of steeds and upon looking out beheld several fine stages each having four horses which were soon to start upon their different roads. Our breakfast over we with the party mentioned above entered a large convenient coach and just as the clock struck seven left the hotel. Upon reaching the top of the hill above the town we looked down upon as fair a scene as any we had seen in our travels. The town was strewed over the hill below us, while the beautiful Ohio lay like a circlet of silver around a pretty island covered with waving corn and dotted with farm-houses, and then glided away in its course winding among the soft green hills until it disappeared behind one of them. The island is Zane's island, containing three hunded and fifty acres. We had now looked our last upon the lovely valley of the Ohio, and its beautiful river the Belle riviere of the French, and Ohio Peekhanne of the Indian. This valley is from the sources of the Ohio to the Mississippi eleven hundred miles in length, and nearly three hundred miles in breadth. It sweeps down from the Alleghanies at an elevation of two thousand two hundred and thirty feet to the Ohio and then ascends gently four hundred feet to the ridge which divides its waters from those which flow into the gulf of St Lawrence, a distance of nearly three hundred miles. Through this valley winds in graceful bends the noble Ohio eleven hundred miles from its source, and nine hundred and forty-eight from its junction with the

Monongohela at Pittsburg. It divides the valley in two unequal portions, having one hundred and sixteen thousand square miles upon the south-east side, and eighty thousand upon the north-west. This valley enjoys a pleasant temperature not too cold to paralyze exertion, and not so warm as to enervate. Its soil is capable of yielding fruits, vegetables, and grains, of the finest quality and in great profusion, and mineral products of the utmost importance to man; and it is settled by a free, virtuous, and enlightened people; add to this the scenery is beautiful and varied, and I think you will look far to find a region of country uniting so many advantages. The dark clouds of slavery which shadow its borders is the only spot in its fair horizon. The valley of the Ohio is in the centre of a great plain, which as the Appalachian chain was elevated raised up that portion, and consequently the rivers which flow over that division come with more impetuosity and dig for themselves deep trenches in the earth. Many who have carefully examined this region are of opinion the regular hills which border the Ohio and many of its tributaries, are parts of the primitive plain, which the streams have worn down into their present shapes. In this valley lies that great coal basin which is so ably described by Dr. Hildreth in the American Journal of Science. It extends over four or five degrees of latitude, and as many of longitude. A circle drawn from the head waters of the Muskingum to the sources of the Alleghany, and from thence to those of the Monongohela and Kenawha would mark the extent of this deposit, comprising portions of Pennsylvania, Virginia, Ohio and Kentucky.

Adieu to the fair Ohio! It has carried us for nearly

nine hundred miles in safety upon its bosom, unharmed by snag or sawyer ; and I say with Milton,

> " May thy brimmed waves for this,
> Their full tribute never miss,
> From a thousand petty rills,
> That rumble down the snowy hills ;
> Summer drought or singed air,
> Never reach thy tresses fair ;
> Nor wet October's torrent flood,
> Thy molten crystal fill with mud."

Our day's journey was very delightful.   The country is rolling, and alternately pretty hill and dale scenery, and winding rivulets.   The first part of our ride was through Virginia, but in a short time at the village of Alexandria, we entered Pennsylvania.   We drove over the national road, which runs from Cumberland, in Maryland, and passes through the intervening States to Vandalia, Illinois, from whence it is expected to be finished to Alton.   This is a firm McAdamized road, eighty feet broad, carried over mountains, vallies and rivers, crossing the. latter as well as every ravine and depression by well built stone bridges.   This very useful and well executed work was done by government, at the suggestion of our statesman, Henry Clay. We passed a neat farm house, before which stood a bronze statue of Clay, placed there by a widow lady, owner of the place, in gratitude for the benefit this road had produced to her property.   We of course were in duty bound to admire the statue, while rolling so rapidly and smoothly over this excellent road.   At Washington, Pa., we dined ; a pretty town, having three churches, hotels, and shops, with a college, a large building, in the centre of pleasant grounds.   A large court-house, of brick, was in progress.   The

dinner was good, but plain. The hills which we
passed in the afternoon, were covered with rich pasture land, where sheep and cattle were making a fine
feast. These grassy hills are famous for the 'glade
butter,' which is celebrated around the country, and
which we found very sweet and fresh. While descending the side of one of these hills, we were told
Brownsville, Pa., was in sight, and looking down, we
beheld a town in the valley, with the pretty Monongohela glistening in the bright sun, as it wound its
way around the hills. Rattling over a fine, strong,
covered bridge, we stopped to change horses before
the principal hotel. This is a large manufacturing
town, containing five thousand inhabitants. Steamboats are here built, and completely fitted up; and
when the river is high, they run to Pittsburg, sixty
miles distant. The hills are high around, abounding
in bituminous coal, and laid with strata of limestone
and sandstone. The coal here is very rich. Dark,
heavy masses, after we had left this place, began to
appear in the horizon, and we were rejoiced to hear
they were the celebrated Alleghany mountains. We
took tea at Uniontown, Pa., at the foot of the chesnut
ridge, and soon after began to ascend the mountain.
Our mountain ride was delightful, and when near the
summit we all descended from the stage coach, to
enjoy the views. What a glorious thing to stand
upon the top of a mountain! How exultingly you
gaze upon the world below! You feel so proud of
the great feat you have performed; you breathe freer;
the heavens seem nearer and brighter, and the earth—
but do not let me speak against the earth, for never
had it looked more enchanting than when looking upon

it from the summit of the Alleghanies. The fair
fields of Pennsylvania, were spread out below, varied
with herbage of every shade ; with groves and villages,
and streams, whose waters were tinted with rose from
the setting sun; around in every direction was a
green ocean of hill tops, robed in a vesture of purple
haze. You will smile at my heroics upon the summit
of so small a mountain as one of the Alleghanies,
scarcely three thousand feet above the earth, and
think it better applied to the Chimborazo, Popocatapetl,
or even Rocky Mountains; but fortunately, I have
never been upon higher ground, and enjoy the view
from the Appalachian range, as much as if I stood
upon the Nevados of our southern continent, twenty-
five thousand feet above the sea. Depend upon it,
those who have seen every thing, who have been
rowed down the Nile ; climbed the rocks of Petra ;
worshipped at Jerusalem; toiled up the Himalayas;
and frozen in Siberia, are no happier than we, who
have been creeping about the circle of our home.
To everything you call upon them to admire they
answer, ' J'ai vu ;' they have seen everything. If you
praise a song, they turn away with scorn and speak
of the opera at Naples ; if you ask them to visit our
springs or our cities, they talk of the spa's of Europe,
of Paris, of London, and Petersburgh. They have
nothing to do but fold their hands, grumble at the
present, and live upon the past. 1 have not seen,
and therefore may be allowed to expatiate upon the
beauties of the Alleghanies. All that night we
drove up the hills and down the hills, shut up in the
stage coach. We were glad of our cloaks, for it was
very cold, and at every stopping place we found fires,

although at the foot of the mountains the thermometer stood at eighty. We talked merrily at first and kept up each others spirits, but towards midnight we grew cold and weary, and one after another sank into silence. There was much nodding and dozing, but little sleeping; for as soon as one fell into a doze another was sure to ask you if you could sleep, or how you came on, a question sure to put to flight your endeavors. At last, hopeless of sleep, we gave it up by mutual consent, and tried to amuse each other by stories. One of our party was a western merchant who had frequently travelled over these mountains, and met with numerous adventures. He told us of an adventure which befel him twenty years since, when the mountains were little travelled, and only accessible on horseback. He was carrying a large sum of money in his saddle-bags, which he feared had been discovered by two ill looking men whom he had seen in the tavern where he had stopped just at dusk. He for some time felt a little fear, but the night had nearly worn away and he had not seen any one; when, soon after midnight, as he was pacing slowly along, he fancied he caught a glimpse of a man standing by the road side just before him. He gazed intently through the darkness and saw distinctly two men who drew farther out of the moonlight into the shade of the trees as he approached. He knew not what to do; he was not armed, no house was near, and if he left the road he must be lost in the pathless woods. Go on he must, and he determined to put spurs to his horse and dart past them. He gazed forward to see if his path were clear; a deep silence reigned around, when 'Dismount and give up your

23*

money !' resounded like thunder in his ears, echoing away among the silent aisles of the mountain forest. Two men were before him; his whip was wrenched from his hands; he was dragged to the ground; the robbers mounted his steed and rode away. 'Well, there I was in a pretty fix, anyhow,' he said, 'sitting upon a mound of snow all alone, in a wild wood at midnight, my two hundred dollars and my horse all gone. I might have said with Shakspeare's queen, "Here I in sorrow sit,' etc., but I was not in a poetical mood anyhow. Besides, I could blame no one but myself, for I ought to have kept my eye skinned, and not have been so blind as not to see the danger of travelling in wild parts with so much gold. Still, if the parts were wild, we had never heard of any robbery committed here, and did not expect it.' 'Did you ever discover the robbers ?' we asked. 'Oh, yes! I went back to the village, and every one turned out to help me. There was snow on the ground and we were thus able to track them. I was forced to go all the way to Buffalo, however, ere one was caught by the police. He had lived like a prince all along the road and spent his share of the money.' 'What became of the other man ?' 'Why, ma'am, as I was one day walking through Pratt street, in Baltimore, some months after, whom should I meet but my man, dressed in the newest style, parading along as proud as a prairie cock, with a grand lady upon each arm. I knew him, as I had remarked him at the tavern, and by the bright moonlight. He also remembered me, and when he saw my eye so eagerly fixed upon him, without saying good bye to the ladies, or even waiting upon them home, he scattered at once down the

street, and I after him. If you had seen the ladies
stare! Away he went, up street, down street, along
the wharves, in the vessels, out again. At last, thinking he had dodged me, he sprang into an empty hogs-
head. But I was'nt to be did that way anyhow; so I
flung a board over the top, and standing on it, clapped
my arms and crowed in such a tone of triumph, that
all the cocks in the neighboring yards crowed in concert. In short my man was treed and imprisoned, but
my money was gone.'

July 25*th*.—At day-break I lifted the curtain, and
by the uncertain light of dawn, beheld at my side a
wide river, whose opposite shores were green and
hilly. 'Are we over the mountains already? What
river can this be?' I asked. With a smile, one of the
party informed me we were on the summit of a high
mountain, and the deep valley filled with mist, with
the opposite summits for a shore, made my river. A
bright sun soon dispersed the mist, and we were never
tired of the variety of views we beheld upon every
hand. That the mountains are not very high adds to
the beauty of the scene; their heads are not lost in
the clouds, and we frequently see the whole mass at
once. While descending one Alleghany we beheld
another before us, like a high green wall reaching to
the heavens, while a line across the summit showed
the road we were to travel; so high and precipitous it
seemed, that we wondered how we ever should reach
the road. Descending again this ridge, we gazed out
over a great extent of country, or down into deep
valleys, brightened by winding streams, while trees,
and flowers, and vines of every tint and form, adorned

the path. The laurels were out of bloom, but their
deep green glossy leaves shone out continually from
the foliage. The chesnut was also frequent; these
two giving names to the two ridges we had passed,
Laurel and Chesnut ridges. We also remarked the
pretty striped maple, whose green bark is striped
with black. This is sometimes called moose wood,
as the moose-deer always seeks with avidity its tender
leaves and bark. The box elder also occurs upon these
slopes, with the holly, and varieties of the magnolia,
the turpelo, gum tree, besides noble forests of many
other trees. The road although leading over mountain ridges and passes, is not a lonely one, as stages
loaded with passengers, were continualy passing, and
huge Pennsylvanian waggons with the large Normandy
horses, high collar, and jingling a bell to give notice
of their approach. The women of the country we
often met upon horseback, sitting upon their gaily
embroidered saddles. The fine broad smooth National
road over which we were passing enabled the drivers
to keep their horses upon a very quick trot. I
am fond of rapid driving, but sometimes it made me
rather nervous to dash at the rate of eight miles an
hour, within two feet of a precipice down which we
looked upon the tops of trees a thousand feet below.
There is, however, very little danger, as where the
descent is steep, the driver can, in a moment, by
putting his foot upon a spring at his side, cramp the
wheel, and check our speed. After ascending a high
mountain, we found a tavern, whose sign bore the
hospitable words 'Welcome from the west.' We were
much pleased with this kind reception, until upon
looking back, perceived upon the other side of the

sign 'welcome from the east.' I wish the good lady
who erected a statue to Clay, would place a monument
upon the Alleghanies, to commemorate honest Daniel
Boon, who claims to be the first who discovered the
fair western plains. Sir Alexander Spotswood, a
governor of Virginia, penetrated part of the way
through the mountains. There was no National road
then, and the hills were almost impassable. To stimu-
late discovery, he instituted the order of the golden
horse-shoe, for those who could pass the Blue Ridge.
He was anxious to counteract the influence of the
French upon the Mississippi. There should also be a
statue to good old Father Marquette, upon the shore
of Lake Michigan, as, before him, no white man had
penetrated farther in the wilderness. He persevered
and discovered the Mississippi. We passed several
towns, as Smythfield, Petersburg, Frostburg, Cumberland, &c. This last town is in Maryland, upon a
branch of the Potomac, one hundred and forty miles
from Baltimore. The scenery around it is beautiful.
It lies in a valley, through which glistens the Potomac river, surrounded by mountains. We reached it
this morning, after descending a slope which seemed
to rise one mass of rocks above us. The town has
several large hotels, a college, court-house, and many
shops. We stopped here to change horses. Here
commences the transition formations, the Appalachian
range, dividing the transition from the secondary formations of the western valley. So clear and distinct
is this division, that the celebrated geologist, Dr.
Aikin, fixed upon the ground between Cumberland and
Hancock, forty miles distant, as the spot where the
Appalachian chain emerged from beneath, upheaved

by igneous action. The mountain which we descended to Cumberland, is called the Alleghany by pre-eminence, it being the highest elevation, and is the ridge which divides the waters which flow into the Ohio, from those which reach the Atlantic. The rocks which we had observed upon our road, were the usual limestone, marl, and conglomerates of the west, mixed with much bituminous coal, while now we remarked with them, grey wacke and transition slates. The Baltimore and Ohio railroad will pass through Cumberland, and the Chesapeake and Ohio canal. Here also the National commences, and we there left it, but found a very good one which continued, with some failures, during the day. We dined at Pine Grove, a small village. Near the hotel is a sulphur spring, which we were obliged to taste, to gratify the landlord, and which was as nauseous as one could desire. This afternoon we passed some very pretty mountain scenery; none so high as those we had left behind, for we were only upon the steps which lead down from the ridge to the plains below. From Sidling Hill we looked down into a large valley surrounded by a circle of hills, through which a river winding its way formed several islands. In the centre, was a high rounded knoll covered with fields of ripened grain, its bright yellow contrasting well with the dark woods which surround it. They have a curious way here of laying the grain when cut, in squares or circles, which looks very pretty at a distance. We took tea at Hancock, a town upon the banks of the Potomac. The Chesapeake and Ohio canal is finished as far as this place. We were but little over half way to Baltimore here, having come, we were told, one hundred and sixty

miles from Wheeling. Another night was passed in
the stage, only varied by occasional stoppages to
change horses. About day-break we stopped at Hagarstown, a very large, thriving place, containing
churches, academies, and many handsome private
dwellings. The hotel which we entered while the
horses were changed, was large, and seemed very commodious. After leaving it, we found the valley in
which it stands, was very highly cultivated. It is
underlaid with a dark blue limestone ; the soil is very
rich, and the wheat which it produces, is sent to Baltimore, and highly esteemed. We saw some of this
limestone which occasionally cropped out ; veins of
calcareous spar crossed the blue, in some instances.
Quartz pebbles, and large nodules were spread over
the country for miles, between this town and Frederic,
as if a storm of enormous hail had spent its fury
over the land. Rounded pieces, as large as a man's
fist, and white as milk, lay against the fences, or were
piled up by the husbandman. The county to Frederic
is very pretty, undulating, cultivated, and well settled,
while dark masses in the distant horizon told us our
pretty mountains were far behind us.

July. 26*th.*—At eleven o'clock, we reached Frederick
city, where we breakfasted. This is a very pretty
city, having an air of antiquity ; as we now had arrived in an old settled country, and the newly painted
towns were giving place to what are called old, although
not what an European would deem aged. I was
almost too sleepy to see much of it, but as we rat-
tled over paved streets, and looked upon rows of
houses, we seemed quite at home again.

We bade adieu to the stage-coach, and after a good
breakfast, entered the rail-road car, and were whirled
along with a rapidity which was frightful, after our
stage-coach pace.   The cars were handsomely finished, having an apartment appropriated to the ladies,
where reclining upon the blue satin sofas we relieved
our cramped limbs.   The country, between Frederick
and Baltimore, is very pretty.   I think it is about
sixty miles from the one place to the other.   We
passed many good houses, surrounded with fine farms,
having the shining Monocasy river, winding among
them.   We crossed this and the Petapsco, over
several bridges.   The latter river flows between high
banks of granite.   Fifteen miles, from Baltimore, are
the celebrated Ellicots mills, built of the granite of
the cliffs, upon which they stand, where is ground
the excellent Baltimore flour, raised from the fertile
country around Frederick and Hagarstown.   Some of
the deep cuts of the rail-road seem to be through a mass
of debris, of all colours, red, white, and blue, mixed
with talcose slate, aud blue limestone, until near Baltimore, when we entered that granitic belt, which
stretched through the Atlantic, border to Georgia, and
which is supposed once to have been the original
Atlantic coast, before the band of alluvion was formed.
After passing many fanciful country seats, and the fine
viaduct which leads to Washington, we beheld Baltimore, an enormous mass of brick and stone lying
upon the shore of Petapsco bay.   Our western friends
were delighted and surprised at the sight of so large
a city while driving through the street.   We arrived
at Barnham's large and elegant hotel just as they were
eating dinner.   We had infringed upon our Sabbath

thus far, without intending it, as we were told we
should arrive in Baltimore in time for morning services.   In the afternoon and evening, however, there
was opportunity of joining in public worship, which
my husband and some of the party embraced, leaving
us, the weaker part, at home to rest.

July 27th.—As we did not leave Baltimore until
half-past nine, we were enabled to see much of it.
Its monuments to Washington, and to the heroes of
the last war, are handsome, and the fountain with its
cool canopy of shadowy elms, pretty ; its churches
and public buildings very good, but as you are so well
acquainted with it, I will not trouble you with any
details.   We entered the rail-road car at half-past
nine, and reached New York at eleven that night, a
distance of two hundred miles, for which we paid
eight dollars each.   Several long bridges carried us
over Bush creek, Gunpowder river, and the noble Sus-
quehanna.   Our western friends, who had been boast-
ing of their great rivers, seemed surprised at the little
use we made of them in travelling.   ' It seems,' said
our fair Missouri lady, ' rivers here are of no consequence—indeed, are in the way, as you make bridges
and drive over them.'

At one o'clock we reached Wilmington, the capitol
of Delaware.   This State was a Swedish settlement,
named by Gustavus Adolphus, Nova Suecia, since
which time, Dutch, English and Americans, have suc-
cessively owed it.

We dined at Wilmington, and then hastening on,
passed through Chester, and a rich level country, to
the beautiful city of Philadelphia.   Leaving our rail-

road at the depot, we drove through the whole length
of the city, where, at five o'clock, we entered the
cars again, turned our faces towards New York, which
we reached, as I said, at eleven o'clock, the road
being along the Delaware, and through some rich
farms, with elegant mansions and huge Pennsylvania
barns; through Bristol and Trenton, in New Jersey,
when darkness spread over the land and we saw no
more.   And now farewell to the

"Land of the west! green forest land."

THE END.

MID-AMERICAN FRONTIER

An Arno Press Collection

Andreas, A[lfred] T[heodore]. **History of Chicago.** 3 volumes. 1884-1886

Andrews, C[hristopher] C[olumbus]. **Minnesota and Dacotah.** 1857

Atwater, Caleb. **Remarks Made on a Tour to Prairie du Chien:** Thence to Washington City, in 1829. 1831

Beck, Lewis C[aleb]. **A Gazetteer of the States of Illinois and Missouri.** 1823

Beckwith, Hiram W[illiams]. **The Illinois and Indiana Indians.** 1884

Blois, John T. **Gazetteer of the State of Michigan,** in Three Parts. 1838

Brown, Jesse and A. M. Willard. **The Black Hills Trails.** 1924

Brunson, Alfred. **A Western Pioneer: Or, Incidents of the Life and Times of Rev. Alfred Brunson.** 2 volumes in one. 1872

Burnet, Jacob. **Notes on the Early Settlement of the North-Western Territory.** 1847

Cass, Lewis. **Considerations on the Present State of the Indians,** and their Removal to the West of the Mississippi. 1828

Coggeshall, William T[urner]. **The Poets and Poetry of the West.** 1860

Darby, John F[letcher]. **Personal Recollections of Many Prominent People Whom I Have Known.** 1880

Eastman, Mary. **Dahcotah:** Or, Life and Legends of the Sioux Around Fort Snelling. 1849

Ebbutt, Percy G. **Emigrant Life in Kansas.** 1886

Edwards, Ninian W[irt]. **History of Illinois, From 1778 to 1833:** And Life and Times of Ninian Edwards. 1870

Ellsworth, Henry William. **Valley of the Upper Wabash, Indiana.** 1838

Esarey, Logan, ed. **Messages and Letters of William Henry Harrison.** 2 volumes. 1922

Flower, George. **The Errors of Emigrants.** [1841]

Hall, Baynard Rush (Robert Carlton, pseud.). **The New Purchase:** Or Seven and a Half Years in the Far West. 2 volumes in one. 1843

Haynes, Fred[erick] Emory. **James Baird Weaver.** 1919

Heilbron, Bertha L., ed. **With Pen and Pencil on the Frontier in 1851:** The Diary and Sketches of Frank Blackwell Mayer. 1932

Hinsdale, B[urke] A[aron]. **The Old Northwest:** The Beginnings of Our Colonial System. [1899]

Johnson, Harrison. **Johnson's History of Nebraska.** 1880

Lapham, I[ncrease] A[llen]. **Wisconsin:** Its Geography and Topography, History, Geology, and Mineralogy. 1846

Mansfield, Edward D. **Memoirs of the Life and Services of Daniel Drake.** 1855

Marshall, Thomas Maitland, ed. **The Life and Papers of Frederick Bates.** 2 volumes in one. 1926

McConnel, J[ohn] L[udlum.] **Western Characters:** Or, Types of Border Life in the Western States. 1853

Miller, Benjamin S. **Ranch Life in Southern Kansas and the Indian Territory.** 1896

Neill, Edward Duffield. **The History of Minnesota.** 1858

Parker, Nathan H[owe]. **The Minnesota Handbook, For 1856-7.** 1857

Peck, J[ohn] M[ason]. **A Guide for Emigrants.** 1831

Pelzer, Louis. **Marches of the Dragoons in the Mississippi Valley.** 1917

Perkins, William Rufus and Barthinius L. Wick. **History of the Amana Society.** 1891

Rister, Carl Coke. **Land Hunger:** David L. Payne and the Oklahoma Boomers. 1942

Schoolcraft, Henry R[owe]. **Personal Memoirs of a Residence of Thirty Years With the Indian Tribes on the American Frontiers.** 1851

Smalley, Eugene V. **History of the Northern Pacific Railroad.** 1883

[Smith, William Rudolph]. **Observations on the Wisconsin Territory.** 1838

Steele, [Eliza R.] **A Summer Journey in the West.** 1841

Streeter, Floyd Benjamin. **The Kaw:** The Heart of a Nation. 1941

[Switzler, William F.] **Switzler's Illustrated History of Missouri, From 1541 to 1877.** 1879

Tallent, Annie D. **The Black Hills.** 1899

Thwaites, Reuben Gold. **On the Storied Ohio.** 1903

Todd, Charles S[tewart] and Benjamin Drake. **Sketches of the Civil and Military Services of William Henry Harrison.** 1840

Wetmore, Alphonso, compiler. **Gazetteer of the State of Missouri.** 1837

Wilder, D[aniel] W[ebster]. **The Annals of Kansas.** 1886

Woollen, William Wesley. **Biographical and Historical Sketches of Early Indiana.** 1883

Wright, Robert M[arr]. **Dodge City.** 1913